In Praise of Risk

In Praise of Risk

ANNE DUFOURMANTELLE

Translated by Steven Miller

FORDHAM UNIVERSITY PRESS

New York 2019

This book was originally published in French as Anne Dufourmantelle, *Éloge du risque*, Copyright © 2011, 2014 Editions Payot & Rivages.

Cet ouvrage, publié dans le cadre d'un programme d'aide à la publication, bénéficie de la participation de la Mission Culturelle et Universitaire Française aux Etats-Unis, service de l'Ambassade de France aux EU.

This work, published as part of a program of aid for publication, received support from the Mission Culturelle et Universitaire Française aux Etats-Unis, a department of the French Embassy in the United States.

Fordham University Press has no responsibility for the persistence or accuracy of URLs for external or third-party Internet websites referred to in this publication and does not guarantee that any content on such websites is, or will remain, accurate or appropriate.

Fordham University Press also publishes its books in a variety of electronic formats. Some content that appears in print may not be available in electronic books.

Visit us online at www.fordhampress.com.

Library of Congress Cataloging-in-Publication Data available online at https://catalog.loc.gov.

Printed in the United States of America

21 20 19   5 4 3 2 1

First edition

to Clara, Gabriel, and Maud

CONTENTS

TRANSLATOR'S INTRODUCTION: THE RISK OF READING

In July 2017, newspapers around the world ran prominent stories about the death of the philosopher and psychoanalyst Anne Dufourmantelle. Although Dufourmantelle was a profound writer who garnered widespread admiration for her many books, her death became a newsworthy event not so much for the value of her life's work but rather for the courageous act that led to it one summer afternoon near St. Tropez. Writing for the *New York Times*, Benoît Morenne and Megan Specia describe what happened:

> Ms. Dufourmantelle was on the beach when the weather began to change and the previously safe swimming area became treacherous. She saw two children who were in danger and leapt into the sea to help . . . before being caught in the rough surf.
>
> She was pulled unresponsive from the water by two other swimmers, and attempts to resuscitate her failed.[1]

For every newspaper that ran the story, however, it was not simply about a woman who risked her life to save two children. The story within this story, the hook that made it especially newsworthy, was about a philosopher who lived and died by her published words, who put theory into practice. In each and every newspaper that reported on Dufourmantelle's death, the headline touted the relationship between her philosophy and her final act. More than any other organization, *The New York Times* made this aspect of the narrative particularly explicit. Under the headline "Philosopher Who Praised Risk Died Trying to Save Children from Drowning," the article opens with a conclusion that is presented as a factual assertion: "A French philosopher and psychoanalyst, known for her work that praised living a life that embraced risk, died last week *as a result of following her own bold philosophy*" [my emphasis].[2] The book to which these statements most explicitly refer is the one that you hold in your hands, *In Praise of Risk* (originally published as *Éloge du risque* in 2011). The fact that the book now appears in translation is due, likely in no small measure, to the notoriety that it gained from the worldwide circulation of this reportage.

How fascinating and frightening to be able to read the very book that set the stage for its author's death. How awe-inspiring and refreshing to read the work of a philosopher whose words are more than empty words, jargon, or obscurantism—a philosopher who does not just learn but manifestly knows how to die.

Dufourmantelle appears to embody what Simon Critchley calls "the ideal of the philosophical death."[3] The news of her death is the good news that the ideal might become real—that, if all too briefly, the truth walked among us, and she was a woman. Let us now praise dead philosophers. Thanks to the renown of Dufourmantelle's courage, a wider public will have the opportunity to discover her essayistic, provocative, and beautiful prose. All of this said, however, I will use the opportunity of this introduction to dispel the expectations raised by the assumption that the risk named in Dufourmantelle's title is the same as the risk whereby she jeopardized and ultimately lost her own life.

Risk is never neutral. It is always an object of praise or blame, an occasion for celebration or lamentation. Dufourmantelle thus opens her reflections on risk not with a proposition (subject to logico-grammatical analysis) but rather an unconjugated infinitive phrase; and what she celebrates about this phrase is not its truth but its beauty. "To risk one's life [*risquer sa vie*]" she extols, "is among the most beautiful expressions in our language." The praise of risk, then, begins with the language that upholds the place of risk in the world. And what's beautiful about this language is the economy with which it encapsulates the symbolic economy of risk society, without forgetting the dimension of risk that escapes its ritualized system of exchange. On the one hand, the expression evokes the Hobbesian paradigm in which the quiet and routine of everyday life are nothing but the absence of risk, the war of all against all held at bay, a fragile episode of calm purchased at the price of unending calculation, precaution, and surveillance.[4] To take a risk, according this this paradigm, is to abandon peace for war, coverage for exposure, the inside for the outside, illusion for reality, the shore for the rough sea, a comfortable life for a beautiful death. And praise would be the symbolic recognition ritually conferred on the brave individuals who abandon their protected existence within the social order in order to confront the abiding evils that threaten it. It's almost impossible, in fact, to separate the expression, *to risk one's life*, from the rituals of praise that belong to the theater of sacrifice.[5] On the other hand, the same expression says none of this. As if forever suspended in mid-thought, it is precisely the type of enigmatic infinitive phrase, without determinate subject or object, whereby an analyst might intervene during a session. Likewise, the analyst in Dufourmantelle declines to predicate the phrase any further. Where a scene of sacrifice would seem about to open up, she stays silent; or rather, she upholds the constitutive understatement of the phrase itself as the occasion for a question—the question that orients her exploration throughout the book. "How not to wonder," she asks, "what becomes of a culture when it can no longer think about risk except as a heroic act, pure madness, deviant conduct? . . . *How is it possible, as a living being, to think risk in terms of life rather than death?*" [my emphasis]. The same expression, then, participates in the ancient economy of sacrifice, giving praise where praise is due, but it also offers praise that could never be earned, extoling the risk that life is, all to itself, before it has ever been exposed to danger, perhaps before it has been exposed to death.

Dufourmantelle's project is to discover—in a searching and experimental combination of philosophical reflection and psychoanalytic case histories—whether such a "before" is even thinkable. Accordingly, the horizon that orients her approach to risk is not death and sacrifice, devotion and heroism, but rather what she calls not dying [*ne pas mourir*], once again relying on an enigmatic infinitive that invites incompatible readings.[6] "I interrogate risk in a manner that does not permit its evaluation or its elimination, within the horizon of: not dying." There is undoubtedly something provocative about such an approach, which flies directly in the face of the melancholy certainty that the greatest risk to life would be its end. Surprisingly, perhaps, her refusal to understand (or deplore or cherish) life in light of potential loss recalls (the obvious differences of style and culture aside) Arakawa and Gins's matter-of-fact declaration that "we have decided not to die."[7]

Each journalistic account of Dufourmantelle's death takes the opportunity, in her name, to reproduce the very paradigm of risk that she explicitly seeks to displace. The journalists who reported on her death, it would seem, did not pause actually to read further than the title of her book and thereby to take the risk of muddling their own narrative. The idea that made Dufourmantelle's death a good story—that she died young by putting her theory of risk into practice—entails an unacknowledged betrayal of her actual ideas about risk. Posthumously, in homage to her often playful catalogue (for example, dependency, suspense, passion, breaking up, leaving the family, solitude, variation, and the unknown), we might add the risk of reading.

Although the *New York Times* report of Dufourmantelle's death identifies her as a "philosopher and psychoanalyst," it goes on to presume, without noticeable justification, that she died solely as a philosopher. Would her heroic action be less heroic, or her story less of a story, or her philosophy less philosophical, if she died as a psychoanalyst? Is the presumption that a psychoanalyst wouldn't have a philosophy to give meaning to her death? Or that psychoanalytic theory, unlike philosophy, does not uphold an ideal or entail any precepts that a person would "follow" to the grave? In order to begin reading this book (and thinking about the singular death of its author), then, it is also important to remember that, in many of Dufourmantelle's books, but particularly in this book, fragments of clinical case histories regularly cut through her philosophical reflections. Because the majority of the book's fifty short chapters, each on a distinct type of risk, include clinical material, the reader—or at least the philosophically inclined reader—might conclude that Dufourmantelle provides these cases as examples of risk. This would be a conclusion, however, that disregards the uniqueness of the genre of the psychoanalytic case history: that it traces the origin of a patient's symptom or disturbance not to a generalizable cause (which will apply in every case) but rather to a singular history, the idiom of an irreplaceable body. In order to insist on the distinction between case and example, perhaps, Dufourmantelle inserts the histories and leaves them suspended without lengthy explanation of them. She resists any discourse that would soften their disruptive force or ease the transition between philosophy and analytic experience. They function, in a sense, like punctuations of the analytic session, offered in an affirmative and contestatory spirit, at odds with the onrush of speech. In other words, she refuses to do what journalism did with her case: to make these patients into so many faces of risk, to sacrifice their lives (or their deaths) for the glory of the concept and the intelligibility of her own discourse.

Dufourmantelle speaks a language that interrupts itself. Turning to case histories, or fragments thereof, all cut short, she cuts herself off; she acts as an analyst in relation to her own philosophical discourse. Among the most consequential and fascinating—albeit unthematized—aspects of this book, in fact, is the unique way in which it stages the psychoanalytic act and the position of the analyst. Most likely, no aspect of psychoanalysis is more broadly misunderstood, and infrequently theorized, than the role of the analyst herself in the process of the analytic cure. Typically, analysts are judged (by patients and fellow analysts alike) in terms of the opposition between absence and presence, withdrawal and empathy. But Dufourmantelle's brief clinical narratives show us how much more complex and unforeseeable the position of the analyst always is in practice. The often maligned silence of the analyst, she observes, is an inherently paradoxical mode of engagement: *"The silence of the analyst opens a suspense. It is not a nonresponse or a nonreception; it is an engagement with the nonresolution of an act, an invitation to take further risks, to hold unbearable contradictions within oneself and bring them alive."* In other words, the analyst does not occupy the position of what Jacques Lacan called the "the subject supposed to know" (*le sujet supposé savoir*).[8] In fact, as Freud makes perfectly clear in his case histories, the elementary analytic act is to suppose that the *patient* knows everything of any importance to interpret her own symptoms. The first thing that the analyst does is to disallow categorically the patient's frequent claims that she is paralyzed, does not know, or has nothing to say. In *Studies in Hysteria*, for example, the text in which Freud describes his first experiences with psychoanalysis per se, which led him to abandon hypnosis as a therapeutic method, the analyst writes: "Eventually I grew so confident that, if patients answered, 'I see nothing' or 'nothing occurred to me,' I could dismiss this as an impossibility and could assure them that they had certainly become aware of what was wanted but had refused to believe that that was so and had rejected it."[9] This unshakeable confidence on the analyst's part in the simple fact that there is something to know is what, in turn, makes it possible for each patient to take the risk of speech, to assume what Freud called a "moral courage." Often, however, as Freud himself learned in the course of his long practice as a psychoanalyst, and as the history of psychoanalysis after Freud has decisively confirmed, such courage requires more than speech. Although the medium of psychoanalytic work is language, the silence of the psychoanalyst also implies a recognition that not all knowledge can be spoken, especially knowledge of experiences that the subject inherits from her own infancy or even from the unconscious of previous generations. Dufourmantelle, in her case histories, privileges the turning points at which the analytic experience carries the patient and the analyst alike up to the limits of the speakable. Psychoanalysis, she shows, is more than a process of anamnesis that helps the patient to reach an ethical transformation. Beyond anamnesis, in order for access to unconscious knowledge to become possible, it also requires the patient to transform the structure of her life radically, to begin anew, and to discover new resources of expression. Accordingly, moments arise when, in order to welcome such transformations and the risks that they entail, the analyst improvises, breaks from routine, and transforms the parameters of her work with the patient, often to her own great surprise.

Each of Dufourmantelle's case histories depicts a patient who risks his or her life in order to make room for never before acknowledged or articulated experiences, fragments of life never before lived. The first case history in *In Praise of Risk*, which figures in the second chapter, "Eurydice Saved," is printed in italics, like all the others in the book, and appears to be inserted between paragraphs. It tells of a woman who, for as long as she can remember, presumed that she would die at age thirty. She lived her life in the past tense, as if it had already come full circle: *"And since she had kept death in her sights for thirty years, her life came to resemble the yellowed photographs that one looks at like a document from another age; it had always been thought in the past tense, starting from that moment of annulment that should be her death."* She finds an analyst who gains her trust because he listens without trying to convince her, as many others had done, that she probably wouldn't really die when or how she anticipated. After a handful of sessions, however, she arrives at this analyst's building only to discover that he had died and no one told her the news. This contretemps, especially because it involves the death of an analyst, raises difficult questions about the intersubjective status of death—whether it is simply a matter of loss and disappearance, passively undergone, or whether, even when not a suicide, it always has the force of an act. For this specific patient, at least, still at an early phase of her analysis, the death of her analyst, has the effect of an intervention: *"In the street, she knew that death had come to pass, that it took someone else."* At first, it might seem that this analyst died *for* his patient; that he took *her* death upon himself so that she might live. This is not entirely mistaken (although, strictly speaking, as Heidegger asserted, it is not possible to take anyone's death away from them). In part, what her analyst's death enables this woman to confront is the fact that death is never simply one's own. His death, precisely because it is absolutely singular, like all deaths, very well might have been hers. For the same reason, however, his death could not have been an act of devotion, a heroic sacrifice on her behalf: *"In her place? No, not even. It was just that she would no longer be there at the appointed time."* At her own death, too, she would arrive too late. This unexpected but hardly unusual missed encounter reveals that there is not, and never was, any position from which she (or anyone else) could bear witness to her own death and thereby regard her life as a thing of the past. Rather than saving her from death, this event leaves her to inherit her ongoing life for the first time. "It was like an accident, a car wreck from which she was miraculously spared. She should pay attention to this life *not so much given back but abruptly given to her*" (my emphasis).

In *Beyond the Pleasure Principle*, Freud writes that all life strives unto death. But, he adds, the goal of this striving resides in the ancient past. The death drive is regressive. Rather than venture toward an unpredictable end, it seeks the extinction of a time before life emerged. Dufourmantelle, in turn, invites us to consider the complexity of this regressive movement. Her patients bear witness again and again that emergence of life is never a simple, punctiform event. Even at the very beginning, in order to survive, life must hold not only death but also itself in abeyance; it remains virtual. Rather than spiraling back toward extinction, then, the death drive would regress from the actual to the virtual; it would constrain the subject to re-visit the very conditions of their survival. In another case, involving a man who lost his wife and his memory in a car accident, Dufourmantelle gives us a sense for how the psychoanalytic clinic of brain damage might unfold: *He had forgotten his name, his life. His memory was totaled along with his car in an accident that killed the wife whom he loved (so he was told).* What does psychoanalysis have to offer such a patient without access to his own past, who has lost any relationship to his own archive? What is psychoanalysis if not a process of anamnesis?[10]

> *The analysis would last a few years. The memories never came back. But something, out of oblivion, did come. Came back within the very time of what should be called a new life. An other love, an other apartment, different tastes, and a profession that happened almost by chance. Thanks to a passion for scuba diving in which it turned out that he was especially gifted, he became a deep sea diving instructor. There couldn't be a more precise metaphor for what he gave up looking for in himself—the traces, the vestiges, the unexploited, and unfindable resources of what had constituted what is commonly called an identity. What came back, then, was the sensation of having a body. His own—that his, a body that also came from the past, made of images and fears, hesitations, sensitivities, and urges that came from beyond him; and little by little this body took its place within him like a transplanted heart, not entirely foreign and not yet himself. In a sense, forgetting became his friend—a risk run, yes, like a risky hand in poker that you play anyway, to see what happens.*

Even a subject without a single memory left, without any recognition of his own life or his loves, is not entirely cut off from his past or his child-hood. Dufourmantelle supposes that her patient has a knowledge—both *savoir* and *savoir-faire*—of childhood that isn't identified with memories and that doesn't belong to the past. Whereas, before the accident, this man had been a landscape architect, the experience of radical oblivion allowed him to discover a talent and a passion for deep sea diving, and, along with this profession, a childhood before the formation of childhood memories, the unspoken and uncanny history of a singular body, which Dufourmantelle sometimes calls the "uterine body." In such a case, psychoanalysis does not, and indeed cannot, reconstruct memories that have been utterly destroyed.

Instead, as Dufourmantelle suggests, it offers the patient an opening to forget about who he used to be and to build a new life. But this new life doesn't simply impose a radical cut, an absolute break of the future from the past; it entails the risk of giving life, for the first time, to the vestiges of an immemorial past, perhaps nothing more substantial than the "sensation of a having a body." Rather than open toward death, the end of life, risk opens toward the body, which, for Dufourmantelle, is not so much synonymous with life, but rather constitutes a division within life, a life before life, or an unclaimed identity.

This book opens with a case that pivots on the sudden death of the analyst, then, in order to foreground the precipitation that, at times, characterizes the analytic act, the decision to alter the parameters of the work, without forewarning, especially when the framework of psychoanalysis itself becomes an obstacle to knowledge. There is undoubtedly something at least potentially sadistic about such unexplained shifts, since there is no guarantee, in advance, that they will lead anywhere. In the moment, they entail the risk of merely subjecting the patient to the pointless whims of the analyst. At the same time, as Dufourmantelle shows us again and again, the analyst's ability to surprise herself in the act, to proceed without foreknowledge entails a radical trust in the unknown, the fragments of experience that remain repressed because they have never been spoken. *"One day,"* she begins another case history, *"I discovered a different way of working in analysis that had already lasted three years."* In response to the patient's frequent inability to get to her second session each week, the analyst offers that both of her sessions should be scheduled on the same day: first a session at the usual time, then a break, and then the second session. What the patient most appreciated about this arrangement, much to her own surprise, was the break between her two sessions. This delimited space of time, it turned out, opened an empty frame in which the uncanny figure of a lost child could appear: *"Several dreams appeared that revolved around the figure of a child whom she lost in a crowd or cared for so poorly that it died. Intrigued by the insistence of this figure (the patient had no children yet), I will ask her about her family genealogy and the order of births. Had a child been 'forgotten'? What absence of a tomb haunted the nights of this young woman?"* When another patient declares that his money troubles make it necessary for him to stop coming to analysis, Dufourmantelle offers him the chance to continue at no cost until his financial situation improved: *"Never had I proposed such a radical solution to one of my patients and God knows many of them were in more precarious situations than his. But I felt that he was on the edge . . ."* In response to this act of trust, which evokes something in him beyond words, the patient writes and brings pages from a new novel to each session. To borrow the words of Serge André: writing begins where psychoanalysis ends (albeit in the midst of analysis).[11] Later, Dufourmantelle adds, this patient would decide to become an analyst himself. Finally, in the analysis of a young and highly successful vascular surgeon who presented with "the symptoms of recalcitrant melancholy, recalcitrant to life and to death," she surprises herself again: *"And yet, one day I suggested that she write something. Rarely, if ever, did I make such a demand: to solicit a text. But I was at a loss, incapable of helping this woman without any consciousness of her femininity, her fragility, her exceptional intelligence, and without any desire other than to operate (especially life-saving surgeries) — everything else expunged from the chessboard of her life."* The patient's response to this demand—as much to its object as to the departure from routine that it represented—is remarkable. Writing becomes the place for the desire that has no place in her life:

> Her writings were akin to molten lava. Full of a vertiginous conscious-
> ness of the most intimate folds of the feminine heart. One might have
> believed that she spent her life in the waiting room of an analyst, a
> gynecologist, and a highly accomplished sociologist. Short sentences,
> vitriolic, devoid of pathos. She didn't comment on her own pages; as
> first, she resisted talking about them or offering associations, as if it was
> an other woman who expressed herself in them. The analyst's office
> became the place for this deposition and little by little, affects began
> to intervene, like isolated blocks drifting on the surface of a precisely
> regulated discourse. Then came her dreams. Seething, very somber,
> full of murder and madness, amphitheaters rife with assassins, rapists,
> prowlers, open hearts, and eviscerated bellies. Desire here is noth-
> ing but writing. Diffracted in the violence of these imagined, written
> destinies, it begins to be able to begin to be said; and no one can say
> whether the splitting that shelters such passion will one day have an-
> other theater than these proffered pages, which absolutely deserve to be
> published without any further commentary. What does it mean for an
> analyst to be the keeper and thus temporarily the witness to this chain
> of unchained words, to such a fulgurant writing of desire?

Cases such as this one, along with the many others that Dufourmantelle brings forth in this book, remind us that the unconscious comprises more than memory; that, precisely because it entails infantile experience, it en-compasses more than the past, more than lived experience. This surplus is libidinal, not cerebral (pace Malabou). Dufourmantelle reminds us that sexuality itself is older than the subject, that the persistence of the drive ultimately opens the subject to the singular history of her unlived experiences. This is the aspect of the unconscious that Freud encounters in the form of the repetition compulsion, that Walter Benjamin brings to our attention in "On Some Motifs in Baudelaire," with the distinction between *Erlebnis* (lived experience) and *Erfahrung* (unlived experience), and that Lacan formalizes with the claim that it is structured like a language.[12] Accordingly, it is this aspect of the unconscious that compels analysts and patients alike to go beyond the work of anamnesis, to risk calling its own framework into question, to supplement speech with writing and artistic production, explicitly to solicit the future. Notably, Freud encapsulated the process of analysis in three unconjugated infinitive verbs: *erinnern, widerholen*, and *durcharbeiten* (remembering, repeating, and working through), as if to indicate that the progress of analysis opens toward an encounter with something that does not align with the order to grammatical predication. Even Freud's well-known archeological metaphors hinge on the factor of surprise, the potential for an encounter with a past older (or newer) than the past: "Our insight into this early, pre-Oedipus, phase in girls comes to us as a surprise, like the discovery, in another field, of the Minoan-Mycenean civilization behind the civilization of Greece."[13] Dufourmantelle thus highlights the risk, the potential for transformative surprise, that structures this archeological enterprise. Her radical departures from routine—because they display an immense confidence, not so much in the analyst's own abilities, but rather in the future—offer patients a chance to make room in their lives for what, in the unconscious, remains incompatible with the patterns of lived experience.

There is a quality of Dufourmantelle's writing that might be called lyrical because it is always restless, slightly out of joint; it upholds the disjunction between saying and knowing, stages the wandering of a voice at odds with language. The singularity of her style heeds a demand that, in many of the book's philosophical fragments, is articulated as the demand to get ahead of oneself. At one point, Dufourmantelle contends that this demand is nothing other than freedom: "Does freedom teach us anything? Perhaps not. It demands that we risk our desire as if it were something infinitely precious, a unique event, an imperious voice; that, in sum, we go out in front of ourselves [*aller . . . en devant de soi*], go where we didn't know we are, where something unknown to us yet speaks of us and convokes us. Freedom is a convocation." And this convocation appears in various guises throughout the book. Among Dufourmantelle's pivotal concepts, which harkens back to her first book, *La vocation prophétique de la philosophie* (Éditions du Cerf, 1998), for example, is that of "intimate prophecy." It is introduced early in her reflections, in connection with her determination of risk as not dying: "To risk one's life is first, perhaps, not dying. Dying in the midst of our lives, in every form of renunciation, the blankness of depression, sacrifice. To risk one's life at decisive moments of our existence is an act that pushes ahead of us on the basis of a still unknown knowledge [*un acte qui nous devance à partir d'un savoir encore inconnu de nous*], like an intimate prophecy; it is a moment of conversion." Elsewhere, this prophetic haste or urgency becomes the basis for a revaluation of the category of the "visionary," to artistic creation, and ultimately to the singular intelligibility of the unconscious:

> We are afraid of our own capacity to perceive, of the "visionary" in us, of what is commonly called intuition—that is, a knowledge you have in advance of yourself [*un savoir en avance de soi*]; a knowledge from which one would rather deliver oneself even before it can be clearly formulated. Retroactively, our gestures, our dreams, our slips of the tongue, and our bungled actions reveal to us, like prophetic utterances, this capacity for intelligible perception much vaster than the ego. Artistic creation is always at grips with the apparatus out ahead of you [*ce dispositif logé en avant de soi*] that informs you, somehow unbeknownst to you, and that unfolds on the canvas, in the score, or on the page even before consciousness takes notice.

Artistic creation, in other words, teaches us that we see not with our eyes but with the drive that inhabits us. The drive, rather than the senses, is what gives access to objects that are not yet objects, that do not yet figure among the world of perceptible things; it entails a movement not just beyond the pleasure principle, but also beyond the reality principle—and beyond the morality of adaptation that it implies.[14] In accordance with such reflections, Dufourmantelle arrives at the hypothesis that the unconscious itself is incompatible with consciousness, not because it harbors unwanted knowledge, but rather because it is turned toward the future:

> Why at certain moments of our lives are we in advance of ourselves? I would like to be able to think the psychic reserve in us whereby we gain access to the future beyond the narrow confines of our consciousness, our class, our education, our fears, and our inability to confront alterity. This ability would be—such is, at least, the hypothesis that I am developing here—a sort of unconscious turned toward the future, toward the promise, toward what portends itself. What derails neurosis—the "always already known," the "been there done that"—is the possibility within us of opening to something hitherto unsuspected, to a different

time . . . It's the hidden face of this "knowledge without knowledge" that can be expressed collectively in revolts, revolutions, movements of anticipation or the avant-garde that announce a step beyond the present time or generalized servitude, bringing about a secondary "collective consciousness."

The risk *par excellence*, for Dufourmantelle, is not that of death or loss of life; it is the risk of opening to something hidden or, to use her privileged word, something "intimate," such as an "intimate prophecy" or an "intimate time." Guided by the testimony of her patients, Dufourmantelle finds that this "intimate" dimension of life unexpectedly comes into play at moments when the possibility of death is set aside.

The photograph on the cover of this book shows the tiny figure of Philippe Petit in the midst of his notorious walk, early in the morning of August 7, 1974, on a high wire rigged between the recently built towers of the World Trade Center in New York City. The high-wire artist, appropriately enough, is among the central figures of risk to which Dufourmantelle often returns in the course of her reflections. In common parlance, as well, this figure is shorthand for the narrowest possible margin between life and death, success and failure. There is no more explicit and fascinating figure for the omnipresence of disaster, it would seem. And yet, the emblematic image of the high-wire walker does not represent him off balance, teetering above the void, but rather utterly focused out on the wire. Accordingly, for Dufourmantelle, the moment that encapsulates the entire art of high-wire walking is when the artist holds still on the wire. Precisely because this is the moment of greatest risk, standing becomes a distinct event, disjoined from sequence or succession. The high-wire artist risks death, then, not to flaunt his own survival or invulnerability, but rather, as Dufourmantelle writes, to open toward an "intimate time," a risk that does not belong to the time of the performance but to the singular history of the artist's body:

> The high-wire artist risks falling, most of all when he holds still, when he attempts to stand in place, almost without moving a muscle. He must restrain the very momentum that gives him stability. As a high-wire artist, he prefers to attempt this miracle of suspense upon the wire. It might be said that he is waiting—but that is not what is happening. Suspension is not the arrested time that comes *before* something else happens; it is the event itself, the passage into the intimate time where, in reality, the decision has already been made but no one knows it yet.

At the center of Petit's own poetic treatise on funambulism is a chapter entitled, precisely, "The Quest for Immobility," which begins:

> This [the quest for immobility] is the mystery of the rope dance. The essence, the secret. Time plays no part in achieving it.
> Or perhaps I should say "in approaching it."
> To approach it, the high-wire walker turns himself into an alchemist. Again and again, he attempts it along the wire, but without ever entering the Domain of Immobility . . .
> The feeling of a second of immobility—if the wire grants it to you—is an intimate happiness.[15]

The word translated into English as "intimate" in both of these texts on the high wire, in French, is *intime*—a quietly pivotal word throughout Dufourmantelle's book. She asks, for example: "How is it possible, as a living being, to think risk in terms of life rather than death? At the instant of decision, risk calls into question our intimate relationship with time [*notre rapport intime au temps*]. It is a combat with an adversary whom we never identify, a desire that we would never know, a love whose face we would never see, a pure event." Intimacy rather than death, for Dufourmantelle, is what defines risk. Whereas in contemporary usage the word "intimate" primarily designates the close (often sexual) relationship between adults, and this sense of the word has recently been aligned with the risk of psychoanalytic thinking in the work of Tim Dean,[16] the translation from French must rely on the survival of an older sense of the term (*OED*: "inmost, most inward, deep-seated; hence, pertaining to or connected with the inmost nature or fundamental character of a thing; essential; intrinsic"), according to which the intimate refers to a radical or hyperbolic interiority, more inward than the self or the heart, the heart of hearts (or what, in French, is called the *for intérieur*). At this inner limit, for Dufourmantelle, intimacy is also more foreign than any stranger, more distant than any spatial exteriority, and more widely shared than any social bond (such that, as she emphasizes, in the form of revolts or revolutions it can become the basis for a new social bond).

Dufourmantelle often relies upon this sense of the word *intime*. Her chapter on envisaging night, for example, begins: "The night is our secret amplitude. The space of our mute, intimate madness." But her reflections also push the boundaries of this sense to make the word designate the recesses of both space and time. Intimate time is actually a form of untimeliness, the urgency of a past beyond the set of conscious (and perhaps even unconscious) memories that remind us who we are, the swarming background of virtual experiences (combat without adversary, love without fact, unconscious desire) that lend memories their clarity and distinctness. Dufourmantelle writes of the way in which the earliest body of the newborn, before it is gathered up and organized around a small number of predetermined zones and the specific objects that pertain to them, survives into adulthood:

> Little by little, the body of the newborn is desensitized. It is wrapped up. Little by little, it closes upon itself. Sensations become concentrated around the mouth and the extremities of the body, around what become the so-called erotogenic zones. The memory of the body is thereby divided, dispersed, and forgotten; the entire vibrant body of the newborn goes away, effaced upon contact with the real; but it also lingers to watch over your dreams, your fears, your nightmares; it is lodged within the scents you love; it is suddenly exacerbated as you brush against a passerby; it is volatilized. We spend our lives dismantling this body and trying to recapture it, to rediscover its scent, the miraculous draught of an elixir of lost life. We know intimately that it exists, but no longer dare to believe in it.

Intimacy is commonly understood to characterize a narrow, hushed, insulated, and ultimately maternal sphere of experience, perhaps not devoid of ambivalence. The temporal axis of Dufourmantelle's intimacy, however, reaches further back than the erotogenic body that a mother gives her infant; it confirms what is perhaps the most elementary and indispensable insight of psychoanalysis: that our knowledge spans our entire lives, lived and unlived, remembered and unremembered, personal and impersonal, singular and collective. It was perhaps in the name of this insight that Freud, in his altercation with Jung, refused to allow for a psychoanalysis minus a theory of repression or infantile sexuality. Dufourmantelle, in turn, aligns psychoanalysis with the need for an "intimate rupture," because it (and perhaps it alone) offers hospitality not merely to persons but, more radically, to the whole range of experiences that make up life from the very beginning. "In this sense, yes," she writes, "it is a sort of survival pact."

The most emotionally complex and wrenching moment in James Marsh's documentary about Petit's famous walk, *Man on Wire*, occurs in an interview with Jean-Louis Blondeau, when he describes the experience of watching his childhood friend step out onto the wire that they had just spent a long and exhausting night rigging in secret: "I saw his face changing. He was tense. Then something like relief. From that time, I said,

'That's it. He's secure, it's good.'"[17] After these words, Blondeau smiles nervously and then covers his face as he breaks down in tears. He becomes overwhelmed with emotion at precisely the moment he remembers being certain that Petit was *safe*. This certainty, however, does not come at the end of the exploit when Petit would step *off* the wire and rejoins his accomplices but rather when he ventures *onto* the wire, long before he is officially out of danger. And Blondeau's tears bear witness to a traumatic encounter with a horizon of risk that only opens when Petit's fearlessness, together with his joy, have effectively set aside the possibility of falling.[18]

Risk is beautiful. —PLATO

The instant of decision is madness. —SØREN KIERKEGAARD

To Risk One's Life

Life is a heedless risk taken by us, the living.

Our days take place under the sign of risk: the calculation of probabilities, surveys, the gaming of potential stock market crashes, the psychological evaluation of individuals, natural disaster preparedness, crisis units, cameras. No dimension of ethical and political discourse escapes from it any longer. Today, the principle of precaution has become the norm. In terms of human lives, accidents, terrorism, or social protest, risk is a cursor that moves according to collective mobilization and economic investment; and for precisely this reason it remains an unquestioned value.

"To risk one's life" is among the most beautiful expressions in our language. Does it necessarily mean to confront death—and to survive? Or rather, is there, in life itself, a secret mechanism, a music that is uniquely capable of displacing existence onto the front line we call desire? For risk—its object still indeterminate for now—opens an unknown space. How is it possible, as a living being, to think risk in terms of life rather than death? At the instant of decision, risk calls into question our intimate relationship with time. It is a combat with an adversary whom we never identify, a desire that we would never know, a love whose face we would never see, a pure event.

How not to question what is to become of a culture that can no longer think about risk except as a heroic act, pure madness, deviant conduct? What if risk traced a territory even before it even accomplished an act? What if it supposed a certain manner of being in the world, constructed a horizon line?

To risk one's life is first, perhaps, not dying. Dying in the midst of our lives, in every form of renunciation, the blankness of depression, sacrifice. To risk one's life at decisive moments of our existence is an act that pushes ahead of us on the basis of a still unknown knowledge, like an intimate prophecy; it is a moment of conversion. Is it this gesture of the prisoner in Plato's myth of the Cave, his turning toward the true light? Or is it, in Kant's discussion of the moral law, this index within us, of universality, which we might take as a basis to think and be free?

As an act, risk lets chance take hold. We would wish it to be voluntary but it originates in obscurity, the unverifiable, the uncertain. I interrogate risk in a manner that does not permit its evaluation or its elimination, within the horizon of: not dying. How are we supposed to imagine that the certainty of our end might not, retroactively, have any effect on our existence? From the furthest edge of this certainty, we know that one day everything we loved, hoped for, and accomplished, will be effaced. And what if not dying in the midst of our lives was the foremost risk of all, refracted in the human proximity of birth and death?

Risk is a *kairos*, in the Greek sense, a decisive instant. And what it determines is not only the future but also the past, a past behind our horizon of expectation, where it reveals an unsuspected reserve of freedom. How should we name that which, in deciding the future, thereby reanimates the past, prevents it from becoming set in stone? Risk is akin to an acoustic phenomenon, the sort of feedback (or Larsen) effect that causes sound to return to its source. When a sound *loops back*, it provokes a kind of secret intelligence that alone, perhaps, is liable to disarm repetition. Far from being a pure "onward" bent on the future, risk subjects time and memory to an inversion of priorities through a sort of revolt, a very gentle and continual rupture. The instant of decision, the one in which a risk is taken, inaugurates an *other* time, much as trauma does. But a positive trauma. Miraculously, it would be the opposite of neurosis whose trademark move is to capture the future in such a way that our present becomes modeled on past experiences, leaving no room for the effraction of the new, for the displacement, albeit minimal, that opens a horizon line. Indeed, the feedback effect of risk would be the exact opposite. It would be a *rewind* from the future, dismantling the reserve of fatality included in any past, opening a possibility of being in the present—in other words, a line of risk.

Eurydice Saved

Eurydice, a timeless and ultracontemporary figure, is she who for love was sought all the way to death. Taking the risk of *not dying* raises the question of what makes us living beings, but more important, beings like Eurydice with the capacity to call. The myth[1] does not speak of Eurydice's call; and yet this call, and Orpheus's fatal turn back in response to it, is the essence, I believe, of the human bond. Invocation founds our primal bond to the other from our fetal origins unto our end, which traverses and makes us something other than mere intelligent bodies—that is, beings capable of a devastating event: love.

She believed that she would die at thirty. She had always thought so. It would be an appointment no more important than the dentist, an oil change, buying a pack of cigarettes. That morning, she knew, would be just a little more definitive than other mornings. And it wouldn't come from her. Certainly not! She was a stranger to any thought of killing herself, or even praying that chance would do it for her. She simply observed that she had a slight advantage over other people: knowing when the grim reaper would come to collect her. A clairvoyant made an attempt to intercede, saying that it would be no more than a symbolic death, you know, a big emotional shock. Oh really? she smiled, and afterward real life begins, is that it? She always felt a maternal protectiveness toward clairvoyants, as if visiting them only ever confirmed what she alone knew. What she hadn't foreseen, at all, was fear. A tiny little fear that just arose one rainy afternoon, the way one picks up a lost dog wandering in the street, or a cold. She had caught— or adopted?—a fear. A fear of dying. That was several weeks earlier . . . Then she had come to find him. A shrink, chosen almost at random, because of his voice heard on the radio late one night. She had always gone to sleep listening to the radio; it was her special way of not having had a childhood. Which embarrassed her a little in going to see this gentleman. He would certainly ask her to speak of it, her childhood; but there was nothing that she believed she could remember. But this fear bothered her and, in any event, it wouldn't do to die with such fear stuck to her like a shadow. She'd prefer, if die she must, to do it with grace and seren- ity. No matter how little she felt like patching together her memories, she would accommodate the man who was willing to listen her. She had very little time left, having started late, but after all it was just a matter of getting someone to help her understand the fear that had suddenly gripped her. Life would be short for her, so what? Having acquired the name of this analyst from the radio station, therefore, she went to her appointment like it was an illicit rendezvous.

The psychoanalyst was late but ultimately the wait allowed her to tame the discomfort of what she had to say to him.

He listened. So far so good, all the same she was expecting that somewhat.

And then he said: "Perhaps you want to live, a little bit more?"

She almost laughed—at the simplicity of the remark, perhaps even its stupid- ity, its gentleness also.

"Yes, the thought had occurred to me, you know . . ."

"Ah!"

"When you're afraid, isn't it because something you care about is threatened?"

Now it was her asking him questions.

"Yes, no doubt," he added simply.

Then a rather reassuring silence settled in, like a tranquil little breeze in their sails, a navigation to windward. At the end of the session, he accompanied her to the door, supposing that she would return? The following week? At the same time? He didn't specify. He had a sort of contagious goodness, the type that quietly envelops you and leaves you not knowing how to extricate yourself. Clingy, no, courteous, yes, but still with a hint of indifference. It seemed to her that he hadn't taken note of the fast approaching date of her death. They would only have three or four meetings. Well, she trusted in him, she would reflect on the things he had said to her. In truth, she had never thought about the thing like this, since death forbade desire for anything after a certain date. And since she kept death in her sights for thirty years, her life came to resemble the yellowed photographs that one

looks at like a document from another age; it had always been thought in the past
tense, starting from that moment of annulment that should be her death.

He hadn't sought to dissuade her about the fatality of this rendezvous—because
it was a certainty—as everyone else had tried to do: but Eurydice, look here, you
know perfectly well how silly this is, we will raise a glass on your thirtieth birthday
and then the day after . . . She didn't object, smiling inside, right, right. . . . The
truth is a point of resistance in the real of unequaled force. An experience that
functions as a test. It makes the real disgorge itself. And the subject who receives it
knows. Eurydice also knew; and she didn't ask anyone to protect her from it.

The following week, he hadn't responded to the intercom. She had rung again
and again until the concierge was moved to answer: you're looking for Mr. X?

"Yes, we had an appointment." Then she added, "I believe . . ."

"Ah, I see. So you're not aware . . . Someone should send a notice, they couldn't
let everyone know, I understand, but still, it shouldn't be my place to do it!" She
had seemed vexed. "He died three days ago now."

Eurydice froze. It was like at eight years old when she witnessed the Aurora
Borealis in Canada and had believed, standing before this great green curtain that
rattled the entire sky, that it was simply the end of the world.

"Dead?"

"Yes, it was printed in the paper, the burial is tomorrow afternoon. You can call
his sister, I think she's the one who responds to his . . . patients," risked the woman
after another glance at her.

"Thank you," she said, "but there's no need. You are very kind."

And she exited the building, turning her back on the mute intercom.

In the street, she knew that death had come to pass, that it took someone else.
In her place? No, not even. It was just that she would no longer be there at the ap-
pointed time. Nonetheless, her fear remained, like a small animal, a kitten left in
her care. Now she had to do something with it to help her gain a taste for life. To
understand what it was to be alive. An unimaginable event a few moments earlier.
It made her think of an accident, a car wreck from which she was miraculously
spared. She should pay attention to this life not so much given back but abruptly
given to her. This life along with this fear, with his words, and his death.

It sometimes happens that the risk of not dying goes unnoticed, or almost . . . It is not offered as a last resort (to live—still), but rather in what
turns out to be a renunciation, in those instants when not believing in
anything anymore is all you are capable of. The question, then, is how
to change scale? Whether an architect's scale or that of Jacob's ladder, it
will be a matter of losing measure, opening a wide angle [*le grand angle*].
Doing an about-face and confronting the past in a radically new manner.
Light, one perceives, often comes from behind, from the spot that is called

blind [*dans cet angle que l'on dit mort*]. Or else from a voice that whispers, "Turn around!" The voice of this turn, of revolt, is what pushes you out of the cave, the drugged sleep of depression, any sort of betrayal, or deceptive opinions, in order to go toward what seems only a dream, since you always believed, indeed, you would swear, that the image projected there, on the wall, is the real. Turning around is a true risk. What seems to be renunciation, backpedaling, the obstinacy of one against all, is actually philosophical anamnesis, a certain path of psychoanalysis; it is the madness of believing against all dogma that "back there" is an unequalled reserve of freedom. Back there, Eurydice is the one who whispers: down this path you will confront death, nothing less. If we construct microphilosophies, little fragments of thought around Eurydice, will it help to understand how to climb from death toward life?

Death, we know, is what is risked in us. Holding it imaginarily in our sights is no guarantee that we'll be more living or more loving. If risk is the event of "not dying," it is beyond choice, a physical engagement at close quarters with the unknown, night, nonknowledge, a wager in the face of what, precisely, remains undecidable. It thus opens the possibility that something unhoped for will happen.

Would it not suffice less dramatically to think, with Spinoza, what makes us persevere in being? To think patience instead, this measure of time that, in the face of urgency, cauterizes wounds . . . The patience of being—a subtle, forgotten, uncolonized art of the self, in which emotion is entangled with thought, the cuisine of all creation. But it would have to be a patience neither in the service of waiting, nor especially in that of depression, compromise, or fatal renunciation. This risk—the risk of being—cannot be envisaged or evaluated. The grand machinery of the economy is what promotes the evaluation of risks.

Sometimes, we have mere moments left before it's time. And in the intensity of what's lived in those moments is an infinite surplus of time. A grace, *a Mercy*.[2]

Minuscule Magical Dependencies

"Addiction" is a fashionable word; the Anglicism lends it an aura that the word "dependency" [*dependence*] has lost. Indeed, "dependency" has received very bad press. One grants it a degree of danger in proportion to its level of attraction. Toxic in more than one sense, it arises in the form of any number of more or less powerful substances commonly designated as drugs (which might include the present-day pharmacopoeia of anxiolytic medications) but also the various fruits of biotechnological research, an endless source of fascination. Dependency—we all cozy up to it in secret and demonize it in public.

To be dependent is to be ill, necessarily, because that's what you're told . . . To be dependent on a body, a liquid, an object that becomes fetishized, a ritual, a game, a screen—it's all suspect. And yet, this is where we all start life, in the most naked dependency. Violent, in fact. And our anxieties or our fears sometimes restore us to this newborn's body at the mercy of hunger, thirst, cold, waiting, pain, and the unknown. The sensations that we experience during the first weeks of life are still there, intact, and a particularly strong wave of melancholy is enough to conjure up this body and bend our adult body back toward it. The newborn is handed over to the other, not only to the good will of her caresses, to care lavished with more or less attention (I avoid the word "love" by design), but also to the moods of her parents, her eventual siblings, and her nannies, no less than to what traverses her from inside, since, just after birth, most likely she remains less detached from the mother and the uterine world than her body is. And when she looks at us with this gaze that, we are told, doesn't yet "see" us, what does she actually perceive? When an adult in an abusive relationship lets herself be treated like garbage, the body of the very little child is what speaks in her and thereby reclaims the attention that no adult is able, or was able, to lavish upon it.

This state of primal dependency, we constantly seek it out and flee from it with the same energy. We play hide-and-seek as grown-ups, having forgotten our childhood somewhere along the line, with the pillow fights, the secrets, the narrow escapes; but who knows what we are looking for, there, among the faces and the nudity of bodies in the openwork weave of landscapes.

To take the risk of dependency is a sign of friendship for this body from just after birth. But this is not all. It is also to think, much like a vaccine that cures a body of a virus by inoculating it with a small dose of the same virus, letting it declare and construct its own defenses, that it's better—even enjoyable—to let our dependencies grow, as in an English garden that keeps wild grasses mixed in with the thyme and dahlias. Not to flee but rather to apprehend them, to lend them our intelligence. Love—now I risk the word, a bit apprehensively to be sure—is an art of dependency. It supposes that one puts oneself at risk. Admitting defeat, senseless expectation, the despair of brusque rejection from the other, letting oneself be devastated by a pain that, it seems at the time, will never end. This acquiescence to dependency is something other than resignation, which suffuses the soul with a fatal venom that sets up any subsequent depression, as when a river dammed up for too long dumps into a swamp. Love is the event that makes us capable of transport into the other, of the act of desertion whereby we choose the adversary over ourselves. Love happens in spite of violence, stupidity, style, envy, and our dreams; it is also constantly ill-timed. In ravishment and disgust, it is a self-dispossession, a disavowal. We have no idea what chimeras are imprinted within us from the first hours of life and that will remerge later, for instance, in the attachment to a certain color of skin, to a certain odor, to this person's gesture, that person's poise, this accent, this slight movement of the hips, this spacing between words.

If dependency is temptation, then we have it to thank for bringing back the figure of the devil. The tempter who engulfed Job in trials speaks the human condition. Provocation is that to which we might succumb. I mean that even if we resist temptation, if we keep our sights on the tempter as the very special enemy to whom "no" will always be the answer, this refusal is still a form of dependency because he, too, thereby holds us in regard, obliging us to think about him a little every day, if not at every instant. Each of us, in our own manner, deals with the devil. Each has an ongoing conversation with him that she tries to keep totally secret.

In addition, we are not aware of our own dependencies . . . You can know yourself dependent, more or less remorsefully, on condensed milk, on the swallows' cry above the Roman rooftops in springtime, on the adrenaline rush of climbing a rock face with ropes in the midst of a summer sky at three o'clock in the morning, on high heels that carry the ankles like a light handle, on a certain perfume, on porn videos, on lavender honey, on the color red, on bad wine, on staying up all night, on knowing how someone's skin feels before touching it, on B-movies, on fly fishing, on dreaming. But this is only a sketch of the familiar landscape of our addictions. The rest is immersed in night. The night of our humanity. A night that no analysis can penetrate but only skim and perhaps learn to name as one learns words in a foreign language. Because this night is given birth within the uterine body that we no longer remember at all but that still constitutes and carries us.

It is dangerous to underestimate the devil; it is vain to believe that the sheer force of will is enough to ward off temptation—we know this much. It is naïve to imagine that one can be rid of temptation by giving in to it. The hold temptation has over us is strengthened no less by refusal than by the act of yielding to it. Bulimics know this perfectly well, no less than their anorexic kindred: the temptation to reach the limit of the hunger that overwhelms them at every instant ultimately leaves them drained and disgusted with themselves, a state from which they will never be delivered by a pact with hunger, in whatever form it takes. But perhaps it is simply not a matter of wanting to be delivered . . .

To depend on another is not necessarily to surrender body and soul. There is perhaps in this vicinity a "weak" ethics to be found, a minimalist thinking that would attach to the details, the conjunctures, and the minuscule signs of acquiescence of which we are capable in our conversation with the real, and at that moment we can invent eras of microdependency, very tiny landscapes of very violent attachments, with a few bubbles up in the air, as light as dragonfly wings.

Voluntary Servitude and Disobedience

Never will servitude have been so voluntary. How did we get here? To will our servility with all our might, to cherish our bonds, indulgently to regard hierarchies, obedience, and diktats knotted for our own good around our lives like pretty colored ribbons destined to make us forget the iron padlock that fastens them.

Of course this servitude borrows other carefully chosen names. Just as we no longer say "maid" or even "cleaning woman" but rather "household assistant," so we speak of security standards, of public surveillance for a more tranquil life, which everyone hopes for, of increased juridical protection, of elementary safety precautions. It is a question of living better, ergonomics, noncontamination—in brief, maximum security. Oh yes! We are free, of course . . . Free, first of all, not to subscribe to any of it. It is like a damage waiver,[1] the never-ending and migraine-inducing calculation of probabilities, which you countersign, heeding the little voice that urges you to do it. Taste dictates that one extol the principle of disobedience but act like a well-behaved, patient citizen, complacent but not ungrateful to a democracy that does the best it can. "A century ahead of time," writes Annie Le Brun, "Alfred Jarry identified the things that our world seeks to liquidate: my singularity, love, and recklessness. However, he also foresaw the monstrous way in which this liquidation would occur, *with the manufacture of soul.*[2]

Taking the risk of disobeying supposes the capacity to obey—an other obedience, if you will—at the behest of something other than the conscious ego. Otherwise, disobedience becomes mere caprice, nothing more than bravado or unpremeditated acts under the sway of drives that are more or less justified after the fact. To obey is first to be able to speak. To have entered the grammar of a language, to have espoused its codes the better to subvert them, to retread the path that goes from Joyce back to Bescherelle. Language is the first place of our obedience; it is the nonciphered arithmetic of a memory, a civilization, a transmission—the first condition of our possibility for disobedience. Like any true ethics, language opens many passageways, but, above all, a certain relation of otherness to oneself. Understanding that obeying is reflexive, the English say *self-obedience*, coining a term that we lack in French. Self-obedience would be to respect the fact that we are not entirely subjective, that the ego is only a part of ourselves, albeit the part that governs us and founds our identity. But certain experiences do not demand the consent of a subject; they simply "happen" and happen to us, that's all, and we happen to be at this specific place for just a moment, just for an event of this world. To be obedient "to oneself" is to recognize the existence of an inalienable place that the subjective does not entirely contain. In the Middle Ages, the "heart of hearts" [*for intérieur*] perhaps designated, albeit with manifestly spiritual overtones, this "other" space inside of oneself that, even under torture, cannot be surrendered—by which I mean that, even in confessing, a person does not have the power to offer up to her tormentor this impregnable and universal place of her freedom.

Would disobedience merely be second obedience, in the Kierkegaardian sense, far from the blind loyalties that urge us to renunciation and compromise? Perhaps one should begin there . . . to act upon this self-obedience that makes it possible to say no. We are human because we are beings of language and promise, but we are also in large part immersed in the immanent experience of the world. Disobedience is the traversal of mirages, a manner of lightheartedly breaking bonds, because one has agreed to lose everything, including life. Yes, there is a gentleness of insolence that is stronger than any tyranny, but it is also the breeziness of humor. In the face of the ineluctable, wit abides. Another response is possible; one can step aside, no matter where one happens to be. To disobey is among the greatest risks because the cataclysm that it triggers is incommensurate with what it opposes. There where resignation is demanded, it remains possible, not to settle, or to argue, but simply to "prefer not to."

In Suspense

Desire is knowledge deferred, but made visible in the
impatience of the suspense in which it is held.

—MICHEL FOUCAULT, *Lectures on the Will to Know*

To be in suspense is to hold your breath. And to look with as much attention as possible at what is simply there, at what offers itself to you in the
presence of things.

The ordeal is in this balance conquered above the void: at every moment, it could be lost. The high-wire artist risks falling, most of all when
he holds still, when he attempts to stay in place, almost without moving a
muscle. He must restrain the very momentum that gives him stability. As
a high-wire artist, he prefers to attempt this miracle of suspense out on the
wire. It might be said that he is waiting—but something else is happening. Suspension is not the arrested time that comes *before* something else
happens; it is the event itself—the passage into the intimate time where, in
reality, the decision has already been made but no one knows it yet.

Taking the risk of being in suspense is rather acrobatic, therefore. We
admire the force and suppleness of the trapeze artists who open their arms
into the void, and their particular way of attempting the leap. Brief glimpses
of takeoff. When it comes to philosophy, the expected qualities are the same
. . . except that there are neither platforms, nor trapezes, nor people to catch
you; you proceed blindly with a certain idea of truth to delimit the arena.

13

Suspending judgment, from ancient Greece to Descartes, is the moment of crisis, the place of the *epoché*. Of philosophizing itself. It is to be suspended upon a conceptual swing without ever really touching ground, and to choose *not to* . . . Not to judge, not to decide, not to act. Not yet, not right now. To remain as long as possible in this untenable posture that internally commands you to remain at the disposal of . . . And not to trust any prefabricated or predigested concept. To remain as far as possible from thinking calcified into postures, responses, and certainties, but still to think.

Suspense is a negation of action that would be action itself, as Far Eastern civilizations have perfectly described. To suspend is not to wait, to delay out of fear or indecision. It does not imply an eventual passage to the act; it can also erase itself, dissolve into its own withdrawal. It is already the event itself in its effective "nonaction."

Cameras produce suspense in the form of still images. Their function: the pause.

What risk do we take when we suspend a decision—a marriage, a dirty trick, a craving for sweets, a decision to die? Do we wager that something else will intervene, that an inner determination, a sort of slow upheaval will carry our being away down an imperious path? The die is cast and we wish to be relieved of fate, joyous (more or less) marionettes in a world of dupes. Suspense causes us to doubt our very identity, Descartes tells us in *Meditations*. Doubt is the acolyte of suspense—its gravedigger, its messenger. The subject of doubt claims the right not to believe what she sees, to examine the very thing that she doubts, to encircle the enemy's territory. Does suspending the faculty of judgment offer the same refuge or is it merely an unconscious maneuver to delay the inevitable? If doubt is the actualization of thinking itself and not only a triage station for sorting what stays or goes, what must be thought or not, then we should apprehend a mode of being in suspense that is lighter, more metaphysical, and more overwhelming than any belief.

This, we might recall, is a function of what Kant calls the aesthetic Idea: through it, imagination does violence to understanding by forcing it to "think more," even though this surplus of thinking can never be grasped in an adequate concept (cf. *Critique of Judgment*, §49). If the aesthetic idea manifest in a sensible form remains unreachable, it is because there is no way to make it correspond to any determined content of consciousness. Is the aesthetic idea, mobilizing a supposedly deceptive emotion, a suspension of the true? Is this risk, solely represented in an embodied Idea, enough to awaken a different relation to what commonly we call the real?

In our latitudes, the imaginary generally calls up an age-old mistrust. It is reduced to a subaltern function, a cheap escape for weary minds. We take flight, so we say, into an imaginary world. In Pascal's most beautiful pages on distraction, once again he presents the faculty of imagination in the guise of escape from self, flight beyond the world, and the mirages of attachment. Yet this "suspense" of the imaginary gives rise to creation as creativity and not simply—as too often thought—as the capacity to produce illusion, chimera, and disavowal. In our relation to imagination and the possibility of suspending judgment, the will is what finds itself thwarted from acting and must undergo, with the wire walker's step that I evoked a moment ago, its own essential passivity.

It is dangerous to undermine the belief that the subject might regain her "self" and construct herself through an immediate decision. This belief forms the armature of our myths, the very root of the political. But it is mere fiction that the subject will find herself in action, a greater fiction than anything else. But it is attractive. We have such a strong desire to recognize ourselves in our acts, our judgments, our assertions. Whereas, in fact, metaphors, nebulous images, and uncertainties describe us best. Being in suspense returns us to the penumbra, to a point of relative blindness, and to a certain manner of holding fast to this point. Holding fast, something else appears, another limit, another shore.

When the subject does not succumb to the mirages of intentionality, when she attempts to disengage from her acts, from her projections, from her movements of identification, she ends up, in a certain sense, disgorging subjectivity itself. A sort of universality is experienced at this threshold. The wire walker's step, suspended so close to the void, is perhaps not so much that of the person walking but rather of a whole body become balance. The suspension of judgment is difficult and highly artificial; it is an exhausting exercise, because what the subject risks encountering is something heterogeneous to its nature. Something that cannot be absorbed into her identity, arriving from the unfamiliar, untamed borderlands of the real. This is what horrifies the ordinary neurotic, whose principal impulse is, at any price, to make the unknown known again. Philosophy, by essence the first space for questioning, is an art of suspense.

"Tell me what I should do. I just don't know anymore. I don't understand anything anymore. I obsess. I haven't been able to sleep. What should I do? Give me an answer . . ."

The silence of the analyst opens a suspense. It is not a nonresponse or a nonreception; it is an engagement with the nonresolution of an act, an invitation to take further risks, to hold unbearable contradictions within oneself and bring them alive.

"You do not answer . . . then why do I even speak to you? Why do I come here each week to hurl myself against your silence? And yet, if you weren't there, I wouldn't still be standing. I just wish so much that you could point out a somewhat clear path to me, a direction to go in . . ."

To suspend, this is also what the analyst attempts to do. Not to judge but to let resonate in herself the patient's speech, her asphyxiated dreams, her devastated expectations, her renunciations—to listen to the tyranny that lies under the complaint, the onrush of tears beneath the façade of happiness, the terror before the unknown. Again and again. In this suspense for two, the ordinary limits of the ego are skirted into a vaster space where there is no need to decide but only to let happen. To suspend, yes, but together. In a common space, an instant is set aside in which nothing need be decided, nor learned, nor expected, nor (above all) renounced. To let a thread of a truth bare itself, a truth that cannot be demanded. Even less could it become the object of a deal or a debt. A truth evinced that arrives just like a letter arrives, one day. The "in suspense" is contiguous to the space of the love letter, to an inner retreat, necessarily spiritual, whatever these words designate. How to take the risk of protecting this retreat without haste or violence? To linger there where thinking—which is also to say, emotion—moves. Not to destroy anything, to observe, to pacify. To let thinking unfold, extend, and emerge from its errors. Then the world gets lighter.

At the Risk of Passion

Nothing takes care of passion but passion.

—CHARLES FOURIER

Passion is not advisable. And yet, everyone keeps watch for it; everyone secretly wants to catch this mortal illness. Ruin of the family, destruction of a slow burning and true love life, little factory of amorous mirages, toxic source of attachment, illusory imprint, machinery of a desire that wishes to be eternal but always turns out to be ephemeral and essentially narcissistic, throughout history passion has been accused of every ill and awaited in secret by all.

And yet, passion is a risk we all take because our will is so paralyzed when the conjugated effects of the flesh and the heart overwhelm our affects without possible escape. At a minimum, it arises and launches us into the strange ballet of misrecognition: tell me who I am and I will love you . . . this truth that one expects from the other is a weapon that can easily be turned against us.

But how can passion be a risk if it proves inevitable? It is a one-sided wager that commits you to chance, luck, or any other face of the unpredictable. This wager convokes you, in return, to exist within it—by which I mean that it takes hold of you, it is a state of being, a precipitate of time and the act in which you are wholly gathered, with unparalleled intensity.

This intensity is the brute name of passion. One can refuse it, close the
chapter of the book that Alice cracked open, not run after any white rabbits, and return to everyday life. Nothing is easier. Show over. But once
swept into the movement whereby everything lived takes on a different
quality, there is no going back to the language you used before; no word
retains the same flavor, the same sense; you no longer have the same body,
the same hunger.

Passion is the very substance of risk. It is the remainder of a passivity
within us that flares up with the least abrasion, with the possible inversion of night into light, of ice into torrent, or of silence into a cry; it is our
capacity to imagine, to be astonished, to be disappointed, impressed, or
undone by something inside us that compels us to love this skin, this gaze,
this accent, every detail of this being astir right in front of us, a brief apparition of naked life.

Etymologically speaking, passion comes from *passio*, the action of un-
dergoing, the fact that to experience passivity at the cardinal point of our
being is also to accept being left in the unknown, losing your points of
reference and sometimes your very identity. One can choose a path but not
tell the wind where to blow. You attempt to master your heart or at least the
acts that issue from it. Believing it possible is enough most of the time.

Elie During says it remarkably well: "If love has never been what makes
'one' of two beings, but rather, on the contrary, disjoins them from one
another and each from himself, then its condition is the impossible self-
coincidence in which desire is conjugated with death."[1] Everything is a
matter of consent, or of refusal. This is our responsibility, to say yes or no.
And how do you love and never forget that you have loved—in spite of the
betrayals, wrongs, denials, nobility, generosity, and yes, even in pain? To
hold fast. The pure enchantment of this light . . . like joy, you can either
delve into it or not let yourself be affected. Passion is not possession. It is
espousing a movement that dispossesses and reveals you at the same time.
Against the common wisdom, there is a terrible truth in passion. *A sharp
edge.*[2] It is accepting the inadequacy, the discrepancy, the inequality that
inhabits any fusion and is delivered from it; but it is a birth for one who
really gives in to it.

To abandon yourself—who among us is capable of this? I mean truly
abandon yourself, for once in your life, unreservedly. Abandon yourself
supposes an other to whom you abandon yourself, an other who does not
demand as much, who is also afraid, and who protects herself. To abandon yourself is to confront abandonment, the fear lurking deep within us
that never lets us out of its sight. Illusion—but of what? Of promises of

forever, of fidelity? Yes. Of peaceful life, of forgetting, of violence against the family? Yes. Passion is torturous. It makes waiting an infernal ordeal. Delay lends itself to a thousand imaginings. Any breach of trust becomes a potential terror in which betrayal already looms. What passion gives us to live comes only at such a price: exorbitant.

Passion brings us back to the ancient opposition between nature and culture, to the primitiveness that Kierkegaard describes, to an unclaimed terror without language, and to savagery, as if murder and passion were always bound up with one another. And what if, on the contrary, passion was liberating, if it *broke us free*?[3] What if, inversely, passion elevated us— in the sense of a paradoxical education of the soul—and was extremely troubling? What if it convoked us to refinement, to the lovable, to the instant, to the wisdom of the body, to be grateful for what is given rather than what is owed? What if its value resided in intensity rather than in anxiety, in penumbra rather than in daylight? The most painful thing about passion is that it drives us to betray our promises, our attachments, and our moral principles, or to hurt those we love. This is why we often prefer to renounce passion, to turn away from it.

She could not stop speaking and sobbing. Her words got lost in her tears and came out scrambled, or blurred, giving the impression of an incredible mishmash. A cloying and sugary stew. She lay on the couch and spoke almost without taking a single breath, spoke of him without stopping, of missing him to death, suddenly interrupting herself sometimes for a second to say, straining back toward the analyst, up on one elbow, "There is no way you can understand, this is all pointless," and then she curled up again, the dark stain of her body on the worn velvet, her voice distraught. She spoke of the man who left her for reasons that she found absurd, and yet she said he would never come back; the very ridiculousness of this reason made getting back together impossible; everything was ruined, permanently. Nothing other was imaginable anymore. In this breakup, she became a pure reverberation of the pain of lack. The sessions went on like this until, one day, the psychoanalyst noticed a particularly beautiful pigeon at her window. He became absorbed in contemplation of the bird while the patient unfurled her suffering, the impossible suture of a devastated love. As a result, he missed the last few words. After which, she fell silent. This abrupt silence was upsetting. He very quickly sought to reconstruct what had just been said, but to no avail. He returned to the pigeon, which had flown off. And she wasn't crying. She said nothing.

Petrified, he no longer even dared to look at her. The silence was supernatural. But what did she say, finally, to put an end to this blizzard of words against the background of a war that had been lost?

So he remained silent as well.

Six minutes went by and each minute seemed three times as long. The bird didn't return; but the analyst kept watching for it, as if the bird's reappearance could bring back the memory of words lost to an attention that was not only float-ing but above all distracted by an animal with a fine white border that had the privilege of flying off over the rooftops.

"He didn't love me anymore, I think."

Her voice was no longer the same. As if she had climbed out of an immense sadness, dragging with her a fund of empty sobs, she was clear, articulate, and precise.

"I was crying over a phantom, a love that no longer existed. It was killing me. I had even filled my pockets with rocks in order to drown myself. Look, I kept one."

From her pocket she took a medium-sized stone, of a slightly irregular shape, light gray and white like those found in Bretagne.

"I have a lot just like this one, oh sure! They wouldn't have been enough—but with the cold and the dark, who knows? To whom would I have given all this love, can you tell me?"

The silenced analyst hardly dares to breathe; he has trouble believing what he is hearing; he doesn't recognize anything, as if it's from a forbidden radio frequency, with unknown acoustic signals. This woman, his patient for nine years, he no lon-ger knew who she was . . . All of a sudden, everything was effaced—her history, her tears, the mad and devouring passion that left no room for her life. He only said to himself that the bird would never return, nor would she; that he understood nothing, heard nothing; that something unprecedented happened in the lapse of time—a few minutes, seconds?—when he got lost in contemplation of the bird; that speech can sometimes return all at once and along with it freedom.

Each of us hopes for passion; each hopes for it and runs from it, al-ways keeping our guard up in the face of this imaginary enemy who makes us abdicate everything in favor of a violent servitude. Inextinguishable. Hours spent waiting, crying, falling to pieces. There is a sort of astonish-ment from which one never recovers. A quality of presence that Virginia Woolf, in *To the Lighthouse*, transcribed almost blindly, a light dusting of vacuity, things superimposed on one another, on the horizon, gossamer layers of insomnia, skin against skin, forgetting, dreams, memory, highly saturated life.

We want intensity without risk. Which is impossible. Intensity is the leap into the void, the unknown part of ourselves that has yet to be written and yet awaits us, some precise thing. Passion is a disposition born within us since childhood that can be enlarged or diminished—but totally altered, never. Like Kierkegaard's knight of faith, it demands passage to the infi-nite, a hyperbole. The path is not defined, nor the how, nor the conventions, nor the reason that might show the way. Love harbors such risks. And yet it remains plagued by so many repetitions . . . For, afterward, so soon after the initial vertigo, fear takes over, and then it's just the same old patterns that don't take long to register the defeat of feeling. What then? Must we not believe in renunciations, alibis, oaths, mirages, and yet love? Knowing that desire is what wants, everything falls into place around it, more or less secretly. And desire is attached to the body—but a body outside the body, which is the soul as well, impossible to gather in a word, in a vision, or in an act. No pact can determine its limits or duration, except for sex that does not exhaust itself in *jouissance* or in repetition. Who would wish for such deliverance?

But there is another passion, or at least an event that goes by the name of Passion, that of Christ. The passion of incarnation, of a god made man. Does this Passion simply designate martyrdom, the tormented body of he who let himself be condemned and betrayed by a friend? Or does this word designate another event that gestures, amidst humility and betrayal, toward another possibility of the most sacred, that evokes acquiescence to an absolute elsewhere? Whether we are believers or not, this Passion belongs to our memory, to our relation to the world and language. Every passion, in this sense, pays tribute to this other, Christic scene, which offers us the possibility of turning savagery into grace.

Leaving the Family

The bourgeois family, thanks to the combined efforts of the Napoleonic Code and Hegelian philosophy, has received the justification of an ethics grounded in economy and the assurance of its perpetuation. From the simple social contract that ensures the cohesion of the species and the name, to the transmission of a heritage and culture, from one war to the next, the family saw itself increasingly freighted with an ideal whereby what one persists in calling "love" is measured in terms of specific facts and weighty responsibilities. Since then, times have changed it seems. As family bonds loosen, however, haven't we seen the ideal become more firmly fixed? And a certain idea of love perpetually brought back within the familial fold? Starting a family, indeed, remains the supreme commitment. We prostrate ourselves on the altar of an immobile eternity in which Prince Charming embraces Snow White under a leaden sky while the weeping dwarves promise they will have many children. We applaud. Entertainment magazines such as *Gala* and *VSD* have replaced the Brothers Grimm but nothing, or almost nothing, has changed. We say goodbye to love or to children but not the family; we confine ourselves to narrow circles of artists or doctors and with studied behaviors, we produce eternal adolescents, little clones seriously committed to replicating their elders, all the same.

To leave one's family, origin, city of birth, the déjà vu and the assurance of seamless familiarity—what singular life does not come at such a price? Being unfaithful—psychically, genealogically—to what has not been handed down with love but ordered, psychologically, genealogically, under threat of destitution. The initiatory ordeal of a second birth is always, and more than ever, necessary. We must depart, extract ourselves from our codes, our allegiances, our heritage. Any work comes at such a price. And any love, I believe. Depression is the flipside of departure. It is not being able to disentangle oneself, to dispossess oneself, or to disburden oneself in time, to ditch everything in order to risk one's life.

To leave the family is also to mourn an originary place to which one belongs by right or even in fact, a place that would hold the key to our intimate belonging, to our ability to be recognized. This standard measure whereby—alas—everything else is evaluated will never restore what has been lost (a childhood, a first love)—that is, the burden of a debt that is incommensurable with all else. Nothing could ever erase this expectation; the verdict will always be adverse; Kafka will always be sent to his room, far from Felice.

Leaving the family behind opens toward the risk of love. Toward a certain coldness of heart. For love is no downy nest, nor is it a tangled web of hatred and envy in which we seek to curl up over and over again. No, love is often frigid. It arises with the irreparable, wounds, remorse, jealousy and forgiveness, expectation, and solitude—everything contrary to what goes by the name of love also comes with actual love. This freedom gained at the price of blood relations can also help us to love our family members, but from an *other* place, not more detached, but free of the debt that commands obedience and compels acquiescence to all violence. The risk of leaving the family is an unrealized elegy to the fugue, to distance, to evasion. To that in us that is capable of being disoriented.

Why is the family so often a hell, forgiven each time it begins all over again, whose singular imprint or flavor we seek to regain throughout lives? What should be believe? We are fortune tellers, soothsayers; we are afraid of being abandoned so we create refuges the better to destroy them, abandon them, or let them perish. There is no end to leaving the family except by recreating friendship and intelligence with blood relations; it is a movement without remorse, passionate, slightly mad, to find elsewhere what makes of us beings capable of love and joy, liberated from the scenarios of a past outside of memory.

Forgetting, Anamnesis, Deliverance

> So we beat on, boats against the current,
> borne back ceaselessly into the past.
>
> —F. SCOTT FITZGERALD, *The Great Gatsby*

To remember is to forget. We live in an amnesiac epoch that venerates memory as never before. Digitized, formatted, and extolled, but contracted out for a fee, we want to protect it at all costs, to construct altars to it, and be able to access it at any time. Everything is a pretext to struggle against forgetting: museums, foundations, archives, recordings, posthumous publications; whatever means are used to exhume, to postdate, to rediscover, to date, or to classify, they will become necessary. More than ever before, our civilization seeks to commit to memory—definitively, technologically, and unassailably—its past betrayals and omissions no less than its glory. Any effacement is suspect, likewise any distraction; and the irreversible disappearance of a clue, or even a memory, is graver still. Even in psychoanalysis, the issue has been decided: one never forgets anything. Somewhere in the obscure chamber of memory, it is ordained that everything will remain engraved. It will be returned to you. Keep your hopes up, even forgetting won't last forever. For, such effacement is the mark of a sterile lack, a grave inconsistency. Yes, the possibility of forgetting—yourself or the world—is more and more intolerable to us. It confronts us with our incapacity to learn lessons from history writ large, or even from our small personal histories . . . as if it permitted the endless repetition of the errors, the failures, and the blindness that presides over crime. It legitimates in some way our guilty amnesia. And the repetition that it authorizes forms a strange litany.

In early childhood, forgetting is acceptable. With lassitude, like an overtaxed mother, we abandon this past since, from these early years, almost nothing remains but scraps of memory that might have been altered, decomposed, and recomposed by design. And this remainder makes a past that suits our needs. Nietzsche writes: "A thing must be burnt in so that it stays in the memory: only something that continues to hurt stays in the memory."[1]

Safekeeping, today, is a matter of urgency. Everything, no matter what, just don't let it get lost, for pity's sake. Come on, still not enough. Not only must we rescue the endangered species on our planet, we are also summoned to fight like a prostrate army against all forgetting. It is necessary to understand . . . Forgetting is an attack on the work of memory—that is, on humanity's duty to itself to remember. Magical fiction. Utopia against disaster. And the living past that this humanity—ours—would like endlessly to archive is a storehouse of testimonies to genocide, to attacks, to unprecedented forms of violence, retrieving from silence the destiny of the sacrificed. The desire for archives is important; it is indeed a duty to remember; but no "archive fever" will relieve us of our responsibility—collectively and singularly—for what happened. The struggle against forgetting has been extended in a troubling way to all forms of safekeeping, perhaps helping us to avoid a different, savage relationship to our past. The cheap, globalized discourse of guilt that surrounds big events, their anniversaries insipidly solemnized in the media, becomes a front for the distraction, in the Pascalian sense, that has taken hold of a civilization haunted by its past but dancing on its dead.

We are, we will be—the accusation is hereby leveled—guilty of non-memory, of self-possessiveness: by name, by identity, by genealogical traceability, by address, by milieu. Forgetting sows disorder; just imagine, you might almost forget yourself . . . From the viewpoint of social, moral, and personal conscience, forgetting is treated as a sort of suspect free zone, in the image of countries that harbor off-shore investment schemes. Amnesia is tolerated only if judged politically indispensable.

Forgetting slips between our fingers like sand, or smoke; it thwarts closure, certainty. Strangely, it has much in common with ecstasy. Forgetting unsettles everything that sustains the subject—her objects, rituals, certainties, discoveries. It has capricious affinities with death, like the effacement of traces, of everything that constituted an existence. It gestures toward the groundlessness from which we emerge, reminds us that, four generations from now, at best no more will remain of a single life than an anecdote, a piece of writing, a bad photo, and often nothing at all. Must we acknowledge, then, that erasure is met with erasure? To forget is a verb. A verb as paradoxical as can be, because it just takes from intelligence a share of its past and offers only night in return. To forget opens a space of availability to the unknown, to something whose possibility hasn't been safeguarded but that will still be delivered to us.

He had forgotten his name, his life. His memory was totaled along with his car in an accident that killed the wife whom he loved (so he was told). There were a few photos of her in their apartment, but they evoked nothing for him, except perhaps the admiration he could muster for her unaffected beauty, now shattered. Otherwise, he was unscathed, as people say. He would have preferred to leave behind a chunk of his body or to have a scar on his face, something that would at least attest to the shock that left him without a past, worse than someone born with X for a name. An adopted child can at least dream of his family, or grapple with his disgrace; he can concoct a story, hope that something will happen—be resolved, be revealed. He had nothing but scattered archives, the basis for a bad screenplay. Photos in two more or less unfinished albums made up the collage of a couple's life that he didn't understand in the least: a first marriage, no children, and then this apparently beloved woman who died right next to him, an old-time beauty, a type of very pale blond, her body bent out of shape. None of this managed to elicit any feeling, any emotion, an inkling of recognition . . . He had had a profession, as his papers bore witness: an architect (not so bad) of gardens (bizarre), and recently (according to invoices) he had even specialized in golf course design, which today could not seem more absurd (since he wouldn't even know by which end to grip a club).

He was sent to a "shrink." To ask what . . . ? To bring back emotions that he knew were irrecoverable? To attempt to piece together lost images, patiently, one by one, while going over each clue from his past or to invent himself a new past? To help him connect to something, no matter how slight, that might provide a trace, furrow the violent waters of forgetfulness? He didn't believe it. He went to devise a formula for survival—for now.

"But," I ask him, "from what did you wish to be so brutally delivered?"

He seemed tired. Possibly drank too much, with rosacea and white hair, but otherwise he had a rather handsome Roman appearance. Of Italian origin, judging by his name. But the origin is precisely what escaped him, and especially to feel it as his own.

"*Delivered? But from nothing! In any event, I couldn't be now, right? I'll always lose at this game because I have forgotten who I was. I only have scraps of dreams to tell and they make me want to vomit. It was an accident, I mean truly an accident. The other car ran a red light. He was ok, not us. That's how it is. Nothing to blame but chance.*"

"*And now*"

"*You are asking what I expect from you, right? That you give me back the desire to invent an identity, not just any identity but almost... provided that I feel something.*"

"*If you don't feel anything, then it's not just forgetting. Forgetting manages only memories, not the sensorium, and even less the emotional register. Whence my first question . . . which chance alone cannot answer.*"

"*And so no more than chance can, you can do nothing for me. It would seem that you're a manager of memories, you oversee clearance sales, wholesale and retail.*"

I smiled.

"*You know perfectly well that you will not find an ad hoc identity here, but at most a new manner of gaining access to the elements that compose you, to what keeps you together, what animates you. Burnt skin, grafted skin, continues to be your skin, and remains organically bound to your body, otherwise it would die, rot, and so would you. You need to find a self-graft that takes.*"

"*I could begin with this woman, try to understand who she was, how I loved her, what we did together. She was alive not so long ago.*"

"*Instead, look there where you—you died*"

"*Is that a hint? Advice? A path to follow?*"

"*It is what I feel.*"

I thought that feeling was precisely what he was exiled from; that return-ing to what in him was cut off from all feeling would be impossible; that in this distressing zone where everything was blank, undifferentiated, there would be an imprint, a thought that would tell him not who he used to be but rather who he might perhaps become, like the core of a rope around which the strands are braided. To discover whether a small remnant could be saved, it would no longer suffice to wander around looking in the penumbra; he would have to follow to the trail of crumbs that he had relegated to the hallway, there where he was today, he who wasn't so dead.

What can you, what do you *want* to save from oblivion—that is, what do you want, among everything that has been forgotten, not to find again but to make come back as if by miracle to the surface of the world? To enact this sudden grace that, suddenly, renders present what had been subtracted, then erased. Along with the impossible return to self whose price only amnesiacs know.

The analysis would last a few years. The memories never came back. But something, out of oblivion, did come. Came back within the very time of what should be called a new life. An other love, an other apartment, different tastes, and a profession that happened almost by chance. Thanks to a passion for scuba diving in which it turned out that he was especially gifted, he became a deep sea diving instructor. There couldn't be a more precise metaphor for what he gave up looking for in himself—the traces, the vestiges, the unexploited, and unfindable resources of what had constituted what is commonly called an identity. What came back was the sensation of having a body. His own—that is, a body that also came from the past, made of images and fears, hesitations, sensitivities, and urges that came from beyond him; and little by little this body took its place within him like a transplanted heart, not entirely foreign and not yet himself. In a sense, forgetting became his friend—a risk run, yes, like a risky hand in poker that you play anyway to see what happens.

Isn't forgetting a reserve of time—of love—afforded for what remains? A civilization that refuses to forget anything condemns us to live as amnesiacs, given that all recording gets exported outside of us, outside of our control, decreeing that it will now be taken care of for us, like so many other things. "But it is necessary to ask," writes Emmanuel Lévinas, "whether the proper meaning of consciousness does not consist in being a vigilance backed against a possibility of sleep."[2] Forgetting, like sleep, is a deliverance, not only an agency of repression, avoidance, and misrecognition. What it delivers is not the same thing as that from which it delivers *us*.

Incurable (In)fidelities

It is the faithless who know love's tragedies.

—OSCAR WILDE, *The Picture of Dorian Gray*

Infidelity is a wound, for each of us, often incurable. Infidelity to whom, to what? The term supposes, implicitly, more primordially than all else, a promised, supposed, or wished for fidelity that forms the horizon of our attachments. But what if being unfaithful was the risk, who knows, of the greatest love?

Juxtaposed instants. A garden, a river—the river. Literature, the river again. Gentle evenings like orgies in which nothing happens. August nights, planets in slow revolution. Slow rock 'n' roll, friendship. But a friendship that would just be love, nothing other. Two little girls in white dresses lying in the too big hammock. Their shining eyes, their lust for life and their insouciance. A ribbon of music unfurling the whole time. The death of a very old and beloved lady, interred with a psalm and the whole memory of generations—in her, with her, carried away. Other mornings, the river yet again, the noise of branches lapping the water in summer. And what if all this happened to disappear? To believe that it will last indefinitely, with slight and loving displacements of things, the planting of linden trees, a basin carried from one house to another, old garden lavender and roses, a sour lemon tart, duck confits and wine to get slightly drunk on evenings when, like lost children, you promise to grow old together and stay in love forever.

I listen. The evocation of that summer sends me back to my own life, to summers long gone, to the laughter of children not yet grown, to the diffuse warmth of August mingled with the torpor of bodies, to interminable siestas, and to boredom as well. The patient continues her evocation and there is a sad quality in her voice that I would like to be able to grasp, protect from a more brutal attack. From a fracture? She tells me that everything happened because a door slammed shut. Just like that, a gust of air through the old house not far from the river. It was on the second floor; she had gone upstairs to close the window. That's where she heard his voice. He was talking to someone, on the telephone, in a voice that she didn't recognize. In spite of herself, she stopped. The walls were very thin so she even heard him whispering. Which is when her heart started to beat violently, like when a child's emotion is so strong she seems about to faint. And yet it was nothing serious, just the tone of this amorous voice that had broken into the old house. His voice was so tender, that was it no doubt, she heard the words that he uttered to another: "I wish you were here, with me." And then the murmur again, which bespoke the desire to make love, at once arousal and gentleness. She entered the room, the conversation had stopped. Interrupted as an effect of her own arrival, of her obvious distress. He had understood right away, had not hid anything, had not defended himself. He had remained silent.

"How do you accommodate such a thing from someone whom you love—another love?" she asks me. "I was the one who loves and who cries. I was the one who waits and who didn't want to interrupt anything, the one who seeks to know and who prefers not to know, who acquiesces and at the same time violently refuses. I understood that he wanted to live a hundred lives, that he sought excitement against boredom, not a boredom from childhood but the boredom of life itself, of being alive in spite of everything. This woman brought her sorrow and her vulnerability, with her lively sensibility and her queenly bearing. I had seen them together and yet I had seen nothing. Life isn't possible for him any other way, I know. He wouldn't want to hurt me, he just wanted it to be possible without inflicting pain . . . And I am devastated."

The session was almost over but I couldn't bring myself to say a word to signal the end, not then, not like that. When I don't know what to say and yet I feel I must offer the rescue of a word, I think of the Greeks, because they had the genius of their language, but also because in this detour and the avowal of my own incapacity to respond to the scandal of this woman's pain there is a link that I am trying to weave; because others have felt and thought the same thing; and there is no such thing as total isolation, even in the absolute solitude of the feeling of betrayal. I told her that the Greeks distinguished two movements within desire: the desire to consent to a choice and desire as desire. But do we know who stops at wanting and who desires? "We are women," writes Euripides. "Sometimes we fall prey to hesitation; sometimes our audacity is unsurpassed . . . Nature wanted someone with absolute disregard for the laws; and this is why woman was born."[1]

She turned back toward me and this *"turning back" pleased me. "You understand," she said, "I fought for him to speak to me, not to extort confessions (which confessions?) or to make him talk about her, or for myself, but rather for a precise risk, the risk of the truth of love. I don't care about the possession of bodies, nor vows and the lies that necessarily come with them. And he did speak, a little. The next day I wrote a very short message to this woman and she responded very simply. Just a few words that avowed her own love, with an infinite respect. I would have liked to write to her again . . . But I didn't. Do you understand? I became haunted. I was no longer at the river, I was no longer in the starry night, I had been caught up in this rupture that makes you disgorge such a strange ungraspable pain that no word could then nor can it now, even as I am speaking to you, here, render its madness. Its absurdity, its disorientation, its idiocy. It's a strange shipwreck, but why? Why this sadness, I don't know . . . I wanted to join them, to be with them, and I couldn't. Same as when I was a child, all the time."*

I thought that she, too, wanted to experience several lives, like him, or else why would she have sought this man before all others? Is it really believable that life strews our path with beings who are absolute strangers? What we call infidelity is a form of exile outside of oneself. We are castaways, stranded on islands as large as childhood from which we return utterly drained, full of nostalgia and terror. We want to be alone but in the midst of a party, together but also alone in the breadth of life; we want dreams in touch with other bodies, other desires, other lives, but we are afraid and sometimes we die, slowly, suffocated under the weight of loyalties we prefer to know nothing about. And when we discover that the other, the beloved is unfaithful, the world suddenly loses its meaning and its human measure. The very possibility of attachment is withdrawn, and speech along with it, its trustworthiness, its aid. Everything becomes a vector of possible betrayal. But love comes at such a price. Unfaithful we are, all of us will be, sooner or later. Neither skin nor sex impose a limit. Only spirit does, and the ties of the heart. The obsessive presence of an other, suddenly, within us.

"Doesn't infidelity begin with oneself?" I ask her as gently as possible. "Doesn't it begin with our own infinite misrecognition of ourselves, with the lies, the alibis, the pretexts, and the excuses that are born, with language itself as a weapon of desire?"

It is necessary to have loved, and betrayed, and suffered, and despaired of a love, and to have been undone and taken back and saved, in order to envisage, perhaps, that there is only infidelity where love is the greatest, but that, at the same time, love can only be risked at the price of truth—that is, of an impossible promise to belong completely to yourself and to

the other but as far as possible from any possession. We have to respond to
the other and for the other, wrote Lévinas, but no one belongs to anyone,
no more than we belong to ourselves, as psychotics often recall in their
violent and astonishing entirety.

Our incurable experiences of the other's infidelity take us back to the
primary tearing apart of the world that occurs after birth in which the separation from the mother and then her absence are imposed for the first time.
When does a nursling understand that she will no longer be "one/two" or
even indissolubly "with"—within the fetal fusion that was her life up to
this point—and that, from then on, a certain solitude will arm her days and
nights? What does she do with this knowledge? How does she transmute
this impotence (to make the other come closer to her, continuously) into a
desire for solitude? For, precisely, this incurable wound is fertile with the
possibility of any future amorous attachment. When does infidelity begin?
With an idea, a kiss, nudity, or a clandestine life? Doesn't it rather begin as
soon as it is represented, as soon as a thought of the other insinuates itself
within you in nearest proximity to your soul and your desiring body? No
matter what you do with this thought and this body, it never leaves you
and will live its own life and death, and won't necessarily coincide with
your acts or your will (many loves die before separation or resist it, going
well beyond—with a sort of animal life of their own). But our fidelities,
for their part, haunt us like so many imperatives whose purpose we ignore
while we bend to them as if our lives depended on it. Confronted with
this categorical imperative, we must invent true infidelities—open, fer-
vent, fertile lines of flight like those that Kerouac speaks of in *On the Road*,[2]
an immense metaphorical text about a wholly other freedom than that of
travel. And thus, taming our own necessary infidelity, we will perhaps discern in it a traversal that is not only betrayal but rather a manner of getting
lost in nearest proximity to yourself.

What is truly incurable is fidelity.

Zero Risk?

In a society where insurance is imposed on us in every domain, because no one is allowed to decline coverage anymore or simply make do without it, it has become useless to promote zero risk; it is a matter of course. Zero risk has become the obligatory horizon of our collective and individual decisions. A little money is all insurance seems to demand for itself to protect us against the occurrence of any type of accident. In reality, our perception of reality has been, as we say these days, reformatted. In her remarkable book *The Test Drive*, Avital Ronell recalls that the category of the test is universal. Humans, throughout history, have put at risk their freedom, their reason, their courage, and their limits, to the point of conceiving the Test itself as the force behind courage. The necessity to be insured only expanded in proportion to the logic of self-evaluation and the "testability" of things and beings.

The zero risk we end up with is deadly. It strips the subject of responsibility for her acts; it divides her from within into a being of the drive who risks anything and everything, a being who therefore must be protected by consent or by force against herself, and a being of reason who is never sufficiently reasonable. She is thus potentially a deviant or on the way to becoming a pathogenic individual. It is strange to think that no era has ever been more "secure" than ours and that nonetheless we all suffer from an ever growing disquiet that is incommensurable with any event, or I should say, any risk of an event. In the future, no doubt, we will be weighed down by genocides committed in wars so radically dehumanizing that, as of yet, they are inconceivable. Zero risk—in armed or diplomatic conflicts, or even in conflicts of interest between industrialized powers—tends, in contemporary wars, to be imposed as an ethical law. It's taken for granted that no one wants to "risk" losing human lives; war, from now on, should paradoxically be able to do without death. No longer allowing for death as a possibility or as a strategy, but only in terms of the necessity to avoid it, the first belligerent who agrees to go beyond this "zero risk" will prevail. It is kamikaze logic. You want to fight? Go ahead, put your life at risk. Hegel elaborated this logic a long time ago, but no doubt he hadn't anticipated the barbarism of our "clean" contemporary wars whose so-called "collateral" damage will henceforth entail more dead among the civilian population than the ranks of the military.

What remains, then . . . is a very narrow margin, empty space, time for nothing. Just sign, right there, on the dotted line as expected. For don't forget that your options aren't only about you but others as well. Risk is an outdated romanticism for adults who refuse to grow up, to assume their share of responsibility and compliantly entrust it to others who, in turn, will proceed to capitalize on it and save you from your own recklessness. Nor will delinquents the world over tell you otherwise, they who are summarily criminalized, in spite of their economic distress, the lack of education, the mismanagement of social services, plain ignorance, the defunding of schools, and the collapse of what's called order. Indeed, as Foucault describes so well, others impugn these delinquents in order to remind us every day what we have escaped. Nowhere are delinquents accepted anymore except in the highest echelons of the State, where they arrogate the privilege to be beyond laws and rights. The law has proliferated with so many edicts, amendments, and decrees of every kind that no jurist, qualified as she may be, could claim comprehensive expertise. All she can do is *interpret the law*. Cynicism and denunciation are de rigueur, tempered by a serenade of noble sentiments whose only value is that they go unquestioned. In our climate of ballyhooed economic austerity and political torpor, the prime necessity is to ensure against risks that, in concentric circles, domestic or planetary, create an atmosphere of diffuse fear and distilled anxiety for which we have no one to incriminate but ourselves, always underinsured.

The very utterance of zero risk is an absurdity because its actuality would annul the very reality of which it attempts to speak.

Peril must be faced head-on. This is the least among the forms of courage that might save us. We can always recover from pain, catastrophe, or mourning, but evil will always claim a share. We will never be saved in advance.

How (Not) to Become Oneself . . .

There is a profusion of books, seemingly, whose purpose is to show us the best way to "become oneself" and how to reach that goal. The *how-to* manuals that have met with such success on the other side of the Atlantic and now here in France as well (How to be happy? How to succeed in life? How to find happiness?) fuel the global market in re-assurance. The formulations designed to attract clients might change, but the discourse hardly does. Almost always such books deal with this gratifying search for self-realization—that is, the blossoming that neither you nor I will ever attain but that we all seem to expect from existence as manna from heaven.

But what does it mean, in reality, "to become oneself"? Aren't we already burdened enough with ourselves to look for yet another secret idyll with this fictive character that one keeps trying to know better? Doesn't it come down, once again, to the question: Do you love me? Unable to exist enough for others, we must recognize ourselves . . . Inclined to doubt and fragility, values today stigmatized as negative, we are offered teaching, courses and seminars in self-reeducation. Even psychoanalysis lends itself to such a project, although in more glorious times (I mean in less fainthearted times) it would have refused to support the artificial construction of narcissism, judging that the world already has more than enough of it, and that those who complain about their meager self-assurance have more than others.

Immanence is a concept without object because it includes, in advance, the whole of the given. It is a horizon line, at the junction of heaven and earth, a mute line that invites our gaze to reach beyond. The necessity for transcendence is undoubtedly the surest mark of the immanence of this world, of its very materiality, the imprint of its profuse prodigality. We move about in the face of events that infinitely exceed us, not because they come from a hither world, or an other world, but rather because they come together and apart without our help, like big animals at play; like ciphers that never cease to overflow the visible from all sides, to inform it, to give it form, image, and time; like the cinema that inscribes an inverted image, albeit in real time, of lives that might be our own. An event has its own density. When it happens, it is above and beyond—that is, without any place set aside for it within the skein of the real; and the occurrence of this pure accident creates a new life. Sometimes, the event anticipates the movement of an entire people; sometimes, as well, it creates something shared, a veritable communism of thought, together with the resolution to live rather than to die, to make die, or to let oneself die. To take the risk of immanence, wouldn't this mean that you begin to give up becoming yourself? In the sense in which this "self," which we are supposed to have recognized at any price and loved better, is still and always remains an imaginary projection born of our attachments, our fears, and our expectations . . . The most powerful experiences that we are given to live dissolve the "self" more than any negative resolution. Within the enlarged perception of the instant and of the world, within the instantaneous joy that they infuse, within the inner upheaval and the alleviation of all anxiety that they provoke, there arises a strange reconciliation, as if the real no longer offered any opposition.

We want insouciance at the expense of servitude. And without having to think such servitude. Psychoanalysis has attempted, for its part, to explore it—at least the pioneers did, Rivers, Freud, Ferenczi, Tausk, Lacan, Winnicott, and a few others: they reminded us that we are the inheritors of a history that traversed us but whose origin remained unknown; that we were infused with desires we would prefer to know nothing about, with obsolete and comforting ideals, and with a baby's skin turned upward to the firmament of adults, wrapped around our hearts up to the instant of our death; and that, in addition, we *wanted* all of it . . . We drank it in with delectation and imagination, and sometimes fanaticism. Whereas we never cease to forget and to receive untimely reminders of our being mortal. To admit that we can do something other than be victims of circumstance, not because chance wouldn't exist (which is magical or religious thinking), nor because the real would no longer break into our lives, but rather because the manner in which we let it infringe upon us, no matter the degree of its gravity, or even ferocity, depends on us and our manner of negotiating an open, moving, accident-strewn, and, in a certain respect, unrepresentable world . . .

And what if you made an effort "not to get hung up on yourself," to throw every familiar thing overboard, and to enter into non–self-conformity? To break things off, but through a modification of your own internal, subjective chemistry? A vertiginous descent toward the place where I am no longer "me," dissolved, confused with perception itself, a psychic space become night, rock, and space, the echo of an animal in the distance, claw marks on the ground. Traces of self, unrecognizable, hacked up, without possible translation. To this end, to self-desist (and not to regain yourself)—that is, *to get lost*. "Getting lost," writes Adam Phillips, "is the best defense against the feeling of being lost, in part because we have the impression that the problem is within our grasp, as it were . . . You get lost because you are not lost. So we can say: we are lost when there is no object of desire; and we make ourselves lost when there is an object of desire."[1] All of the fundamental experiences of our being—including, and perhaps above all, joy— cannot be contained within the boundaries of what we could define, even in a vague manner, as "self"; they make coexist states of the world and subjective perceptions, but also pieces of the body, images, representations, and affects. To take the risk of immanence is to refuse any hither world, as Nietzsche insisted, to bet only on this world, which infinitely exceeds our perception. Sometimes, *not becoming yourself* is precisely like not dying, not being already locked in a strait jacket—existence, identity, or rule of life, which serve as reference points, as a fragile enclave where the ego perdures. "We will say of pure immanence that it is A LIFE, and nothing else," writes Gilles Deleuze. "It is not immanence to life, but the immanent that is in nothing is itself a life. A life is the immanence of immanence, absolute immanence: it is complete power, complete beatitude."[2]

Being in Secret

In what sense is the secret a risk? The secret is much more than something kept. It is also an essential dimension of being because it allows the heart to fortify itself, to welcome this inviolable "heart of hearts" [*for intérieur*] A body can be tortured; your eyes can be scanned by a lie detector; you can be hypnotized; but it will never be possible to force entry into the secret of your soul. Torturers know it well. Even during the Inquisition, the condemned could refuse to talk by invoking the "heart of hearts" [*for intérieur*]. The door of the heart would not be open. The mystics have given us the most beautiful pages on the *secret heart*. In French, to be "au secret" means to be consigned to a dungeon, a place of the most radical withdrawal of the living before death. The capacity to keep a secret is an aptitude to resist power. This is the political and spiritual dimension that, in these times when we are told to reveal everything, it is perhaps important to defend.

Truth is an exit from the crypt, a laying bare. Can everything be unveiled? Must we tell everything to the other? What is the relation between truth and the secret? The secret does not exist without the possibility of being shared, without the word that defends it or that betrays it, without the promise to keep it, without the confession that unravels it. If the secret touches on all the facets of the human experience, there exist, in history, at least two domains where—as a discourse—it will have served a dominant function: sex and prayer. Sexuality is a sphere in which intimate discourse plays a central role. What goes unspoken has no other function than to underscore the gap between what is said and what could be said. The erotic is a function of the secret that reaches into language. The other dimension of intimate silent language is prayer. Invocation, meditation, hope: all the forms of inner religious discourse betoken a secret shared exclusively with God. Today, however, this token has no currency. Sex and prayer, to take only these two examples of internalized discourse that essentially belong to silence and the secret, were radically "exposed" during the last century. Perhaps it's time to recall their essential complicity.

Prayer is a state of waiting for a word that you know will not come, but that, at the same time, is there inside you, deposited there from time immemorial. Speech is linked to this lack of the other, this absent other who does not respond, who will not respond, who doesn't know and yet welcomes your voice unlike any other, in the absolute opening to the unhoped-for. Does another similar space exist? You need only believe that an other might hear you, with the most intense hope against the background of night, such a paradox . . .

What space exists today to risk the secret, not the "miserable little pile of secrets" of occulted vices or jealous possessiveness, nor the political secret, I mean the secret that must transpire between self and self—the density of an infrangible night?

The secret is the other side of shame.

Befriending Our Fears

We live in fear without knowing it. We are surrounded by fear as by a ghostly presence, an apparition. Fear unsettles and bewilders us, and yet . . . why not risk befriending it just as, at night, we approach certain large animals? Going right out, and at night, to meet it. We believe that our fears hold us back; we believe we don't have enough strength to confront them, because this would be to know them, but also to love them, even to grow attached to them. Our fears present the face of our future amazement, the beginning of all creation. They are the crystallized scraps of our tiniest emotions just beyond our fingertips; we let them slip away, then regret not keeping them. We confront our fears and, silently, we are held back inwardly by the memory of ancient hopes. We live under local anesthesia, wrapped in cellophane, desperately seeking the substance, or the love, which might wake us up without frightening us.

We are caught up in the wrong war, lost soldiers fighting for a forgotten cause. The desperate cause, always so urgent, of childhood. The pure perfection of childhood whose very wounds make us feel nostalgic. Then our first terrors were invented, our first drawings of ogres and heavens, sleepless nights armed with promises that won't be kept but that we will claim as our due for years on end without anyone able to do anything about it, not even the attentive psychoanalyst who listens without interrupting you, for years on end, from whom the path of white pebbles eroded by wind, birds, solitude, and forgetting, also slips away. The mystery is that it never leaves us. The territory delimited, very precisely, by our fears. To take the risk of being afraid in order, finally, to enter this territory, to dissolve into it, to dive into the river and, holding your breath, to reach the bright stones on the bottom and to bring them up to the surface where they won't have the same sheen or mystery, and to observe them up close, brushing them with a fingertip. Where do you come from? What is your name? What do you want from me? One is afraid of being abandoned, betrayed, afraid of not being loved anymore, of not being capable of love anymore, afraid of being cold, hungry, sick, or alone, afraid that life will pass and nothing will have happened. Fear enfolds each event as if to protect its chrysalis, eventually unfurling all the words that circulate for holding, for making bend, for sex, for the momentary impulse, for treasure believed lost, for betrayal, for making suffer, for loving, for creating. At odds with time, almost at odds with life, leaning on terror and standing against it, how to keep your eyes open, just a little longer . . . how not to remain at a remove from the most beautiful things?

"*My heart, she says, is dismembered. I am a terrorized child, in pieces. I never take a plane or a train; I don't sleep; I don't swim in deep water; I avoid crowds. I am on hiatus. I exist within a somnambulistic fear that cramps my movements, inhibits my desire, asphyxiates my life. I am afraid of you as well, and of wasting my time here, of unreasonably expecting that something will happen . . .*"

"*You are afraid . . . here, now?*"

I look at her attentively, my gaze never leaving her body, like a fisherman when the fly on his line drops very gently on the ripples of the water.

"*Yes, I want to run away, never to have come.*"

The silence spreads out for a long time, a bright calming fire, and then little by little I sense her breathing otherwise.

"*And what if you loved your fear . . .*" *I risked, barely a question.*

"*This horrible fear is suffocating, you don't understand, that's clear . . . I can't say anything about it, only flee from it, think about it as little as possible. Curl up in a ball when it comes and wait. As a little girl, already, this is what I'd do in my room . . .*"

I repeated: "*And what if perhaps you love it?*" *This is all I said, that perhaps, indeed, you love it . . .*

She turned her head toward the window. The curtains let in a filtered, meager light. The silence took on the quality that it gets from surprise, or at least from something that slips into the rhythm of the dialogue, at the split second when the response is lodged exactly where the other is waiting for it, expecting its arrival.

"What if, perhaps, I loved it?" she repeats.

Words, when they are repeated, sometimes assume a talismanic value, as if reprise conferred on them an unparalleled power, a sort of internalization of their power to name the world. With this mere repetition, simple as a child's rhyme, fear became embodied, a vector of desire, at once distant and incorporated. It became thinkable, a very gentle surface of projection that might uphold the word: love.

"Why would I love it since it prevents everything, including putting an end to my stupid little life?"

All of a sudden, she glimpsed the infinite power invested in the fear she donned in order to stay still, curled up in a ball, waiting for someone to come looking for her. Her mother or some other person who would deign to love her. Poor hidden thing, no voice or body or desire, just a ready alibi.

"Why?" she says. "You know why, so tell me . . ."

"There is no why . . ."

There is a certain lassitude in my response. No why . . . no. We so much want that to be it, a key memory that surges up again and makes it all come together, a single word, an event such as the tiny pea in the fairy tale that keeps the princess from sleeping. But the why remains a bluff, a rearview mirror in the blind spot. There is only the how, Kierkegaard said, the specific manner whereby we invented a path to the event of love, of fear, of death, or of the effraction of beauty within us, along with many other fugitive bewilderments that we have trouble recovering from. I decided to talk to her, to deal with her fear as best as I could . . .

"This fear that you shelter within you is perhaps, who knows, your sole refuge, or perhaps you have believed in it for so long that it's now difficult to mourn it. It is painful to renounce renunciation because, from the instant you do, you realize that the damage has been done, that time has been lost, that blindness and alibis and the poverty of self-deception are gone as well. When blood returns to nearly frozen limbs, a terrible pain sets in that makes you long for the deadly anesthesia of the cold; you wish never to have had to awaken. To welcome fear is also to welcome the possibility of joy, the effraction of alterity, of the unknown, and of the living; it is to leave renunciation behind and this is what's terrible. Fear protects us from such a risk like an anxious, unhappy mother, whom you will never appease."

"You are sending me back into unhappiness . . ."

There was a blankness to her voice infinitely vaster that any sadness. I leaned forward, toward her, surprised by wanting to embrace her, to take her hands in mine like you would do with a child who is grieving but doesn't know it yet. I would have liked to be able to imagine that my words touch her, reach her.

"I am sending you back to the place of your unhappiness, yes, perhaps, you'd know better than me, I am sending you back there as to a deadly shelter you still believe it impossible to distance yourself from, to free yourself from. The point is not to prove you wrong . . ."

"Forget my heart, forget my head, forget my reason, forget my fear, forget my words, forget my childhood terror, but keep me close to you."

"I will not replace your fear, I will not guard you against it, I can only listen to you, and with you, very gently, wait for the strange chrysalis of your fear to sprout colorful wings, delicate and shimmery, suffused with light. In Greek, the name for this butterfly is psychè.*"*

She stood. Time was up. She staggered as if the room was listing slightly. "It will pass . . . I have vertigo, it happens often, I don't even notice anymore."

I helped her to regain balance.

"You never say sorry," she said.

"Yes I do, it happens like your dizzy spells. I say sorry, my mistake, apologies."

"But you are sure you're right . . ."

"I am neither right nor wrong, just as there was no why, it is what is happening at this moment that might change everything, in a second, in your life and in mine as well, because we are in each other's presence and it's an event that, if we are there for it, if we accept being there, is absolutely overwhelming, like any encounter."

"You don't have the right to speak that way, you are an analyst."

"If analysis is not an encounter, what is it? A pact? An alliance? Yes, that too, an alliance with whoever in you no longer wishes to love this fear to death, to die of it on your feet, upright like a soldier at the front; and also with whoever wants to leave and feels dizzy. I am just saying that this fear is the same as your desire, the very same, and that you are right to love it because there where it is, your desire is as well."

"I don't understand a thing."

"Yes, I believe you do, and that is even why you are here." I went to look for a book and handed it to her. It is one of the few talismans against fear that I know of . . ."

She lingered on the cover and smiled at the title. "Thank you," she said. "Most likely I won't be back, but I will keep it." Then she bent down to cross the threshold, the low door, and made her way down the stairs. Another person was waiting to be let in. I was running late, nighttime already.

A fear does not come undone; it coexists with a perception of the world to which it adheres, indissolubly. Each of our voyages, our attempts to escape from boredom, everydayness, the same on an indefinite loop, sustains a relation with fear that, at the exact place of the heart, the heart that remembers, digs a front line. What appears in our fears are the disparate pieces of a puzzle, which potentially contains what haunted us, disappointed us, made us dream, or totter, what constituted in filigree a possible world for us. To take the risk of our fears, then, is perhaps simply to tame their naked voice and, like children do with the menacing darkness that surrounds sleep, to tell ourselves stories, knowing that for each fright there is a tiny magic spell, a fugitive talisman as limpid as a Bach cantata.

At the Risk of Being Sad

Sadness leaves us caught between two worlds. Neither despair nor indifference, it is a stroll on the edge of catastrophe, but with elegance, like a child running along a cliff with no awareness of danger, eyes on shards of blue sky, the design of the clouds, the gentleness of the wind. Sadness has no density of its own, no echo. It delimits a shifting, unreasonable, internal space where you are always both on the verge of tears and of a strange appeasement. Sadness can engulf but also calm; it possesses an enveloping power that swathes the body with a cottony feeling of strangeness to itself, like a heartbreak that suddenly deprives one of sense, but not nostalgia. Sadness is unproductive, we are told, which is (also) why it is condemned.

What is sadness good for? Not a true cathartic outburst (into the bargain), not angry or transgressive, it has an unassailable gentleness that is unsettling. And yet it is fecund, make no mistake, but not in an organized or stable fashion. It detaches, it harbors a subtle force of unbinding; but it is in the meshwork of broken links, of disparate thoughts, quietly disheartening emotions, that true thinking appears. What I mean is an other, unrecognizable thinking—the thinking of mad love, for example, or of the future, like a stroke of lightning that you see flare up on the horizon and then disappear. A restless (that is, philosophical) thinking or a vision, who knows, something that takes form in space before your eyes and that you can suddenly transcribe with ease—something obvious.

Sadness has in common with forgiveness that it bears upon an unknown fault, an intolerable act, an offense, applies a balm that, at the same time, reignites pain. Sadness appeases what, at the same time, it sharpens like the blade of a samurai. Nothing more acute or less certain. Sadness clears the slate of time, the tranquil expanse of time, and gathers it back up in the form of pointy little stones and rubs them together, which makes a bizarre music; the past reemerges mingled with tiny instants of life that would otherwise be forgotten. Mingled with sadness, this patchwork of time is not merely nostalgic, even if sadness is often accompanied by this combined feeling of regret and expectation toward our own past. It is also a folded time, bundled upon itself, with its own throughline, its own echo chambers parallel to ours. Sadness is not tragic; it spaces drama out as landscape; it diffracts pain to make it bearable, scatters it into several points of the body and soul. Sadness is never entirely one's own, which is what makes it a rare object. Felt by oneself, it does not belong to us; it never manages fully to sink into us; and this gap is precisely what binds us to it. You are sad about never having dared to give your name to that woman you talked to for a few minutes and whose beauty, five years later, still overwhelms you; you are sad about missing an important meeting, about being forgotten, about no longer loving, about going by the wayside, about being in exile. You are sad as you would be in the solitude of a foreign land when no familiar things lull your gaze. There is a cruelty to sadness because of its limitless expanse, the impossibility of assigning it a threshold, of deciding when it ends. But the moment when sadness has finally released you is ungraspable, like sand. The sadness has left you, that's all there is to it. And you write, you love, you dream, and you fall asleep with loose arms and a clenched heart; sadness will have left you free, but different. Whence its risk. You can avoid it, cut yourself off from it, step away from it, or ignore it. Or else you can take the risk of sadness and open yourself to the inner exile to which it subjects you without violence, impossible to imagine beforehand. And in this unmapped and unmarked territory, you can linger awhile . . .

Sadness is very close to fatigue, this contemporary illness. Fatigue is a vital process, Blanchot said. It is a state of being on the outskirts of yourself that, in a certain manner, steps in to take the illness of life upon itself. It arranges things for you as well, providing a ready excuse: "I am tired"; and in the withdrawal that it authorizes, its underlying gravity escapes you, so that it becomes almost intangible and ultimately incurable. By sparing us the need to recognize an even deeper illness, fatigue is a capricious affect that is liable to take bodily form in an instant and never let go, opposing our life force with unbearable resistance, and denying us access to the world of healthy people who never seem to get exhausted. Fatigue bears a foretaste of melancholy that is attributed to stress, lack of sleep, or time for oneself, all things that we could easily bear in the throes of amorous effervescence. Fatigue levies the "for itself" that seems so lacking today, feeding the ogre (work, family, and so on). Here we are by the sandbox, grown up too quickly, and alone. Without imagination to persuade us that anyone is waiting for us. Fatigue makes imperceptible the pain, although acute, of not being recognized. It is difficult to give up waiting for recognition, to deliver yourself from it except by distributing it among the shallow friendships crammed into impossible schedules and long "vacations." To gain access to sadness, then, is to delve into the truth of this fatigue. To extract its active or vital principle, its urgency.

To take the risk of sadness would be the opposite of entering into melancholy; it would be to understand that sadness is the secret underside of beatitude, and of the enlargement of being unto which it beckons us, makes us remember another possibility of being toward ourselves and in the world, in hospitality to what comes.

At the Risk of Being Free

To philosophize is to trace freedom back to what lies before it.

—EMMANUEL LÉVINAS, *Totality and Infinity*

Freedom is undoubtedly the most banal among the usual ways of understanding risk. Who doesn't desire more freedom, to move in a vaster space,
to open everyday life to the unexpected? Who wouldn't wish to be delivered from constraints? In an existence besieged with obligations, prey to all
sorts of stress and pressure, who wouldn't want to have a voyager's latitude?
And yet, whether freedom is an object of desire, nothing is less certain . . .
Freedom is a movement of emancipation, not a stable state. It supposes that
we become conscious of our shackles, of what holds us back like Monsieur
Seguin's goat, penned up—with our consent, to boot—in our fantasies.
On this score, psychoanalysis is unequivocal. Freedom is almost always illusory; it relies on the multiple conditions of our desire, our education, our
culture, our world; it is rooted in an ideology that offers the subject only a
beautiful escape route . . . into an extremely cramped space. The space of a
sequestered self who willingly arranges for its own surveillance.

What would a "self" do who wasn't bolted shut from the inside? Our
capacity to act takes into account, at each instant of our lives, an unbelievable number of parameters, certain of them conscious, others less so. To
risk more freedom is necessarily to leave something behind, a quietude, a

community, a familiar world that offers, many frustrations certainly, but also solid points of reference, footholds. Does freedom teach us anything? Perhaps not. It demands that we risk our desire as if it were something infinitely precious, a unique event, an imperious voice—that, in sum, we go out ahead of ourselves, go where we didn't know we are, where something unknown to us yet speaks of us and convokes us. Freedom is a convocation. But how do we respond when it can't be willed or its outcome hastened? Perhaps it's a disposition of being—or an "inclination," to use the lovely expression from the seventeenth century—a disposition to the right moment, a *kairos*, to the intensity that designates the moment when we are utterly and truly alive. What is called chance, or destiny, is undoubtedly but one possible interpretation of this intensity of presence to others and to the event. For freedom hails us from the greatest distance (seemingly) from ourselves; it puts up very little resistance to our objections, takes leave of us, and disappears. It arises like a blind spot in a rearview mirror, so that you must turn around to see what's back there. But nothing in the annals of our past corresponds to it; no more codes of conduct here, no more heritage, only the raw future yet to be written. Fears above all are what precede us, far ahead of our acts. Depression is just another name for this refusal of freedom or, more precisely, for the radical impossibility, unbeknownst to us, of believing that any liberation is possible, any emancipation from the "objective" limits upon our existence. What divides within us, here, is the field of an endless battle because the risk of being free touches upon the most ancient loyalties that we carry; our armor on this battlefront isn't of our own making but that of other generations, other memories.

Is freedom exercised at the risk of truth? To think freedom in terms of subjective will is to discount everything from well before our birth that forbids it, forgotten oaths, coerced promises, unburied dead, meager and violent secrets. To take the risk of being free is to make the Pascalian wager that freedom will be discovered to the extent that we venture out to sea. The boat that carries Virgil and his friend into Hell restores its passengers to their exilic condition as human beings, for only at such a price, Dante tells us, will they be witnesses to what they have risked as subjects— namely, the truth. "The distinction between free and non-free," writes Lévinas, "would not be the ultimate distinction between humanity and inhumanity, nor the ultimate mark of sense and nonsense . . . Has not the Good chosen the subject with an election recognizable in the responsibility of being hostage, to which the subject is destined, which he cannot evade without denying himself, and by virtue of which he is unique?"[1] Herein we recognize the ethics of Lévinas according to which the Good comes before

Being and in the infinite responsibility of the subject for the other, which alone founds the (finite) possibility of her freedom.

The freedom to act is but infinitesimal in relation to the freedom of being, which is what properly constitutes our humanity. Under terror and torture, each human being remains free to the bitter end to risk her truth—that is, something that no one will ever be able to take by force. Because the human is a spiritual being, this freedom, which founds her in turn, she alone can abdicate it. If the human and the inhuman diverge along the lines of a humanity in which the relation to the other, never risked enough, folds into pure suffering, what do we make of this surfeit of freedom? Will we sacrifice again and always more to our rapacious appetite for power and technological mastery? Or will we have the audacity to take within ourselves the responsibility for a difficult freedom that can be risked only to the extent that it's in danger?

The Time They Call Lost

Time, inconsiderately, is as difficult to think as to experience as such. Constituted in the imaginary but arming the most unrepresentable real, it convokes us to an impossible figuration. The time that we eternally seek to make our own, to recapture, seems never to stop defying our expectations. True time is never anything but lost. Diverted, destroyed, detached, fragmented, or even indefinitely deferred, time lost is of no use. It gets lost in us just as in the acts that it will not anchor. Decision, choice, function: everything happens in detached bits and pieces, nothing remains but an indecisive stretch of time on the threshold of which we exist. We revolve around our lives in the oscillating rhythm of more or less fictional schedules, overfilled by the real but also by the impossibility in which we exist, from birth, to be on time. Time took nine months to fashion us, without us—that is, without anything for us to do, to decide, or to vanquish—nine months of wrapping our fibers with time, of our being in becoming, of our nascent, not yet subjective freedom . . . What to do with this time from before our history as subjects?

We like to say: I gained time, as if such a gain could satisfy us, delivering us into a sort of economy without money or exchange, gained from a nonquantifiable surplus of life that would amount to a supplement of being . . . This imaginary gain is distilled everywhere, but unnoticed, making us believe that we have a surfeit of desire at our disposal. Propelled into activities, the accumulation of goods, and the busyness of urban life at multiple rhythms and counter-rhythms, we imperceptibly lose touch with ourselves. At odds with the movement of interiority that opens our ears, the floating attention that is not only to be had in an analyst's office but also in existence, and that, close to meditation, would be a manner of envisaging the real without violence while letting it affect us. In this movement, time is indeed lost. Inevitably so—lost in flânerie, boredom, and insomnia, all of the intervals that serve no purpose and yet translate into states of being, into disquiet, at times into aimless wandering. Familiar strangeness, *Unheimlichkeit*, temporal translation of the copresence of a mother both vertiginously close and faraway. The close and the faraway here serve as an initial measure (or immeasure) to express the irresolute temporality that fabricates our relation to the world, to inner time, and to finitude. Does losing time merely mean accepting that we never had it to lose but had always been within it as within a time before time, within a genesis that wouldn't yet belong to the history to which we are returned, for example, by trauma but also jouissance? Such a risk obliges us to think the possibility of being "without outside," perhaps what Rilke called the Open.

There will never be a way to recover from being born of an other and yet being alone, having to die alone; between these two enters an impossible dialogue that fabricates a time that is literally, as Maurice Blanchot wrote, impossible: "Prophetic speech announces an impossible future, or makes the future it announces, because it announces it, something impossible, a future one would not know how to live and that must upset all the sure givens of existence."[1] This impossible future, however, is that which speech affords us, and which links us. To lose time is thus perhaps to attach ourselves to the fetal "outside of time" when we were two, one in two, two in one, memory, affects, and sensations, linked indissolubly to the Other who carries and nourishes us (the mother, but also language), and this outside of time that will always resonate within us because it is matrix of our being, spirit, and body. "Time has more than one dimension," Elie During writes. "It is not a form of interiority because it is what, on the contrary, envelops us. Time cannot be inside of us, far from it, because it is we who inhabit time; it is we who move within it as a virtual milieu in whose obscure depths coexist all the degrees of duration."[2] To wander randomly, to get lost even in a city that you know well, to make time for a conversation that never stops coming together and falling apart, to forget all about an appointment, to stay up until morning, to be reconciled for a time with our ghosts—such are the moments that we extract from the economy of bonds that we wish to keep as regular as our schedules; and this grueling inability to manage time imperceptibly sends us back to early childhood, to the time of play and awakening, of building forts and crazy laughter, and of disquiet as well, when time strains the confines of the day, in an ungraspable projection of duration. What does tomorrow mean when you are only a few months old? Tomorrow and yesterday are continents where the promise, "I'll be right back," is the only fixed point (the voice, invocation) that makes sense for the child, giving her the strength to wait and make of this waiting time into a refuge, a chamber of dreams and writing whence she can, like Victor Ségalen, explore the world.

Dead Alive

Death and life tear apart from one another like silence and thunder.

—GEORGES BATAILLE, *Les Mangeurs d'étoiles*

No one wants to die anymore. Formerly obvious, everywhere present, death has become a scandal. It is an unacceptable affront to our effort to find a cure, or eternal youth, and to access the instantaneity of virtual and fantasy worlds. Death is a thing that shouldn't encumber us any longer, that we hide and avoid. The dead, today, go up in industrial smoke, without ceremony or ritual, or only with shoddy ceremonies that hardly seem worth the effort. Soon, there will be no cemeteries left, too much useless space. The economy of death resides in so-called life insurance and in the funeral industry: leave it to the professionals, you will get a reasonable mourning period, three or four months for next of kin, any more would be indecent, any less shocking.

To risk not dying, then, how is it a risk and not the most widespread fantasy in Western society? For, dead we are, quite often . . . Dead of a quiet little death—obvious, even charming, a death that includes a garden and a landscape, diverse amusements and pleasures, nothing easier, everything will be provided as long as you consent to it: oh yes, all that's required is your soul, but no, there will be no Faustian bargain. The devil has left the building; he has lost interest. Since what torments you is life, get used to the fact, give yourself a little peace at last, sign right here, Hell won't be a problem, we take care of the rest. Children, life stress, sex and love, hand it all off, lighten your load, sign out for awhile, let your yourself go, dying amidst your life is not such a bad thing, you'll see . . .

To take the risk of not dying might resemble Micro-Miniscule Almost Undetectable Refusals. Even if there is a pill to replace complaint, avidity, and anxiety, straining the limits of illusion and expectation—and just like that, thanks to this sophisticated biology (antidepressants, morphine, anxiolytics, hashish, or other drug therapies), no more boredom, frustration, envy, or feelings of isolation—you will be granted what the misrecognition of your desire, in the end, still allows you to grasp. No, in fact, there is no object that will bring an end to your hunger and your tears. No object will give you back a desiring body. And whatever substance you swallow—because, here is another (object, drug, artifact) and another. . . you will gradually forget what you were waiting for, your desire will get lost in the web of a world taken over by readymade operants and performance enhancers . . . Why persist? You need only lay down your weapons, elaborate gestures and pretexts, misunderstandings and excuses, very quietly follow your path without fury or freedom, without sharp edges, shadow, or light. Almost nothing will be asked of you. Even sex will no longer be a problem. And if the pain of living remains—for, ultimately, you will be clinically alive—there are other somniferants to vanquish your last scruples, your persistent anxieties, whence you will find deliverance, no attachments left, merely bonds as light as champagne bubbles.

You will be enshrouded alive, asleep in light tombs. You will lie there, yes, allowing the world to offer you the ugliest, most grotesque, unstable, and vulgar objects, the right ideals in response to your appetites. What does it matter? Deracinated, disinvested, you wander without compass or territory, tethered by nothing but an artificial fixity—work, family, religion—which includes the clandestine side of your story, walking the same walks, at the same hours. How to disembalm already dead bodies, formatted minds, while forgetting that it's possible to invent a life of desire and joy? The risks are serious—collapse, vertigo, isolation, rejection, even open hostility. No one likes to be reminded that freedom is right there, right away, ready for the taking. Not tomorrow, not elsewhere, here and now. Or to recall that we are the first to dig our own graves . . . Reread Kierkegaard. Our migraines prevent us from thinking that, already in the midst of life, we are wound in a sheet. We are entering an era of gentle glaciation, continuous light anesthesia with organized leisure, administered thinking, life in bits, more objects to numb us, to prevent, from one instant to the next, any feeling of wonder, any step aside, or step back.

The obsessional neurotic reminds us every day of all of this. What a perfect patient! With a velvety voice and steady gait, he plays the loyal butler who ushers you with utter quietude into Bluebeard's castle and the chambers of horrors that it conceals. He will come to you, a little obsequiously, of course, but sure of his right to be cured. Might betray a hint of irony, just to see whom he's dealing with. And so the analysis will go, always on time. Attempting to seize control of the frame through the use of reason and to manipulate the transference, he will point from afar to the chaos that inhabits him, obliging you to bear witness to your own impotence along with his. A clock in apparent working order but with a faulty mechanism, he invites you to stand by and watch with him as time passes on the way to death. Smooth and unbreakable on the outside, devastated within. The obsessional neurotic has constructed a few refuges, hobbyhorses, and routines that he is willing to share so long as you don't tamper with them. He tells you that he is already dead and wants you to raise him from the tomb without changing a thing about his existence. He will keep pretending to be alive all the time. At times, he might even be eccentric, but he alone knows what crypt withholds his sense of festivity and friendship. To disentangle him from death is no easy task for the analyst that you will be led to be. I say led to be because you must invent a path not found in any guide.

History is frozen, time as well. There is no reprieve. Now or never. Tomorrow is not the beginning. The more people grasp this fact, the more they sink into melancholy before our eyes. As if existence were solely a question of accepting renunciation without sacrifice, without heroism or sublime cause, whatever the price. The obsessional neurotic encloses within the vice grip of surveillance the vital force that threatens the equilibrium that he has patiently constructed in order to avoid a nameless anxiety. Risk is the untimely baring of ancient wounds, without fortified archives where memory abides. These memories that now seem to belong only from a great distance to the one who suffers from "non-life" remain no less suffocating. The temptation, for the analyst, when faced with people embalmed alive, is to alert them that waiting is over, now is the emergency, no time is left. But she must avoid falling for their panic, and for the criers of tempest and disaster whom they echo, knowing full well that arming themselves with fear never makes them any freer. You probably have to travel back in time, return to the wild afternoons at ten years old—to your first ambushes, your first hard knocks. Your secrets wrapped in scraps of paper. To venture back to the impalpable night of childhood that makes you weep noiselessly. To take images of little bits of life and put them together one by one, slow-motion vibrations: seesaw, betrayal, falling, slight vertigo, a juxtaposition of the unhitched certainties of the real. At the finish, almost nothing is left to hold onto, a handful of memories, a few places, two or three first names—somewhere among them your own name, softly whispered. This name doesn't belong to you; you don't know it. It founds you and traverses you. Some call it the unconscious. Others don't believe in it at all. You think that you might have glimpsed it, but it is what holds you fast. To know anything about it, you must tread step by step back into the realm of the dead. Traverse where there is no registered territory, where no maps are permitted, no passports, and no excuses. In order to return from death to life, quit the loop of obsession and the permanent surveillance of the inner eye that never quits he who suffers from anxiety, and go down and cross paths with souls for whom no one weeps.

Once back, we discover here, in this darkness peopled by the dead, something to put our faith in. Something in the face of which courage has a meaning. Desire comes from a very pure, enchanted form of wonder unhampered by terror. All of a sudden it opens up within us. Numbers, a piece of music, a chord, a light, a skin, or the taste of the fruit of darkness, our senses encounter the world, which suddenly responds to us. But we forget. We lose everything down to the thread that would lead us back—down to the memory that it ever existed, within us. We build towers in order to protect ourselves against imaginary enemies without seeing that the apparatus is coiled inside of us, that the adversary is an inner principle whereby we are persecuted by ourselves better than any other could ever do.

Of a Perception Infinitely Vaster . . .

Is perception feeling and seeing at the same time? Perception reveals us to be plural, preventing us from coinciding exactly with the self-image that we carry around. Perceiving undoes us, dismantles thought, which never protects you as well as expected, each sensation just as legitimate as the judgment that contains it. It is impossible, I believe, to run the risk of perception without giving up a bit of our reason for being, of our sovereignty. In *The Waves*, Virginia Woolf returns us to a language that evokes the wonder and terror that inhabited us early in life, but on the basis of a pure sensation of the world. Novalis said it thus: "To every sensation man adds another sensation as soon as he begins to think." At the very end of World War Two, Merleau-Ponty echoes this thought: "In the present and in perception, my being and my consciousness are at one, not that my being is reducible to the knowledge I have of it or that it is clearly set out before me—on the contrary perception is opaque, for it brings into play, beneath what I know, my sensory fields which are my primitive alliance with the world—but because 'being conscious' is here nothing but 'being-to . . .' ['*être à* . . .'], and because my consciousness of existing merges into the actual gesture of 'ex-sistence.' It is by communicating with the world that we communicate beyond all doubt with ourselves. We hold time in its entirety, and we are present to ourselves because we are present to the world."[1]

Our perception is much vaster than the boundaries of what we call "I." My body, my voice, the thoughts that visit me, the visions that traverse me, "it" in me that sees, breathes, and hears, feels more broadly than I do. If perception is carnal and makes itself visible to us, it is also, in part, what in us remains in a relation of immanence to the world. Paradoxically, the more we are a perceiving body, the less we are conscious of our singularity. What we are thereby given, from the specter of a perception so vast that it overflows consciousness on all sides, remains encrypted, registered down to the smallest detail. "It" in us that Freud one day decided to call the unconscious, remembers, recalls everything, for us, in our place. And we—like a dancer frozen in place—turn upon ourselves, wild eyed before the void, trying to stay upright like good little soldiers full of certainties. There are certain moments when bits of this pure perception occur in the interstices of consciousness and threaten us with imminent danger: the ego cannot confront this influx of perceptions undigested by consciousness that come from nowhere, from a region within us where we are *terra incognita*. Risk is a matter of opening up to this liberating amplitude. And of losing control. Of suffering where we seemed to be tranquil residents of our psychic space, because we often prefer consciousness of pain to the unknown.

There is a child, within you, who doesn't forget being held in such contempt, treated with such coldness, with such anxiety she was forced to confront all alone nights rife with ghosts (hers and others'), within the oblivion of the secret that enveloped her like a shroud. What have we preserved of this savage solitude to which we were consigned? Whom to trust? What can be done with these disordered words: commands, maledictions, promises, interdictions, deposited in us at random . . . What creative fervor will deliver them from our body, and at what price? Deposited within us there is a slight terror of the world spread like a film over the world to make it habitable. These words, then, translate the dread that the world is not in our hands. The greatest risk, we've known since always, is to love. To quit the enclosure, the belly of solitude, the haven of the familiar.

You might believe that you let yourself dream, be distracted, that you love being in love, and that you enjoy being alone, but no one would be duped . . . We doubt our own perception just as we doubt our desire. We are tyrannized by anxiety about not actualizing ourselves, by the fear of missing our life, as if "true" life was right there, ever so close, a meaningful existence just waiting for whoever knows how to grab hold and take full advantage of it. This doubt is our double, which persecutes us with a strange and insistent gentleness. To let ourselves be inundated by perception, by images from a perceptive capacity infinitely vaster than the ego, is to allow everything in us that records, comprehends, captures, hears, untangles, and intertwines, or that contains information about many generations and intelligence about multiple persons, of many genres, including animals, and doubtless vegetables as well, to think and to dream. Fine, then, but where is the risk? It is the risk of entering a penumbral domain, of apparent indistinction, of confusion among senses and genres, of what we sometimes attain through drunkenness and drugs and insomnia and being in love and in panic: a hyperlucidity that lifts the burden of one hundred thousand lives.

When he questions the Delphic oracle, Socrates obtains from her the maxim, *gnothi seauton* ("know thyself"). The "care of the self" to which she refers him is not a little egoistic apparatus but rather a capacity of being unto yourself that relies upon a perception that is inseparable from the intelligible. "Emotion does not say 'I,'" Deleuze writes. "It is very difficult to grasp an event, but I do not believe that this grasp implies the first person."[2] To understand what our perception is capable of, beyond the limits of mere subjectivity, always and once again we must deconstruct what we believed our self to be. Not to "become" yourself, but rather to go unto yourself like you go out in search of love. To construct white with light, to abandon childhood debts, the rigged dictates of the roles we assume, and the whole economy that wishes to put need in place of desire. To experience "the derangement of all the senses,"[3] as Rimbaud wrote. For whom is it their heart's joy to break the boundaries of perception at the risk of losing the boundaries of their own identity? To tarry with destruction, the abyss. The question of addiction comes up more insistently than ever. Dependence catches hold of us with the first breath our lungs take, with the tearing of the placenta, and fixates itself within us as a principle that is prolonged, whether we like it or not, in the search for substances, objects, bodies, sex, or ideals that are identified with life. "Expanded perception is the aim of art," Deleuze writes. "Such a goal can only be reached if perception breaks with the identity to which memory binds it . . . Extending perception means making forces that are ordinarily imperceptible sensible, resonant (or visible)."[4]

The experience of reanimation, Pierre Guyotat attests, is the traversal of a beyond, a terrifying echo chamber where the ego is dissolved, "as if each of your background thoughts was immediately echoed . . . it's terrible, you are ripped apart, and when you get out of there, you are wretched, a little humanity still clings to you, but almost none . . ." Everything becomes both terribly carnal and obscene: "You feel like going away, you can no longer say 'I' and yet you must come back and start all over again . . . you have to plunge back in, into affect, while you inhabit a world that risks becoming pleasant, detached . . . impurity, that can only begin again, plus the fatigue . . . and you have already gone well down the road toward disappearance, after the big terrifying dreams calm sets in and 'they' would prefer that you be left in peace . . . And so this is what happened. Obviously, I love life even while I think it's unimportant . . . You'd like to be able to live, which is what drives everything, it is the absolute desire, the absolute in this world."[5] To come back from these territories between life and death that you might not have escaped alive—body shredded, mind lost, deep depressions, schizoid states, paralyses, and so on—is, as Guyotat bears witness, to experience the edge of the world where I am no longer "I," the edge of the self that is nothing but an open wound. Pure perception is not a simple state of presence but a region where there is no "person" to ensure a serene adequation with I, with self. Those who have explored this borderland between unbearable pain and the dissolution of everything that tethers them to life only rarely speak of their experience, and even when they do make themselves its witness it is only with an infinite modesty that could never be breached, imagining in their place what they lived through and whence they returned.

We are afraid of our own capacity to perceive, of the "visionary" in us, of what is commonly called intuition—that is, a knowledge you have in advance of yourself; a knowledge from which one prefers to deliver oneself even before it can be clearly formulated. Retroactively, our gestures, our dreams, our slips of the tongue, and our bungled actions reveal to us, like prophetic utterances, this capacity for intelligible perception much vaster than the ego. Artistic creation is always at grips with the apparatus out ahead of you that informs you, somehow unbeknownst to you, and that unfolds on the canvas, in the score, or on the page even before consciousness takes notice. Only upon rereading does it become aware.

Anxiety, Lack—Spiritual Hunger?

Anxiety is proper to man, a secret weapon without which humanity would founder. Is someone who is anxiety-free completely human? "How does spirit relate to itself and to its conditionality?" asks Kierkegaard.[1] "It relates to itself as anxiety. Do away with itself, the spirit cannot; lay hold of itself, it cannot, as long as it has itself outside itself. Nor can man sink down into the vegetative, for he is qualified as spirit; flee away from anxiety, he cannot, for he loves it; really love it, he cannot, for he flees from it . . . Here there is no knowledge of good and evil etc., but the whole actuality of knowledge projects itself in anxiety as the enormous nothing of ignorance."[2] And he adds: "Dreamily the spirit projects its own actuality, but this actuality is nothing, and innocence always sees this nothing outside itself."[3] Anxiety, the Danish philosopher recalls, is primarily a spiritual affliction. Throughout his work, he unceasingly explored the abysses of anxiety with the genius of his language and thought. He risked this exploration on the basis of his own history, beginning with the night when, as he recounts, his father cursed God. He didn't seek so much to understand anxiety as to describe its ordeal, without reducing or falsifying it, much less psychologizing it, which was already the rage in his epoch. The "nothing" that he describes as innocence or ignorance enlarges the space of our spiritual hunger; for, such is anxiety, it speaks of an unquenchable desire, but also of our freedom. Anxiety does not always speak its own name, nor even that of despair. It is oppressive, clamps our hands around an imaginary support, causes migraines and vertigo, sparks intimations of an impending and ever deferred catastrophe. Mornings, it is a terrible malaise and the groundless expectation of some irreparable event. It takes place in our lives, in our sleepless nights, without ever unmasking the conflict that underlies it. This is the conflict that I call spiritual. Although spoken in the body, it will not be appeased unless the hunger that it combats is recognized as an aspiration that no substance could ever satisfy.

Anxiety is a smokescreen that spares consciousness the obligation to shed light on things it doesn't want to know anything about. The truth that anxiety shields us from, most often, is that of a combat raging totally unknown to us. To expose it requires that we distinguish between two orders of indefectible loyalties—that which stems from childhood experiences, from secrets and truncated genealogies, or from interdicted or unreachable memories of war and sacrificial silence; and that which beckons us to a freedom wholly cut off from any past. Anxiety is akin to a layer of snow atop a devastated landscape: everything, at first sight, is white, intact, almost unreal. Only with the thaw does the broken terrain emerge. Anxiety, like the snow, allows for nothing to be revealed, for all to remain enshrouded beneath the light anesthesia of the deadly cold. And yet an unease surges up, the stomach is tied in knots, the head swims, cruel and pointless insomnia sets in. Anxiety can't stop the conflict from spilling onto the territory of the body; it can only attempt to keep it unknown. You have no idea, at bottom, why you are reeling. The sense of failure, for instance, is not enough to explain why tears well up each time you try to say a word. Anxiety attacks the body to keep spirit afloat, to give enough strength to go on a bit further. Anxiety feeds on spirit, but our body is what it demands. Knotting the stomach or stealing our very breath, it churns gently from inside, never offering us any chance to regain life. Anxiety is an almost entirely immaterial hand-to-hand combat. The battlefield is psychic but the fighting is mainly physical. It extends the life of the living while leading them gently toward death.

Anxiety is the risk that none among us wishes to run, because it attacks the very meaning of what it is "to be." Spectral, it is a nocturnal visitor who prevents sleep. Witness to the conflict we wish to forget, it inheres in the memory of the event, of a childhood that we have surmounted by leaving part of ourselves behind as a hostage, at the mercy of an enemy unknown to us. Thus it always requires its collateral. Anxiety reminds us that being alive does not come without a price. That the price is exorbitant—beyond all measure. That we will never have enough to pay it. And that perhaps we will always have to remain an other's debtor. Its action often deferred, anxiety never belongs to the time in which it operates (as in, for example, a panic attack); it comes from a previous time, perhaps even previous to your own existence; its rights hail from an other scene. A theater of shadows cast by light from an inaccessible source.

We are houses haunted by complaints that we have made our own, not knowing to whom they first belonged. What we are thus left with, of our own, is a raw, heart-rending complaint. And the daily stabbing pain of lack, which we attempt to float within reasonable limits. Depending on the circumstances, it might be a lack of love, of gentleness, of recognition, of money, of a child, of freedom, of pleasure, or all of them together in an excoriating mix. The sole witness to this lack is the child we once were. A child who demands reparations times a hundred, always for the same reason, at the same place, and becomes the adult's tyrant, her daily tormentor. We are haunted by the same thing as the child because her time does not pass. Never will pass again. This is the frozen time that Françoise Davoine and Jean-Max Gaudillière discuss so well in their magnificent book, *History Beyond Trauma.*[4] Even if this lack is ill-named, or displaced, it happens that analysis might welcome it. In this protected space, the adult in distress names her persecutors; analysis offers words for terror, frustration, anger, envy, or impotence; it opens a laborious path through the wicked forest. The phantom child is recognized; she agrees, for a time, to defect from the infernal economy of debt, its impossible settlement.

The path of spiritual freedom, Kierkegaard wrote, is repetition. How to tell this child that she will never obtain reparations, not full, perhaps not any? To disenchant the haunted house that we are in is not to pretend that nothing happened there, that there were not mass graves in the vicinity, that a secret hadn't been sealed between its four walls. Can the child within us accept this? How not to give up, but rather to help her give thanks for what is?

The melancholic, as Derrida reminds us,[5] is the one who refuses to forget. Against any reasons for appeasement and forgetting, against time's gradual healing of all wounds, the melancholic upholds her pain despite and against everything. Which impels Derrida to assert, "Melancholy is therefore *necessary*."[6] And thus it is necessary to make provision for all melancholy—to accept the incurable and thereby perhaps to welcome it as an unfillable void, suffering that cannot be alleviated, such that lack becomes the very matter whereby desire is elevated, the place where life might re-launch, not just a seed of hope, but a movement that carries life forth. Welcoming lack thus protects the space of desire, its very restlessness. When the trauma that devastates psychic space allows for the upsurge of a lack, it already opens toward life, the touch of time and the very beginning of metamorphosis. To confront the possibility of radical loss is to change subjective position; it is not the same thing as staying strong or being resigned. Both lack and anxiety are forms of spiritual hunger. No experience of them spares us their negativity, or even their morbidity; but they can always become a vector of power also known as freedom.

Farewell Magic World:
Beyond Disappointment

The world of childhood is a nacelle hanging in wait for something to happen . . . When everything is still possible. Disappointment is the stumble awaiting in each event and the mad hope that it sparks in us. The so-called adult world has yet to shut this Pandora's box. Disappointment, promise: it's as if neither exists without the other. You promised me love and you disappeared. Does life consist of anything but the succession of our defeats? The collapse of our hopes? Isn't disappointment ultimately a shadow theater, a make-believe world, the puppet strings that you discover tugging behind the gold-painted decor?

The experience of disappointment supposes having believed in a magic world, with fairy wands and dragons up in the sky and fantastic creatures everywhere you look. It is having played the game, having taken risks and in a certain respect having lost, but without regrets for having believed. If this world is not your dream come true, at least it contains your expectations and the promises I make to you. It used to be our shelter, our refuge and our freedom. And then it was shattered. Disappointment first belongs body and soul to childhood. Children are constantly disappointed and always find some way to regain hope—such valiant little soldiers! The movement of expectation is what, *in spite of everything*, constitutes children in the very fiber of their being, because they are almost entirely, at every second, hope. They belong to the dreamworld far more that we realize. During the initial months of a child's life, the contours of the world are not yet directly real; they only become real little by little, very slowly. But, then, no parcel of everyday life escapes this world. Day and night her reveries will meet her with overheard and whispered words, even words kept secret, far away from her. Reverie, expectation, and what the child makes of our promises are the very matter of her body, her desire, and her gentleness. Adults cannot begin to imagine the amplitude of a child's disappointment, her capacity to be disappointed. Disappointment is a very gentle monster who swallows her up and spits her out into darkness, beyond the reach of sleep. A forgotten promise is enough to wreck an entire swath of her life, and no one notices. But right there amidst the wreckage of these ruins, she has already regained breath; she has begun to build a secret language, her refuge. This liability to disappointment is, paradoxically, an untapped reserve of imagination (a child cannot be broken, totally disappointed, without inflicting huge violence on her), which makes it possible for her to tame the real and to lodge herself in it; it is like a secret apparatus, her horizon of expectation.

Disappointment is the overturning of the magic world into the so-called real world; people say that it's the same world, but for oneself, it will never be the same—or it would be only if one were able to adopt the language of madness once and for all, and this would be too sad. To disappoint the other—lover, wife, child, friend—is to deceive expectations and attempt, afterward, to redeem yourself, in hope the bond remains intact. The one who disappoints would like to be forgiven for a transgression that doesn't exist because it rested on a promise. Unless the promise is more real than the real itself. To disappoint is to encroach on another person's dream in order to mine it with a miniscule time-bomb, in hope of still being loved after the conflagration—as if it was possible to forget speech and to begin over again.

One does not have the right to demand that a promise be kept; one can only hope it will be, by virtue of a primary ethics, because promising already entails a gamble on time, on the permanence of a subject who won't have sunken into madness or succumbed to death. But promising is also believing that you must abide by language and that the truth is at stake in everything said. Or not entirely in what is said but rather in the manner and moment at which it will have been said, in the intention of the body and the voice, in concentrated presence and the silence around it.

To disappoint is to have been disappointed during a savage, unremembered childhood. To have emerged from it supposes a great past experience
of something hoped for and never renounced; to have traversed the collapse of the madness of childhood expectations—which doubtless passed
unperceived—and survived. Nothing is more difficult to discern than disappointment; it is no more than the lightest flaking of paint on a wall, a
mere hairline crack; and yet, it is a fall from which sometimes you don't
recover. There are suicides that are appointments kept, forty years too late,
in memory of a disappointment so slight, so subtle, that very few ears had
perceived the shattering.

Life—Mine, Yours

What binds each of us to one another, and to risk, is our own lives. In fine, it is as language says: to risk your life. But where does the possessive pronoun, quietly slipped into this expression, come from? What does it mean to say "your" life—that is, your very own—and not simply "life"? What is the status of the possessive: *your*? To what extent is your life truly your own and what do you possess exactly when you say "my" life? In her very beautiful book on the La Borde clinic, Marie Depussé writes that possessive pronouns are all little ramparts that you erect in order to guard against the real, or desire, which are sometimes the same thing.[1] In any event, it is a matter of what tramples on the lovely order of our world, our trusty alibis, the memories we worship and those we pass over in silence, the edges of boundless shame and anxiety.

To speak of "risking your life" is to be alive in "your" own life and to envisage it as event that might be catastrophic or wonderful; that is, to envisage the possibility that death will come to bury life, cover it up, turn it away from itself or from yourself. It is a matter of risking the impersonality of a certain risk of what is most your own—that is, the possessive of "my" life; for, what else do I have in existence, in fact, except my life, because all else can be taken away from me: beloved beings, objects, corporeity (or at least certain nonvital parts of my body that make my body not solely and entirely my life).

Nonetheless, this risk isn't entirely subjective, or personal, or even voluntary; it is that by which we constantly exceed ourselves. It is that in which we are lost and exchange the feeling of irremediable loss for the desire to remain on the move in territories where it's possible to explore desire. How do we lose what is not ours? Life is given to us, this much we can admit whether or not we are believers. And yet it's scarcely ours, this life, which is the last thing that properly belongs to us, the last event that we live, and the last solitude that we experience, and also our place of greatest hope. There, perhaps, is this layer of intense life, bound up with the dead along with the memory and history of those who will never possess the words to transmit it. There, perhaps, lies the risk of "your" life—the fact that it is absolutely singular and yet not your own . . . Like any crushing experience, this life does not belong to us and yet we alone have lived it and have been transformed by it. We are transformed enough that, after the fact, in the future anterior, we can judge that life will have been risked up to that point, perhaps, in us; that this hospitality, like that of madness, or amorous delirium, was a violence that we ended up surviving, for good or for ill, and returned from; that it will have been life that thus risked us— against death and with it, against attachments, loyalties, defenses, families, shame, and the burial of all memory; because at this very instant we have been *passeurs*, most often unconsciously—that is, in an incandescence, a sadness, a dependence, a revolt, an imagination, a love, or a silence that remains unknown to us and yet found asylum within us. To say, "I risk my life," is almost impossible. Only at rare moments do we coincide with ourselves to such an extent. But we must believe it possible to say: life was risked in him or her—that is, as a witness, to recognize this risk in a painful fraternity, perhaps, but a true one.

At the Risk of the Unknown

At the risk of asking a woman to get up and dance and whispering to her: "Close your eyes."

At the risk of taking the car into the city for dinner and ending up in Rome the next day after driving through the night, just because you changed your mind.

At the risk of seeing your husband wave off the little Pakistani seller of (crumpled) roses for the fiftieth time and you buying his whole armful and offering them to everyone in the room.

At the risk of sleepless nights.

At the risk of writing a letter to an unknown man or woman just because of a slight feeling that coursed through you with an intensity you never knew before.

At the risk of making love over and over.

At the risk of praying without the help of any God, or even with it.

At the risk of hidden, mad, hopeless, infinite friendship. Worse than love.

At the risk of boredom, and loving this boredom without recourse.

At the risk of walking alone in a city and expecting at any instant to happen on the whole meaning of life, knowing that tomorrow it will be gone again.

At the risk of listening to Bach's *Saint Matthew Passion* on repeat.

At the risk of assuming all of someone else's responsibilities, without taking the slightest precaution.

At the risk of gathering pebbles of glass polished by the sea and then, the same evening, scattering them on the beach.

At the risk of a communism of thought.

At the risk of joy.

At the Risk of Being Carnal

He watches as the body of the dancer rises into the
air and asks himself: "What is your secret?"

—ALAIN DIDIER-WEILL, *Lila et la lumière de Vermeer*

To have a body, to be a body, to take bodily form . . . How do we navigate
among these three locutions? Having a body supposes that it might be possible that we don't have one, that the body is a place where we never fully
are. Being a body identifies us with this animate matter that we call a body
but still remains hardly namable, especially given that the body is also the
emotions that traverse it, the ideas that affect it, the unquantifiable pain
that shatters it, or the fulgurant jouissance that infuses it. "No one knows
what a body can do," wrote Spinoza. Where does a body, or the capacity of
a body, begin and where does it stop? In what sense is my identity entirely
captured within this so-called carnal envelope? Does embodiment designate the act whereby we make the body we have into the body we are? Does
taking bodily form mean entering your body just as having is transmuted
into being, the thing into essence, or the object into subject? Being carnal
is at one and the same time having, being, and taking bodily form . . .

In jouissance, you lose your body in an ordeal of a joy whereby you are at
once delivered and incarnated—*embodied* is the word in English. Antonio
Damasio says that the body is contained in the soul and not the reverse.
The body itself is traversed through and through by something that infi-

nitely exceeds it, that opens it, that exposes it to the unlimited. In song, the human voice is both the most material and the most immaterial thing—*das Ding*, the "thing" itself, Lacan would say. What it gives us to hear is a plane of immanence in the body that is infinitely vaster than what is perceptible, palpable, or visible. The voice gestures toward something in which we were bathed as children, something that most definitely constituted us as far back as the embryo's first cellular divisions—that is, the amniotic sound carrying with it the maternal voice, but also the voices of the father and siblings, as well as the sonorities that become the agents of love and hate, repulsion, attachment, and disgust, sonorities ceaselessly adjoined with food (from the umbilical cord), the movements inside the mother's body (felt by the fetus), and audition. This passage between the inside and the outside is constantly assured and reassuring, ushering in the whole of the possible, the burgeoning space of a subject to come. Our carnal being is an entity that goes infinitely beyond the perceptible body; it must be adjoined by the thought body, the imagined body, the dreamed body, the body of the voice, the body of taste, the affected body, or the body overtaken by fever, jouissance, drunkenness, the body that migrates beyond the body in order not to suffer, for example. Descartes will remain the father of Cartesianism—that is, the consummate divorce between the thinking subject and extended space—and yet, for his whole life his first question will have been what constitutes the union of the soul and the body, and how can this union even be thought. Biologists today seek answers just as urgently to the same question.

To be a body, to have a body, is also to be nude. What a strange risk nudity is. With age you forgive your body for not being perfect; you sometimes reconcile with it when it begins to slip away from you. Nudity is always scandalous because it lets be seen what cannot be seen; it offers what precisely cannot be offered; it supposes a sharing, delimits a territory open to sight and touch when, in reality, it has no extension, remains out of reach. Nudity can be photographed, delimited, and constrained; it can be caressed, avoided, and hidden, but what it offers cannot be taken. This is certainly the reason why it is so arousing: covetousness, hatred, desire, horror, compassion, the wish to remove every last veil. "Bodies (and souls) are forces. As such they are defined by their chance encounters and collisions (state of crisis). They are defined by relationships between an infinite number of parts that compose each body and that already characterize it as a 'multitude.'"[1]

What does it mean to risk nudity, today, when it is offered up everywhere all the time, on every possible platform, retouched and not? The risk of nudity is the unveiling of intimacy, an unmapped territory that separates me from another body with whom I am not (yet) one, before whom I create a space that is not simply that of my proper body. This is the space of my body from which, in a certain sense, my nudity is split off. This unreachable nudity is what's proper to the soul, a word that Freud himself used all the time, which people don't realize enough, because it tends to be translated as "psychic apparatus." This soul he envisaged has no other surface than the body, its essential nudity. Nudity, like a Moebius strip that makes it impossible to distinguish inside from outside, is also a metaphor. The words you employ to qualify it, whereby you adorn it, or spoil it, or avoid speaking it, naming it, or detailing it, will end up speaking of you, of your most secret intimacy, of your own history, and of history as such, of your fears, of you as a little child, and of you as a future little old person or victim of unfortunate events, of you at the place where your name gives way to this skin that bodies forth, that becomes a loving body, a tearful body, or a combatant body. There is no demarcation and no sign that allows you to say: here is the dead center of interiority, there where you cannot gain access, the place where spirit resides apart from all flesh. No, there is no such retreat, precisely because everything is there; out in the intangible space of nudity, it remains forever unreachable, and even in a certain sense invisible. There is a drive to expose things that keep silent, that are so open to being seen that they cannot be seen, by a rhetorical sleight of hand, precisely because nudity continually outstrips the gaze, touch, and sensation. "But what is caressed is not touched, properly speaking. It is not the softness or warmth of the hand given in contact that the caress seeks. The seeking of the caress constitutes its essence by the fact that the caress does not know what it seeks. This 'not knowing,' this fundamental disorder, is the essential. It is like a game with something slipping away, a game absolutely without project or plan, not with what can become ours or us, but with something other, always other, always inaccessible, and always still to come. The caress is the anticipation of this pure future, without content."[2]

She couldn't stand being seen nude. No more than she could looking at her face. It seemed to her that between them—nudity, face—there was an indissoluble pact, a secret kinship. I asked whether she remembered a particular scene from her childhood or adolescence in which her image might be present. She thought for a long time. Nothing in particular emerged but the memory of uncontrollably laughing with her sisters in bed at undressing time; nothing more. But yesterday she did recall an apparently banal scene that featured an image of her nude. It was summertime, very hot, and everyone was bathing in the river next to their property. Far from any onlookers, or so it seemed, she dove into the water and—

seven or eight years old at the time—delighted in being nude. Once back on shore, she looked in vain for her clothes. And yet, everyone else was gone. She ran across the open field back to the house, not very far, and up to her room to get dressed. None of her cousins or her sisters were there, all gone to play badminton; she had been the only one who decided to stay longer at the river, which is why she went nude. She joined the others and no one made the slightest allusion to the event. She also didn't talk about it that evening and never knew who took her clothes. Never knew whether anyone had seen. Her. Nude.

I listened attentively to her—that is, with a certain astonishment.

"Could it be that I took this theft [vol] to be a rape [viol]?" she asked. "The culprit was most likely someone close to me, I mean it must have been because a stranger would have had to cut across the lawn in front of the house, continue into the woods behind it, onto private, unknown property. But no one was there except my cousins, just silly adolescents and their parents, and another couple who were my parents' friends." She paused for a moment. "It actually could be them, but why? Why play such a nasty trick on a little girl bathing in the river? To punish me, to embarrass me? If so, I would have known, they would have ended up telling me . . . I need for you not to leave me alone with this. I don't understand . . . Would it have been enough to double-lock me in this impossible gaze upon myself, I mean to lock me in outside. I don't understand . . ."

"And what if this scene never took place?"

"Why would you say that? Don't you believe me?"

"Yes, I believe you. But perhaps you lost track of your clothes, for example, because you drifted a bit downstream, with the current? And you might have interpreted their disappearance how you did, as the prefiguration of what you call a 'rape' of your intimacy. This is what we do with our memories, lending them something of a prophetic value."

"For what reason?"

"The river, in dreams, is sometimes an extension of the maternal body, the uterine body . . ."

"This would then be a way of staging the rape of an image, of imagining that someone, if I denuded myself, would come steal my protection, my armor?"

I allowed for a silence. Then I continued: "Perhaps . . . memories are auguries. We place them at the beginning and then return to them because they tell something about what we have become; they are not completely made up, but we do unconsciously sift them, transform them, or mishandle them so that they become shards of a mirror reflecting our future ego, our existence to come."

"It's dizzying."

Nudity is a violence; it exposes us to the gaze, or a caress, or blows, or contempt, or seduction, without an opposing shore to lean on. The river is a state of liquid *fusion where, in the uterine body regained, there is nothing but the pure nudity of being. Do the stolen clothes* [habits dérobés] *mark the impossibility of being "one," of confidently letting oneself go? Perhaps this memory itself—whether true or reconstituted—steals* [dérobe] *from consciousness a more ancient theft* [vol], *a more archaic ripping away, itself outside any possibility of representation. This is what I gestured toward in my words to her. Doubt—which is to say, the vertigo that gripped the adult dreamer, lying there on the couch and in the impossibility that she betrays of confronting her own image, her nudity—thus arises as an effraction within the defensive citadel of forgetting. What is repressed, perhaps, far from this river, is the very earliest body.*

In amorous fusion you hardly feel the other's nudity or your own—by which I mean that these nudities form a third body that is the body of desire. In neurosis, nudity is altered—spoiled. It can be subjugated, confiscated, dismantled, and destroyed like we have perhaps been destroyed or abandoned. This is why the road is so long perhaps before you are able to abandon yourself to it with confidence, with friendship.

May There Be an End to Our Torment . . .

What do we want from an analyst: an end to our torments, a meaning to life, an answer for our fears, help finding love at last? Sometimes you have no idea what to hope for; you only know that someone will be there to listen. Perhaps that is all . . . an ear. There will be a framework posited, for protection: that is, a meeting place and one or two moments during the week apart from the daily routine, for a few months or a few years. It's also expensive for what you get: less than an hour. How can you believe that this would suffice to lift impediments to living? By what miracle will speech be able to conjure a whole generation of silence and misunderstandings? How can it dispel maledictions, despair, rage, mad jealousy, insomnia, amorous fever, or mourning? How much do you ask of a cure that you no longer even dare not believe in, even when you go ahead and entrust yourself to it, almost despite yourself? What will you lose in the process, and what might you discover along the way? In a strange way, they are the same thing: what you lose, what you find, but wholly otherwise. And how it happens is through the almost alchemical transmutation of a language. More than a language, in fact, it is a strange address, a living metaphor. Heard speech calls the analyst to witness as the one to whom it is addressed in secret. Whether silent or spoken aloud, whether a plea to a lover, the absent one, a reproach to a dead person, an incantation toward an animal, or a god, or the memory of a beloved body . . . this address makes language into a living, animate, or quasi-magic thing whose phenomenal power comes from the fact that it traverses at once the body and the spirit, and that it is linked, by breath, to the fact of arriving in life because an other carried you, named you, prattled to you, hoped for you, dreaded you, sung to you, and delivered you—what is called *being born.*

This speech is the space of our humanity, of hospitality to a humanity that, insofar as it is a space of immanence, absolutely overflows our subjectivity. In the voyage into and through this speech, therefore, a strange transmutation takes place that we have called: losing, then finding, and not re-finding, because what's found is a real find, in the sense of something singular, unprecedented, an unhoped for encounter, an overturning, almost a conversion without religion or armature, a pure event. Lacan said it somewhat differently: "How do we recognize one who loves? He has changed discourse." The word "discourse" should be understood in the Greek sense as logos, which has a secret affinity with truth.

Is the patient the only one who loses something in the senseless enterprise of analysis or does the analyst also lose something? At the beginning of an analytic cure, the subject interrogates her history; she explores the hidden byways of this history—its impasses, its secrets; slowly and against the grain she treads back to a past that she believes herself to know in part, pieces together the puzzle, assembles things said, convokes her memories and her buried emotions. She becomes an explorer and, in this excavation, exhumes treasures, vestiges, as well as horrors. She draws connections, forges hypotheses, and begins to detach affects from one another, to untangle fears, to isolate the different parts of her history (parents, siblings, friends, enemies), and in this enormous site, she does the work of reconnaissance; like an archeologist, she classifies, sifts, and exhumes. In this first period of analysis, she identifies guilty parties, those whom she knows and those whom she has misjudged; she will identify harm done, injuries. And naming them, she dresses (and addresses) them, disinfects the dormant wound that contaminated her whole psyche. We are still in a kind of refuge, a place where the work of analysis discovers unusual clearings; and yet, there is as yet no question what she, the patient, has invested in the subtle and permanent interplay between others and herself. This is when the true loss occurs. Little by little, what seemed to be solid ground will crumble; security will give way to doubt and vertigo.

The gambler's greatest fear, which buoys and saves her, is losing. To risk losing is to hold out hope of winning, of being able to make yet another bet, waiting, kept in suspense for an instant as the tiny ball hops around, as the next card peels from the deck, deciding her fate. To risk losing is to forge into the silky black of the shadows, in the belief that all will not close in on you, in the hope that something will reappear, unfold, bend back. Something that was not completely unknown to you . . . But what you lose in analysis, perhaps, is not simply the meaning that you believed it possible to give things; it is the "why," the imaginary cause of your complaint, of your affection, and of the injustice that accounts for it. It is the certainty that this is what has always determined your life. There is no why. Both consciousness and its inscription within the world are bound up and composed with the possibilities of the world. The delicate layering of the multiple events and determinations that produce the real are mixed up with your history, with endless ramifications, well beyond what's perceptible. And so what gets lost, at a given moment, is the certainty of belonging to a world, a language, or a territory of immediately transmissible recognition.

You are the patient who begins to lose your grip and no longer even knows why you came in the first place . . . The lack you used to feel so deeply—a lost lover, the child you didn't have, fleeting beauty, the time of youth, past glory—no longer affects you in the same way; you are prising yourself away from things you used to consider the most precious, your life's safeguards. But another lack will now appear, another sort of lack, such a radical lack in being that it will displace every other lack; it is a spiritual lack, a void that attracts and increases, that allows for linkage and life.

Breaking Up

Is this one of life's indispensable events: breaking up? But what a bizarre idea . . . For example, you'll probably agree that, most of the time, people don't enter analysis for the purpose of breaking up with someone but rather to heal after a break up. After a bereavement, a bout of melancholia, or a divorce perhaps, they come to repair themselves, to air their grievances. Nonetheless, what if analysis were a school of rupture?

Breaking up is oh so tedious, always the same old story. Nothing is sadder, today, than a breakup. Chronicles of unlove foretold, they seal the demise of an attraction that fell apart before it had a chance to develop. Pointless emotional burdens, vulgar feelings of despair, vague death wishes, the ingredients are always, or almost always, the same. In the case of a couple, the children become helpless onlookers of the carnage, forced to bear witness to a story that began well before they came on the scene and already wrapped up, digested in a necrology hastily composed for judges tired of listening to the same quarrels. There is a generalized lassitude about breakups because no one has a choice in the matter, as if the only thing we know how to do marginally well is break up. Or threaten to . . . and then do it anyway in a bout of unescapable melancholy. The thresholds of tolerance have been displaced, especially among women, whereas men are disoriented . . . To all appearances, breaking up has become a matter of style. Because it's bound to happen, the only question is—when? And then—how? After things get back to normal, it's like nothing happened. Life goes on, they say. But breaking up remains a rather grave thing to do, perhaps because no one really takes the risk of breaking up for real. We let breaking up act upon us like an ill wind of revolt, a "too late" converted into a now, a flurry of sad thoughts that end up gently laying waste to everyday life, nothing left unscathed. But, in the end, is that all it takes? Because we don't have much idea what we're looking for. New freedom? You've got to be naïve. Revenge, perhaps? The satisfaction fades so soon. Maybe, then, it's that you wanted an end to incomprehension, boredom, fatigue, recriminations. All of it, yes, no question, and yet a breakup happens between beings without really changing them; it wafts over them, undoes bonds, exhausts past hopes, and creates new and unanticipated obligations, all of it rather outside of oneself, as if, in the end, it happened out of bounds.

Nonetheless, I maintain that we must take the risk of breaking up. At least once. This is something you encounter in analysis, without knowing it. Breaking up, not with he or she whom we claim to love, or to hate, but rather with the more deep-seated pact whereby we are beholden to a debt older than our very lives, a debt that makes us inherently *obligated beings*. Why are we willing to pay such an exorbitant price to recommence the same scenario over and over again? Why do we prefer to hold on to our poor little miseries in place of the joy that might arise from the unknown, from the open sea? What keeps us here on the opaque side of things, closed off from memory, as close as possible to the regions where we suffered abandonment and lack? Still, we must—always and again—save our childhood from disaster, as if it behooved us to rescue it from an imminent shipwreck, sometimes fifty years after the fact. But what is the truth that frightens us so much as we shift the pieces around the chess board until all players are exhausted? "We believe that some novelty in our lives will turn everything upside down, make us unrecognizable, and enliven fossils; but we soon realize that what actually fascinates us about the new is the element of déjà-vu that it harbors," writes Maurice Terence. The same pieces along the same diagonals, from breakup to breakup, the same game is played again and again.

He left her before the summer. Like a dog left by the roadside. Just a note stuck to the fridge (the fridge!): I can't anymore. She had gone to her dance class, bought flowers for once, and arrived home in a carefree mood. They had lived together for a little less than a year. A perfect bliss, as it were. No intimation of disaster. Now she had to play the whole film in reverse. What's the meaning of this? She puts the flowers down, unfolds the red tissue paper . . . "I can't anymore." She has a fit of mad laughter and then collapses in tears. Hours pass. No sign of him. When the day finally turns to night, she has lost the ability to think. Nothing, there is nothing in her head. It's empty, as if no one had ever been there, ever. Nothing has any weight anymore. All is fuzzy. No hunger or cold has she now. No body.

At the hospital, they ask her name. She's at pains to remember. Finally, she pronounces it, very slowly, as if making sure it's right. The doctor is young, the psychiatrist on call one Sunday. He had anticipated harrowing emergencies, feared that the day of rest is particularly hard to bear for those who are locked out in their nausea and their dread. But he was not afraid of this frail woman. On the contrary, he felt like taking her in his arms and speaking gentle words to her. He can't. What happened to you? She said nothing, and so he began to speak, a bit at random, of himself, his likes and dislikes. And little by little she regained her color, in front of his very eyes. She took root and came to life like the plants in E.T., a movie that he would watch on Sunday afternoons as a child, a memory that couldn't but make him smile.

"Who brought me here?" she finally asked.

"You don't remember?"

"Your sister. You called her for help."

"Where is she now?"

"Home. She said that she couldn't leave her children alone. But she'll be back tomorrow. She signed the papers so you can rest. Do you know why you were brought here?"

He doesn't know whether he's allowed to say this. But he says it.

"My boyfriend left me," she responds. "That's not so serious," she adds, watching him. "Right?"

How to answer? At this moment, what's his role? He no longer knows. Should he tell her the truth? But what truth? That she was brought here because she became delusional. That her sister wanted to unload her as quickly as possible. That he is just the intern on call; that this is his first emergency; and that he no longer understands much of anything. Except perhaps her suffering. The biggest fear in this place is that the lovelorn will attempt suicide. We can't take that risk, they would answer (he knows already) if he requested same-day release for her (which makes her a prisoner?). She will have to be medicated and show that her wits have returned. In our day, it is scandalous to love too much. We are entreated to love within the limits of reason alone.

She slept. She stayed for a few days and then went home. There was mail at her door. But from him, nothing. She thought it was better that way. It seemed that she had the body of a newborn who barely knew how to breathe or to move, that she would have to relearn everything, slowly. She often thought of the intern: he probably didn't know that he saved her with his small talk, his awkward patience, and all the time for nothing that he devoted to her that Sunday night. She who loathed hospitals, crybabies, and Sundays . . . Under other circumstances, she might have fallen in love with him, but now she would always think of him as the young doctor too young for the task at hand, a little perplexed, lost amidst his too weighty function, and yet . . . To learn to break up, for this woman, would mean to accept the unthinkable, to proceed as if she'd taken a new name, opened herself to another gaze, and to reinvent everything.

The risk of breaking up, truly, for once, we have all actually taken it, at birth. When we breathe outside the womb for the first time, when new air fills our lungs and makes us cry, and we enter the world. Why should we have to be born anew? Why isn't one time enough? The risk of breaking up is the risk of revolution in the stellar sense of the term—*revolverer*, to turn around an axis. Such revolt isn't without wounds, but it is sovereign.

At the Risk of Speech

> We truly incline toward something only when it in turn inclines
> toward us, toward our essential being, by appealing to our essential
> being as what holds us there. Through this inclination, our being
> is called forth. Inclination is address. This address speaks to us
> from our essential being, calls us into being and holds us there.
> What keeps us in our essential being holds us only so long,
> however, as we for our part keep holding on to what holds us.
>
> —MARTIN HEIDEGGER, "What Calls for Thinking"[1]

Speaking and keeping silent, throughout the history of humanity, have always been two paradoxical figures of our liberation, our salvation, as well as our loss, and our night. Can I gently take my turn to speak? Can I speak without *taking* a turn? Without violence, without abuse? Instead, the question would be: can speech coexist amicably, fraternally, with me, with us? Very quickly, very soon, the exercise of speech becomes an exercise of power. From childhood on, obviously. The cry, in this sense, is what comes before speech. The cry—that of the child still an *infans*, or that of the prophet—is an impatience, a desire for speech. The cry shatters the voice without words. The will to speak is heard as early as the cry, as early as the first call. Speech gives form to the call, to the voice, to desire, to our engagement within existence. Confession is primarily avowal because it is the act of abandonment through speech to the Word. From Socrates to Augustine and up to Freud there is a continuous revolution that makes the given or avowed word—in brief, inner space—into the place of the truth of being. Its testing ground.

In analysis, it sometimes happens that speech in its entirety comes to grief, gets lost. There are those who make it to analysis only to have speech fail them, those to whom this act is refused, denied. Whose speech has been trampled on. Those who are frightened of speech, encumbered by it, or from whom it escapes. There exist lives that speech devastates, that this act of will and power overturns, and often kills. Are we healers of speech? Can we, in the cradle of analysis, through its slow anamnesis, rediscover a primary complicity with the world that would found each subject's ability to speak of it, to speak it, to say the world? This will to speak is often lacking. The will to hold to the world through speech. We are all plunged in a sort of insomnia that fixates speech within an impossible silence—the patient no less than the analyst. And slowly we begin to stammer, we *are at a loss for words* (another strange expression, abusive, because words are never first ours to lose but always the words of others, or other words, spoken by those who were here before us . . .) but we hang onto the heroic conviction that words will save us if we can just find them. As if our world owed its presence to nothing but a few words pronounced in the dark.

In analysis, we come across phantoms but also old people lost in speech as in a fantastic, black, and frightening world, populated by words without things, faces without names, words without head or tail. A father or a mother whom language drives mad, whom speech has drowned in the world. And those who persuade us, on certain days of distress, when speech no longer passes between them and us, that a great outbreak of Alzheimer's disease lies at the root of all possible humanity: I speak and nothing is created. I create, I make, and nothing is spoken, nothing is said. No longer spoken, life is savage, anterior, overwhelming. Speech becomes like a nocturnal calque on life and its horror. What is lost when speech dies? What can be regained? Is it something that we remember like an ancient event, a lost scent, or a person both alive and dead? Do there exist memories that will never have belonged to spoken life?

"The created world is everything that we can remember through speech," writes Frédéric Boyer. What analysis says is that the simple fact of being alive, of existing and speaking, of naming the world, is endowed with an inexhaustible value for life. It opens an immense freedom for us between life and death. The act of speech is also political: it is invested with a power, a gravity, and a sovereignty that make speech itself a indispensable to existence and power. "It is only our words which bind us together and make us human," writes Montaigne.[2] Often we think that we don't know, that the origins escape us . . . However, the beginning lies in the act of seizing the moment to speak that consists of saying the world, naming it. This is what is lost and what is regained. The same speech, but now returned. Lost in the process is the fantasy of an origin. The created world is never a stranger to us so long as we speak.

Speech is caught up in this analytic grinder: speaking in order to create, speaking to make happen, and speaking to recognize the thing created. The grinder that cycles between creation and recognition, between beginning and memory. Certain people can't recognize anything that their own speech has created, anything that the speech around them creates, does or undoes. There is a negative creation or a negative of creation, when speech no longer recognizes either things or words. When it no longer serves to make the world familiar but rather unsettles us like an other side of the world or an *other* of the world. Can speech also destroy the world? Or rather can the world destroy speech? I desire to speak in order to be because speech itself is the desire to be welcomed.

Words come afterwards. After the intimate and overwhelming certainty of the event, after the real, after birth, after death itself, words always lag behind; always, after the fact, they attempt to explain what can't be explained, to give meaning to what causes nothing but vertigo; they reformulate memories, imprint them with tranquil assurance when they are as evanescent, as troubling, and as new as the very words that retrace them—everything is reinvented, which is what's incredible. No one can recreate the tonality or immense emotional charge of the first music from before our birth. The first vocal tonality remains unavowed, unavowable. Words register our alibis, our requirement that things be a certain way, our need for meaning, fidelity, sharing, our belief that we speak the same language, that words alone might change something; and it's true that, if they have such power, it derives from the primary, definitive emotion that binds them to our body. Our thinking, hoping bodies, our distraught and sobbing bodies as well, free, at times, of words.

Solitudes

Is solitude a secret prefiguration of death? We can accept solitude in small doses, for a limited time, when the other remains within reach and we tremble at the thought of losing her; we play with the idea, frighten ourselves, feel alone, and then cry. But solitude as the space of the world is something other, wholly other. When the known world disappears, when its contours start to fade, when you keep heading down the same endless corridors without knowing where your steps will lead, when the darkness no longer promises light, when no voices seem familiar anymore, when nothing echoes but your own weightless movements above the void, where does one find refuge? Who will hear us, who recognize us? Solitude is sometimes the name for this opacity, for this slow panic that comes over the whole body to the point of paralysis, when you no longer even know the name of love. Here, who knows, there might appear another moment of the world, another name for the real.

In chosen solitude, which comes with joy and lightness of being, nostalgia for what used to be disappears, along with regret for what never happened, and the burden of all repetitions gathered up in the blink of an eye. It is the movement of this yes, to life, to the instant, the child's yes (Nietzsche), the yes that departs from expectations, from fear, from disappointment, from what had been envisaged, stared down, vanquished, from what gives asylum to the living, to the most loving; and suddenly everything grows lighter with a lightness that is not nothing, that is an invisible and swarming world, a whole world set down right here, quivering with ramifications right into you, toward you and beyond, in a strange dance that you never learned and that still opens a path for you through this untamed night. In this quietude, which does not renounce the night, or fear, or horror, in this miraculous quietude that comes to you with such solitude, the regained world is there, and suddenly fatigue is gone and you have ceased to struggle.

"I am alone" is a complaint that we hear repeated, obstinately, especially in this place that is the analyst's den. A vertiginous utterance, Derrida recalls, because the avowal itself supposes that you are not alone. That there is a witness to hear. Only someone suffering from amnesia could tell us, without doubt, what it's like to be locked out, without an inkling of recognition, not even toward yourself . . . What is a solitude outside of language—without a single metaphor or memory safeguarded? How to name the isolation experienced by someone who no longer even knows how to stand up, without any reserves left to draw the strength to continue? Someone at the limits of strength and often unable to express suffering except with her body: insomnia, anxiety, malaise, nausea, vertigo. Sometimes, solitude strips things of their obviousness. The obviousness of the real's copresence within us—like living archives deposited, displaced, reinvested, uninscribed—even this we forget. Just as we forget that one day we were ripped from the fetal state, from the uterine memory that had carried us. One born from two by cellular division. Do we ever recover from this exile? If not, would we talk about it? Would we have this strange obsession with solitude?

There are no shamans left, not many priests, and churches are closed at night. Nothing remains for loners and insomniacs but friends and analysts. The other, there, who listens to us, whom we invest with the aura of knowing and recognition, whom we give the trust necessary for analysis (in the almost chemical sense of the term), is the one who could—who must—heal all of our pain. She is the one to whom we come to pry open the unbearable vise of solitude. And yet a new solitude is what comes to light in the voyage of the cure. No, the analyst won't be there to meet our expectations of finally being saved from being alone, not even to evoke the epiphany of an absent presence. For nothing can suture this solitude except the encounter with the world itself . . .

It is difficult, almost insurmountable, to give up hoping for someone to arrive with the right answer for our suffering, the magic balm of recognition offered at last. It's quite hard for the analyst, too, not to offer the appeasement demanded of her! We seek the other in the place of love even as we don't allow ourselves to believe in it, our negation raised to the level of pain. But who will save us form the search for pure love? The scenarios of our solitude are our principal enigma. How can we abandon them, unravel them? This is the beginning of a long and slow traversal in which taste for the *how* prevails over the search for the *why*.

Solitude on the couch is the certainty of a voice that carries well beyond its own echo, but it is also the nonresponse of the analyst, or at least the gap between the expectation of a response and what is given—or just silence. For the only response belongs to she who doubts and calls out, who waits impatiently, to the point of exhaustion, for a true speech that will come to offer words for her suffering and deliver her. The appeal to God, for some people, is the only possible avenue of recognition out of solitude.

It is not easy to recover from the inner fragmentation that solitude can evoke when anxiety attacks the very possibility of our being in the world. A parent's unhappiness, for instance, prevents a child from perceiving solitude as a possible refuge. Many children of suffering parents, good little soldiers of an unknown cause, are consigned to such a fate. To enter familiarity with a certain solitude is to accept that supposedly reliable bonds are deceptive, and to take the risk of tarrying with yourself as an unknown friend, very gently, as you would enter into convalescence. A regained taste for solitude is so precious that it is preferable to all else. It occurs where thought emerges, where ideas visit us, where sensations begin life. The enlargement of being, here, cannot be subjectified. It is the sorcerer's crucible that undoes our recourse to perpetual avoidance, the regime to which neurosis commits us. Our ancient loyalties deny that solitude can be savored rather than remain a source of affliction, horror, and sadness. Why is it so dangerous? Why the stubborn will to prevent yourself from living it, such a powerful and solar solitude? Because this inner resource goes by way of revolt and resistance: a sort of anticonsumerist ascesis, it is the capacity to resonate with the world without getting ensnared in it.

This is how we will outwit this solitude, to look in it for a new skin, a different gaze that will tell us who we are, even as it delivers us from the burden of being ourselves, if only briefly, one night, for a single moment. This is how we project ourselves into other lives, into other miniscule fragments of dreams where we will believe ourselves recognized. This solitude will be the inner echo chamber of our sensations, our expectations, our ideal. We only offer it refuge by lassitude or default. Such is our intolerance of the idea of living only for oneself. As if we did nothing else since childhood but collect partial imprints, little rhymes, *cailloux chou genou*, eyelids filtering air and light, a caress, the smell of fire, a face leaning in—a whole miniature clockwork universe, but for whom? And for what? For an other who will remember as well? This is a tenacious illusion but one that keeps us upright, up until the bitter end. You will never belong to me. And I too will escape you. And we will love each other without knowing the abyss that separates us and yet brings us together, as close as possible to one another. At evening light, just before dark, is when something appears, is delivered. Very furtively. A certain solitude that wouldn't hurt, which allows for writing, and loving. And suffering as well, but with grace, lightness. Like a dress that flutters in the wind. To accept being in this remainder that nothing will exhaust is to be capable, also, of being in peace. A certain solitude is the saturated point necessary for creation to break through. No work is created outside such a point of solitude.

Laughter, Dreaming—Beyond the Impasse

Laughter is a risk. Dreaming too. You can laugh or dream about anything and this is precisely what is scandalous. Humor is not an authorized path of thought; or, if sanctioned, it will be in the name of every good reason that can be found for implementing ever subtler forms of censorship. Laughter and dreams are effractions; they don't say where they come from. Only after the fact can you form a hypothesis. Laughter carries us all to the edge of a fissure; it tarries within ambiguity, where things take a fall, as in jest or a gag. In the face of the unbearable, laughter is still possible. Both laughter and dreams are flashes of wit that the body renders tangible, the one by spreading concrete joy, the other in the eclipse of sleep. Operators of the real, neither of them traffics in desire or freedom. Each is a singular mode of resistance, a derailment, an instantaneous form of intelligence. A very fleeting solution to the question, "what sustains desire in the face of death?"

Humor is the only real solution to neurosis, Freud said. Dreaming as well, I would add. They are magnificent compromises and not forms of renunciation—indeed, the only compromises with respect to the real that are not neurotic. Laughter and dreams come in bursts: they are effractions that tear apart the skein of everyday life, signs of the resistance of the human in the face of the inhuman. Neurosis is a compromise that primarily hinges on denial: this very painful thing that happened to me, let's just say that it doesn't exist, that it never existed. This thing that I think I know and that causes me anxiety, I'll just forget about it, the conflict that gives rise to an impossible choice, I won't think about it, I won't represent it... This is how we look for ways to escape from the tyranny of the real, from our native helplessness, albeit at the price of distorting our vision, denying our desire, and forgetting what took place. This is how the family romance gets written, stripping us of the ability to suffer, endlessly rewriting a scenario that we are obliged to believe in. But neither laughter nor dreams bend to the law of denial. In a certain respect, they escape censorship, opposing all power with an unquenchable language of truth. In a flash of humor, reality, no matter how terrible, is neither denied nor truncated, but rather transcended, contriving for the subject to rise above it in a burst of laughter.

But humor is not exactly the same thing as laughter. Freud opposes the laughter of humor—in which the one who provokes it laughs with the other and at herself—to the witticism of irony and its cruelty at a distance, its desperate detachment, but also to the metaphysical slapstick of the clown. To exemplify the exit from the impasse of neurosis, Freud cited a phase that has since become famous: "a criminal who was being led out to the gallows on a Monday remarked: 'Well, the week's beginning nicely.'"[1] No compromise here. Since death is the only exit from life, without alternative, what to do in the meantime? The least one can say is that Freud, in this essay, is quite close to Marcus Aurelius. Freud the Stoic finds in the familiar proximity of death a comfort that might be hailed with a witticism. There is no ordeal that you can't whistle your way out of, a woman patient tells me one day while speaking of her father shot down by the Francoists, adding: "What he didn't say to me: from the moment you accept that it will probably kill you . . ." The humor that outwits the torsion of the superego and the surveillance that presses at every instant upon the obsessional neurotic that we all potentially are, such humor is perhaps a form of abstinence; it consents to a radical self-dispossession that makes every situation appear artificial or burlesque. What's odd about Freud's stoicism here is that, in the course of a discussion of humor, he proposes that definitive liberation from the torment of inhibition, anxiety, and the inaptitude at life, can only be won by facing up to our more or less foretold death sentence with a snub of the nose, a witty remark. Along the same lines, Jewish jokes maintain a resolutely metaphysical distance toward death. Such jokes summon wit in order to steel one's patience, definitively, with respect to existence caught up not in the torment of neurosis but of persecution, knowing that it always begins with ourselves. Laughter is not entirely the black humor of the man sentenced to death who Freud invokes in his wish to detach us once and for all from the sirens of illusion; it is both more radical and more simple, because it is also an invention of the body. In this respect, the closest thing to it is, perhaps, the dream...

For, indeed, the other possible resolution, in face of the real, is the dream. Both laughter and dreams are flashes of wit. Each is an incarnation of thought in the body; each is literally the spirit made flesh. Laughter is form of seizure, since, as we say, a person can keel over laughing, or stifle a laugh, or burst out laughing; and its upsurge is most often irrepressible, so that, like the dream, it is a sort of eclipse. It is a form that allows us to slip the shackles of our subject position, to which it opposes a freedom, an intrinsically risky mode of resistance. At the vertiginous edge of the unbearable, it consorts with our madness. Don't we speak of mad laughter, which refers to the demonical aspect of the impulse to laugh that, even in a dramatic context such as a burial or a car accident might break out and seize hold of the whole audience. It is, for instance, the only failsafe antidote to sadomasochistic scenarios. Take an SM ritual and usher in a facetious witness—the whole thing will collapse in a burst of laughter. The exercise of power requires solemnity, which places us in the antechamber of dread; laughter knows fear but does not sustain it, much like the dream that allows us *in extremis* to escape our assailants. It denudes the machinations of power and exaggerates its features to the point of absurdity. Far from Kierkegaardian irony, that redoubtable weapon for felling the architecture of the Hegelian dialectic, far from the vitriolic irony of Cioran, laughter lays claim to a form of stupidity, of innocence. The propagation of drunkenness without alcohol, nor anything else to sustain it but but an image, an imitation, or a funny story, laughter is also communicable. It is shared. Drollery forges a community around an elusive point of impact; what hits the mark propagates all by itself. This light and communicable convulsion has something to do with truth and travesty. It unveils the real by painting its face, twisting a situation to the point of absurdity, signaling its hidden stupidity, sounding the alarm. Nevertheless, indeed, there is a sort of innocence to laughter because it entails the surrender of reason. At a certain moment, intelligence lays down its weapons and the body is seized with laughter. The genius of Chaplin was his use of the gag to up-end logic. Thought, or the image, is no longer an object of examination; it becomes a flash point, literally enters your body. And this surrender is both dangerous and devastating. It is an effective weapon against all power because, to the very end, laughter can stand up to force; but it is also a point of resistance to thought, obliging it to bow down in defeat. Laughter grabs you by the throat like sobbing, to which it's so close; emotion prevails over the examination of consciousness. Like the dream, laughter goes through the body in order to go beyond thought; for, after all, in a certain respect, a joke can't be explained. When you dream, consciousness is eclipsed in order to transmit a message that remains inadmissible; its disguises, its detail, are each precious gems. The unconscious is redoubtably precise; it offers the dreamer a freedom that she wouldn't have—or have any longer—without the dream. It offers her a margin of lightness but also compels her to pass through the fearsome defiles of trauma; it causes her to revisit a time that never ceases *not* to pass; but the image makes it possible to escape the worst, to avoid having to confront it directly, since it is only a dream… Nothing about it is forgotten and yet we end up with only a handful of fears, reminiscences that perplex us upon waking, recalling us to ourselves as never before.

Another way out of the impasse: dreams and laughter are erotic solutions to the neurotic compromise. From eros they derive their brilliance and impact the body like a flash of jouissance. Eros, Lacan recalls, is an effect of the real. In this sense, we might say that it is a metaphor in the body for the libido, not far from the amorous embrace in which erotism unfolds. Even when laughter is not linked to explicit sexual allusions, when it appears in the context of a wholly other reality, one that is "just funny," it remains charged with an erotic energy—much like the scraps of a dream that stay with us, I think, a fragment of desire partially extracted from a buried knowledge, of which we retain a color, a taste, intermingled sensations and impressions. Laughter does not care about being right, nor does the dream. Even after the mechanism of laughter has been exposed—as in a running gag or, indeed, the interpretation of a dream—a part remains unknown that gives it a secret erotic charge. Neurotic repetition is like mathematical fractions; what gets repeated is secretly the same "relationship" but never in the same guise. You are destined to replay the same scenario of abandonment with beings who have nothing to do with it; the relationship itself is the thing that returns; and, in a certain respect, dreams and laughter make their own use of this technique but they expose its workings and thereby become redoubtable enemies of the superego.

One comes to analysis with little scraps of self braided together—tender or murderous phrases jealously guarded like mantras, improvised shelters from fatality—what Tristram Shandy called "hobby horses"; you come with bits of dreams that open onto unknown landscapes, certain qualities of light; all this comes with you to analysis: little magical thoughts amidst impasses—there where things come to a halt, where they are repressed, where they curl upon themselves like a wave, and where their expression is prohibited, struck down.

"I dreamed of 12 yellow wolves," says a woman patient who abandoned a career in mathematical engineering for photography. She was the inventor of a process that makes faces both appear and disappear, become universal. Among her extended family there are suicides that no one talked about in fear of being stigmatized in the village, an ignominious fate. "Twelve, like the 12 times of day, like the 12 months, like time that circles back on itself, time enclosed within ritual and the annual cycle, the life cycle as well. In any event," says this beautiful young woman, "I have always been already old."

Subsequently, she will say "dogs" each time she referred to the threatening animals that popped up in her dream. And when I remind her that she had first called them wolves, she responded: "I forgot... it's a little vague. It's like the time of night when I was born, 'between dog and wolf,' as people say, neither night nor day, the hour of lengthening shadows."

Yellow is solar, but the wolf, as the archaic animal of fairy tales and the frozen steppes, should be black. Is the creativity that photography opens up as disquieting for the dreamer as the apparition of a wolf for a traveler? The dream tells of the uncanniness of an animal become incandescent: the black and gold of an unknown bestiary. Isn't it also said that man is a wolf to man? Dreams bring images that verge on known forms, objects, faces, and landscapes; they are pieces of me/not me, little discoveries that you let drop, as if they had nothing to do with yourself. They are bursts of the real that emerge from a forgotten scene whose form you try to reconstitute. "Twelve yellow wolves": the dream is a visitation, a haiku in our own language. Same as a burst of laughter? "Interpreting a text," Deleuze wrote, "always comes back to evaluating its humor. A great author is someone who laughs a lot."[2]

Sometimes it is necessary to set a dream aside, let it haunt us for a while without trying to understand it, like a nursery rhyme detached from memory—whose isolated refrain sticks in the head but can't be localized in space or time. Freud writes: "There is often a passage in even the most thoroughly interpreted dream which has to be left obscure; this is because we become aware during the work of interpretation that at that point there is a tangle of dream-thoughts which cannot be unraveled and which moreover adds nothing to our knowledge of the content of the dream. This is the dream's navel, the spot where it reaches down into the unknown."[3] The analyst, too, must know how to leave the dream alone, as if forgotten, confident that it will return in its own time. We should stop imagining the unconscious as a reserve, a bag of repression, libido, drives. The unconscious is an act—which assembles, disassembles, and disposes memory, the body, and forgetting in a movement like a shuttle across a loom. Anything integrated into to the canvas of the dream branches out in the session, between the imaginary of the analyst and that of the patient; it is a psychically bound force. The entire creativity of the dream is an attempt to reconnect thought to image and emotion, to recreate new circuits, hitherto in disuse because the old ones had been destroyed. Thought, too, gets frozen in the wake of trauma. Trauma prevents you from thinking, from thinking of trauma itself. It inwardly anaesthetizes the devastated zone and by extension everything that might relate to it. Only the dream, sometimes, escapes this obliteration. Whence the vagueness of dreams, sometimes evoked in analysis, and the difficulty of finding the right words. How to gain enough confidence to open the door to the imaginary without anxiety, to let yourself be guided, to offer hospitality to images and new ideas? The circle on the water opens up; the surface of the mirror warps; the exit from narcissism is the abandonment of something of the body, its very envelope. When you pass anew through traumatic territories, you accept a measure of desubjectification, the "no longer being yourself" that was integral to initiations in ancient civilizations. Such was, for the dreamer, the encounter that night with twelve yellow wolves.

The following night, she once again dreamed of a yellow wolf, but this time there was only one. Staring right at her. That's was all. She remembered a walk she took in the Bronx one snowy winter day, after her mother obtained her divorce. At the Bronx zoo, there was her mother's crying and most certainly . . . wolves. In her most recent dream, she says, this funny wolf staring at her. She wasn't afraid. In the midst of describing him to me, she started laughing, uncontrollably laughing.

"I have no idea why," she said catching her breath, "it was a ridiculous wolf."

The dream has a relation to fright and fantasy. Laughter as well. It manages to turn fright into sweetness, interdiction into an open door, but it holds onto a few traces of the surmounted terror. Laughter is not a simple substance; it is bound up within a complex web that likens it to the construction of a dream that is now gone except for a single fragment or arresting image. The moment when laughter erupts, when joy spills out, is the terminal stage of a subtle process of germination. There is, in what we remember from our dreams, in the fragments deposited in us, fantasy combined with images from the body itself, prohibition imposed by censorship (certain things forbidden from thought not because they are somehow "indecent" but rather too close to trauma), and yearning, the displacement of the essential into the details, as in the art of camouflage. The risk of the dream is to signify to the dreamer that the path forward is always second-ary; it is always, as Kierkegaard asserted, a repetition. It signifies to us, says to the child in us, to this eternal revenant who weeps over the disappear-ance of a lost world: never will you get anything back, not the same as it used to be, perhaps nothing at all. Difficult as this might be, it doesn't lead to resignation; at this point, a new path is invented where none was before. And laughter, this time it allies itself with the dream, to say, in its turn, a strange solution has opened up, a way out of the impasse, a wolf who's not disturbing but absurd. In brief, a silly wolf...

But there is bad laughter just as there are bad dreams. When we join forces with an other in derision, we touch on what is most contemptible in human beings. To laugh at an other is, in a certain respect, a manner of transforming fright into hate. The humiliation of a derided person hits close to home, as in a nightmare: what if that was us, there, in his place? I'd like to recall Bergson's famous text on laughter: "[F]or laughter has no greater foe than emotion... To produce the whole of its effect, then, the comic demands something like a momentary anesthesia of the heart. Its appeal is to intelligence, pure and simple."[4] And he pursues this line of thinking with these famous lines: "The attitudes, gestures and movements of the human body are laughable in exact proportion as that body reminds us of a mere machine... This is no longer life, it is automatism established in life and imitating it. It belongs to the comic."[5] But let us return for a moment to the yellow wolf. This liberating laughter might well be suffused with extreme emotion—like any outburst of laughter, I believe, no matter how futile, fleeting, or mechanical is might seem. The same goes for the well-oiled mechanics of the gag. There is, Vaclav Havel writes, an anatomy of the gag. Its mainspring, he adds, is the sudden and unexpected leap from one generally recognized convention to another. It stages a quick disinte-gration of the body. Immediate disarticulation/recomposition, hanging by a thread. And we get it. The gag shows us our passing moments of weak-ness, their singularization ad absurdum. Indeed, there is a mechanism of the gag just as there is a mechanism of the body. We laugh at it and find it wonderful. Of savagery, we only want to retain its style; of the gag, we only want to know its catastrophic denouement, but as a cause for gaiety. From behind, Chaplin's body seemed wracked by sobs. From the front, he is shown preparing a cocktail in a shaker, agitating it frantically. The cruelty of the gag recalls the cruelty of temporal existence. We are nothing but laughter, falling, and contempt. We are nothing but the surprise of the instant that summons us back to our temporality. Slayed by the instant, the time that opens right beneath our feet. The comic relies on error as a source of energy and representation. It reveals the share of the absurd necessarily engaged in and by existence. "The gag reveals to man his own amnesia," Frédéric Boyer writes, "in the task of existing in the world and unto others. Something of humanity's somnambulism suddenly appears. The waking dream of familiar life incarnated by the pure cinematographic silhouettes of the early burlesque films. Like high-wire walkers upon an invisible wire, stretched out on the ground and thereby above an even more dizzying abyss. The sleepy gaze of Stan Laurel. The imperturbable gentleness of Buster Keaton. The dancing awkwardness, graceful and on point, of Charlie Chaplin. The greatest precision within the vague, a new kind of awkwardness always in the service of a higher catastrophism. A manner of underscoring their resemblance to children."[6]

Laughter liberates, dreams as well. They attempt, at least, to free us from the loyalties that we uphold with all our might, against all odds but above all against ourselves. In a sense, they make us have the experience of a positive trauma. Events with no return, they happen and that's it. A radical risk. Of the same nature as joy, I believe, they are moments from which we don't recover, opening, for a few seconds or hours, a space of psychic openness to the unprecedented. Dreams and laughter blur the boundaries between night and wakefulness, the luminous and the obscure, the precise and the vague; they bear witness to a new possibility of invention and resistance that subverts repetition from an unanticipated angle. For a brief interval, their effraction opens toward what hasn't been already said, already written, already signed, already destroyed, offering us a few magic signs.

Hope No More

We must keep a distance no less from defeat than from hope.

—GEORGES BATAILLE

Hope is a strange drug whose effect begins with the value we accord it: eternal life, nothing less. Of all the poisons concocted by consciousness, it is perhaps the most redoubtable. For the slow and meticulous work of neurosis and its compromises are nothing without hope. But how can we cast doubt on the means whereby human consciousness, gambling on time, exits its own condition in order to project itself into a future freedom? Hope is a strange form of renunciation because it incites us to bet on the future; it offers an exit door out of the present situation and signifies to us: tomorrow will bring relief . . . As the secret motor of our renunciations, hope is what permits us to hold on. And often, we must admit, there is no alternative but to gulp this poison to the dregs rather than sink ever so gently into the abyss. But such is the subtle danger of hope; it makes us believe that without it our life would already be lost. No way to do without it any more than dreams, thinking, and beauty.

How does existence become something we endure, something that we survive? By hope. This is what gives rise to the swamps of ordinary melancholy. Contracts have been signed with the so-called economy of the real;

and, for the price of this resignation, you get the dream of another life. And yet, isn't hope our primary task? That of mystics, madmen, and people on their last legs, living in physical and psychic misery. But they don't even have enough strength left to hope. Wresting free of the possible, imagined to be inexhaustible, only leads us to remain entangled in impossible situations. Fatigue then descends on everything and doesn't even weigh on us. Living in hope leaves the present ridden with anxiety and resentment and ceaselessly puts off any expectation of metamorphosis until tomorrow, for the benefit of an unconscious tyranny begun long before oneself, intimately woven into the history of the generations that preceded us and whose revolt as well as sacrificial power we also carry inside. "True life" is thereby relegated to the accessory aisle of the future. This life endlessly begun anew tomorrow, whose very credibility is in jeopardy, becomes opaque, muddy, reluctant to become a destiny. And the ever displaced, differential (in Derrida's sense) space, which it opens between us and our fantasies, between the truth of our desire and our inability truly to desire, ceaselessly projects its shadows out in front of us.

To internalize a practice of hope should be possible, but in the instant. No temporal rupture. Remind yourself that the combat is right here, right now, without further ado. That things have already started to turn; that always and again it's a matter of being born, of breaking up, of separating, and of being delivered. Of opening yourself to what happens. To the never before of the event—that is, to what might be an event, always, for each and everyone. But then perhaps we need another word for the sort of hope that despairs of the future and refuses to wait, a new type of courage.

Hope is yet another word for consolation. It provides the surfeit of meaning that you can't stop looking for, to the point of madness. The great lesson of the Stoics is that, as we go through the world and continue in life, we should sharpen our perception to the point of indifference. Which is anything but lukewarm, depressed, or resigned. Stoic *ataraxia* (indifference: terrible translation of a magnificent word) is a posture of war—make no mistake about it—of extreme precision. To attain Stoic indifference is to take everything that comes with the intensity of what is given, lived, but without preference, without adherence, and without suffering from it. Not to hope for the future is not to be devoid of hope. Another word is thus needed for this precise risk. It's like a glove turned inside out, the same but with the seamy side showing. The seamy side of hope—not a matter of renunciation but consent to what our desire encounters in the real, here, now. Stoic thought doesn't give us a magic formula to combat the ills that befall us nor a mollifying reading of the world; nor does it coil up in the self-enclosure of a refuge undisturbed by external events. Rather than any of this, it incites you to go for a walk in a rainstorm and not care about the downpour, violent as it might be, and to confront the *hubris* and immoderation that we all maintain in secret.

Neurosis is a logic of deferral, and of power as well. It constructs a patient economy of expectation and renunciation; it calibrates a subtle dosage, leaving you with a little of both. Prince Charming is on his way. We never tire of the Sleeping Beauty scenario in the hope that the destiny of her magic wand might save us. But what if the point was to get lost in the forest without asking anyone for directions; what if, indeed, the point was to get lost on purpose . . . never to retread the same path twice, not to keep desperately waiting for a clearing to appear, but rather for night to fall, for darkness. How do we bend hope toward the heart of the present, enter into the presence of each detail like an entomologist of sensation, of evanescence, of upsurge, of the least thinkable, and sometimes the most equivocal?

This attention to the present, which undoes the alibi of hope, brings to mind certain films by Marguerite Duras, the apparent immobility of a camera that imperceptibly displaces the light and the gaze and causes us to hear an oblique quality of voice off to the side of the word, at an angle, in harmony with it. It's the risk that nothing is there—or, at least, precisely, nothing visible. Still frame. A presence from behind. For example, *L'homme Atlantique* or even *Agatha*. "Living as far from defeat as from hope" might resemble such a space, overexposed and yet secret. An almost immobile space-time, as if suspended in such a way that each movement is cast in particular relief, with its own singular, inimitable accent. Each shot sequence emerges from an unforgettable time, forever fixed within you, you who watch the film without understanding why nothing budges, why so few gestures, so little light to accompany the words spoken with backs turned. How to make a present arise where there is no longer any present? You must set off anew and, in this secrecy, begin. At times life affords us a reprieve, to be present, truly present to what appears, to what unconceals itself. Nietzsche, we might recall, sought to think force as what exposes itself unprotected and thus reveals itself in its own fragility, in combat. Sometimes the real defeats us. Its impact strikes us at the exact spot where we were vulnerable. This might be the death of someone close, but also a friend who betrays you, a devastated love, an unfinished project, an accident. This is also called being heart-struck. We judge the ways in which our life falls short of our dreams, and the only match for our severity is the trusty excuse of the "real," always in reach when an alibi is needed (however shoddy we know it is). It might be even more difficult to live as far from defeat as from hope because defeat is not our fault. It just happens and places us at its mercy. It might take the form of a miniscule event, such as the fall, in Tolstoy's tale, from which Ivan Ilyich never recovers; the ricochet causes an inner death before it becomes visible. A defeat, both silent and light.

You live what you desire to live. A revolting formulation in relation to the poor, the excluded, those whose misery can't be relieved, whom fate has laid low, who have met death on the road one rainy night, broken before they could take another breath, and offering nothing to the survivors but an eternity of crap. Not to recognize that it's a desire that guides us and fashions a life for us in our own image, for which there is no question of finding an alibi or excuse, increases the ranks of victims who know nothing about the despair that holds them prisoner. Defeated in the midst of their lives, such victims are gravediggers of the almost unbearable existence that comes back to them each day, deserted by pleasure or only hastily visited by it, as if by the sheer luck of an unknown grace. You live what you want to live. This is perhaps where, very gently and carefully, we should begin anew. Forget consciousness and the unconscious and their ill-conceived dispute, their heterogeneity; forget about asking why . . . Begin where you already are, "for real," as children like to say. For real does not mean that there is some original reality; it just attempts to articulate the impact of what we persist in calling the real, as if it occurred wholly outside of us. How to examine yourself and identify bit by bit the stuff of our stellar composition, as a very young chemist might do? To observe our dreams and forget nothing, to subject ourselves to no judgment but our own benevolence, and to begin by desiring to be right where we already are, to take what we do and what we love back for ourselves and into ourselves. . . Do we ask what is it that guides our steps, our days, our expectations, what we celebrate or ignore, what we hate, cherish, pursue, abandon, without considering any external cause as valid? At least initially, yes. Everything considered "obligatory"—that is, necessary—or almost. Contemporary Stoicism? Perhaps . . .

Hope comes at the risk of unhope, I believe. The defeat of the hope that has us believe in a better life on the way, soon. A sorrow well lost. How do we not, in the process, give up all hope? Take the time just to sort through what's sprouting right in front of you . . . Understand which species of which wild grasses are interspersed with the pebbles, the mounds of dirt, rodents—which roots foster growth and which suffocate it. With the calm and patient demeanor of an apprentice gardener tending a patch of daffodils sprouting among wild grasses. Explore, watch. Take the risk of seeing, making tiny judgments before laying a hand. Observe it with love. Everything will then take on another color. No revelation, no, just a gravitation.

Once Upon a Time, the "Athenaeum" ... or, Why Risk Romanticism?

How could we have forgotten the night of the Romantics who, in 1800, together in Jena, wanted to remake the world? A few men, and two women, who wanted to share love, thought, friendship, space and time, the future they envisaged, along with the end of terror. At this moment in history, thinking was regarded as an activity of the highest importance. The Schlegel brothers in collaboration with Carolina, August's future wife, and Dorothea, Friedrich's scandalous mistress, launched a journal of immense significance in the history of thought: the *Athenaeum*. They dreamed of a new Athens, and of a new relationship to the ideal and the universal than what the Enlightenment set forth. Through them, it was another relationship to the night that opened up at the heart of philosophy. Hegel, Schelling, and Hölderlin also happened to be in Jena at the same moment, along with Novalis, Fichte, Schleiermacher, and other poets. Venerating Goethe while flaunting him at the same time, the Romantics situated art at the very heart of philosophy, and thereby ousted the pure form of the Kantian a priori, the subject emptied of any possibilities of being, from his enchanted kingdom and convoked man to respond to the night. The sensory night, the night of poets and madmen, the night of exile and revolt, the night of language and its crystal history. Six issues of the *Athenaeum* were published. It was around 1800—or around midnight, as it were. Recall that one hundred years later, in the work of Lewis Carroll, would take place the unbirthday tea party with Alice and the Mad Hatter. Freeze frame. At Jena, too, time had just begun. The German Romantics invented a new language, another way of naming the world, and terror. And this was (almost) all. Everyone else continued on without them; they wrote and taught; something had been born and come to an end. It was like all utopias, undoubtedly beautiful in proportion to their fragility. This philosophical distillation took place while the wider world was embroiled in unprecedented revolutions, the siege of Stalingrad on the horizon.

It is as if, writes Annie Le Brun, "the only aim of poetic consciousness were to give form to a lack that almost everyone feels without knowing anything about it. The whole greatness of German Romanticism would thus reside in its blind faith in the shackle-breaking force of what Schlegel termed *echappées de vue*."[1] It was in the agitation of German intellectual life at the end of the eighteenth century that the group of the early Romantics took form; then will come England, around Shelley and Byron, and France. The epoch that begins with Jena features a return to the magic world of myth. The thought of nature sought to counterbalance the Kantian separation of natural mechanics from infinite freedom. It was also said that the Romantics upheld nature as something other than a pure mechanism in order to reunify terms that Kant left unreconciled. But Kant was not their enemy; Romanticism also took form on the basis of Kant's radicality and his philosophy of the sublime. The utopia that sustained them simply envisaged the nocturnal as the indomitable territory that Enlightenment reason wouldn't politicize, to which even the young Hegel will appoint himself a witness. In the first version of the *Phenomenology of Spirit* (1805), as Annie Le Brun underscores, there is an idea of the nocturnal absolute that is inconsistent with Hegel's ultimate attempt to reprise the totality of the negative within the life of spirit: "Man is this night, this empty nothingness that contains everything in its simplicity—a wealth in infinitely many representations, images, none of which occur to it directly, and none of which are not present. This is the Night, the interior of nature, existing here—pure Self—in phantasmagoric representations where night is everywhere: here a bloody head suddenly shoots up and there another white shape, only to disappear as suddenly. We see this Night when we look a human being in the eye, plunging our gaze into a night that turns terrifying. This is the night of the world that comes to meet us."[2] So wrote the young Hegel whose genius hadn't yet brought his system of the world to a close as the triumphant march of the Spirit through History. This Hegel belongs to the same time that the German Romantics opened up. Beginning from this total night of the subject, thought and poetry come together to invent new alliances in which style and content are no longer opposed. Writes Novalis: "Our language is either—mechanical—atomistic—or dynamic. But true poetic language should be organically alive. How often one feels the poverty of words—to express several ideas all at once."[3] In this desired and sought after unity of myth and philosophy, poetry and a certain mathematics of being, there is, we might say, a quest shared among all Romantics, just as they shared in the relationship of the fragment to the totality, or in a thinking of the future, which, contrary to Nietzsche's a few years later, wouldn't only be figured by the Eternal Return of the Same and the Will to Power. This unity can also be found in the unsettling figure of Eckerman, Goethe's interlocutor in the famous *Conversations*, in which it's ultimately impossible to distinguish what belongs to whom, where the master's discourse begins and where and how it becomes an echo or actually an invention of the discourse of the disciple—that is, the obscure double, the man locked up in his cabin with birds, in the back of Goethe's garden, like his condemned soul. Far from any theoretical purity, what takes shape in Jena mixes the language of ancient lore with that of philosophy, but also with linguistics, history, fragments, and digressions (a path that the Surrealists pursued in their own attempt to recreate the conditions for such a moment of poetic and political incandescence).

Friedrich Schlegel was undoubtedly the most influential theoretician among the circle of the Jena Romantics, and it was he who contributed most to the composition of the "manifesto" and the only six issues of the *Athenaeum*. But more generally, the actors in this history sought to go beyond themselves toward the Absolute through poetic language or, more precisely, through the *poietics* that made it possible to produce the Absolute in its eternal becoming. This Absolute is no longer philosophical or conceptual; it has become literary. Leaving behind the space of the rational concept, which is traditionally the province of philosophy, Schlegel wanted to abolish the distinction among genres in order to qualify their Poetry as "progressive and universal."[4] For the Romantics, there existed only two privileged forms of access to poetic saying and the infinite of the literary Absolute: the fragment[5] and the novel, which Schlegel qualified as "the Socratic dialogue of our time." Commonly defined as a mixture of paradox and humor, irony meant something very precise for the Romantics, as it would later for Kierkegaard; it was a purely poetic negativity that cannot be subsumed in any Totality whatsoever, "reflexive consciousness of the incompletion of the work, but also and above all the infinite recommencement of the work's proper dynamic." Hegel will reproach the Romantic subject for its inability to emerge from isolation, its withdrawal, its abstract and unhappy interiority. The "self," however, is not folded upon itself but situated at the heart of the work. The ironic nature of the relationship between Romantic subjectivity and the work is thus poorly understood when Romantic irony, rather than being conceived in terms of incompletion, is presumed to be the dissolution of the subject in self-reflexivity. This reading has contributed to the assimilation of Romanticism to a negative ontology that comes dangerously close to nihilism. This vision has been judged dangerous because of the imprecise way in which the world, language, and the night are lumped together. What radicalizes the Romantic risk, with regard to the heritage of the Enlightenment that attempts to get rid of all impurity, is the incandescent mixture of poetics and politics. Even in Kant's heroic pages on the aesthetics of the sublime, little margin is left for inspiration or revolt. For the Jena Romantics, the abstract search for a lost world is also proposed as a viable path to regain this world. The poetic logic of the appropriation the objective Absolute is linked to irony, which becomes its method. The Heideggerian idea of the "predominance of the futural dimension" is a direct descendant of the Romantic notion of a Golden Age to come.

But in the circle of early Romantics, the desire is for the actualization of a new world; I'd even say a new language of the world. There is an eroticism in this movement that doesn't simply derive from the presence of women free enough to dare to live in this sort of community of free thinkers whose fervor and audacity laid claim at once to the French Revolution and to a very free interpretation of Kantian theses. There is nothing of the tortured ego that many people thought they saw in this movement nor of a poor revolt without political weapons that would quickly be reprised in the facticity of the new century. What will later become Spleen remains, at this moment, only an exploration, a turn toward the night. It is a constraint turned into an aspiration, an ideal into a hell, love into an impossible appeal, the closest into the furthest, the faraway into exile, and all convention into heresy. It is a strange historical moment when a group of friends delves into the pure, poetic invention of a new form of lived experience (what Dionys Mascolo calls a "communism of thought") in order to experience the world as battlefront where the intensity of living cedes no ground to the ideal. In this respect, the *Athenaeum* fragments are even more astonishing: both dated and incredibly fresh, they are and remain *untimely* in the Nietzschean sense. In early German Romanticism, both hope and irony are the instruments of a new measure of the world—the poetic, philosophical, and political incarnation of an absolutely new language. The future thereby renewed will never be thinkable as before.

Risking Belief

Belief might seem to be the least risky act in the world: the simple act of adherence or acquiescence to something that presents itself or with which we have chosen to identify. Our whole being becomes attached to it; it suffices to give oneself over. Faith is represented with a blindfold on. At best it's an illusion, at worst the antechamber of crime, the justification for the worst passions. We speak of credulity as an especially poor form of stupidity, even devoid of innocent enchantment. Nonetheless, there is a magnificent risk in belief. Pascal and Kierkegaard both spoke of it, and not only as Christians; the philosophical position that they occupied was that of paradox. Of an obstacle that can only be cleared by taking a leap—that is, by venturing into an unlimited theoretical and spiritual space. There is no possible rational continuity. For what does it mean to believe if not to come face to face with what can't be believed? Only in this sense, absolutely paradoxical, can a risk be taken, making a leap that reason refuses to make. But such risk would be the opposite of adherence, of belief in the sectarian sense of the term. It is, on the contrary, an exposure to extremes. Believing would thus be a matter of dispensing with all beliefs in order, that way, to remain face to face with the unbelievable and yet not turn away. This is what sometimes makes psychoanalysis a space in which madness can be spoken without fear and nearly without judgment. In which delusion can be disclaimed and disengaged without much harm.

The Pascalian wager is not contrary to reason, but does put faith in the unverifiable, or at least in what can be verified only if gambled—that is, lived. There is a sort of future anterior to Pascalian wager that, by a "reasonable" sleight-of-hand, invites each of us to prefer offering asylum to God rather than to indifference. Today, however, verifiability is the only recognized form of trustworthiness. What can be reproduced or results in reproducible, teachable knowledge subjected to publicly accessible tests. Absent this criterion, no valid knowledge. How many lives would be saved if only we could hurdle over our familial schemas, our antediluvian repetitions, and our deepest ruts? But how to believe in what will never happen, in what there is no reason to believe? This is perhaps the risk. Not a matter of finding hope by the roadside back where we dropped it, but of gambling on the unhoped for.

If risk is an event, then it defines a before and an after, a *crisis* in time that renders impossible any wise, guaranteed return to "how things used to be." Isn't this what the patient in analysis expects but has so much trouble believing in, that the unforeseeable might appear, arise, manifest itself, and come to transform her life? She leads us to believe that this is what she expects to happen, but if she couldn't take this risk in the first place, perhaps it's because she couldn't even represent it as a possible real, because in a single blow, it would shatter her previous life, rendering it obsolete, useless, or vague. Risk and the capacity for the unhoped for are one and the same thing. Antigone defies all human law because the dictates of her heart abide by the unbelievable: for her, respecting the law of the burial of the dead is the basis of all other laws, and her obstinacy leads her to death, a death that all reason declares madness, the abdication of possible life—and yet remains for her the one possible choice. To risk believing is to surrender to the unbelievable, to surrender in the same sense that one surrenders weapons or to the authorities, to surrender not to reason but rather to the share of night that inhabits us when it rises to the height of the symptom, in that it rises above and obliges us to lift our gaze on high. An eminently uncomfortable position, obviously. Better to sharpen the edge of critique and be maligners, as Nietzsche said, of other worlds, ready for them to crumble right before our eyes. But also, to open a horizon line that touches the unlimited, to embrace the risk of believing that everything familiar, known, or lived can be subverted, knowing that there is no going back. This is the path of Socratic irony, which arrives at the aporia and must radically bifurcate. To believe—yes—but in an absolutely aporetic sense. A sense that takes a scandalous turn, which is a stumbling block in the real and always will be. To believe, of course, at the place where thought, paradoxically, falls silent, where as such it offers no further resistance. To believe is a dissidence, or rather an abdication. As dissidence, it carries toward a horizon that it doesn't envisage, that it can't envisage, because the overflowing of limits, which it incarnates (might believing also be an affect? a form of transport?), opens zones of creative resistance, literally "deranged," untamable spaces.

Because believing is not necessarily being credulous or duped by the imaginary—which is indeed what Kierkegaard sought to think. To gamble on the unthinkable. To take a leap. To commit to discontinuity there where everything always seeks to restore us to continuity. To be absolutely unreasonable does not suffice. The horizon line must be displaced . . . We must change discourse, parameters, angle of vision. Redirect our gaze toward the edge of the painting, finally see what is happening on the margins, there in a single detail, change parameters, alphabet, history, and memory.

Risking Variation

What is a variation? It is an art and a risk.

Neurosis complicates things, makes compromises, gives and then takes back, negotiates; the symptom is a usurer who expects repayment of a debt that it won't let the debtor forget. Neurosis dislikes variations, on the suspicion that they entail a dangerous audacity, as if it were nothing. In music, variations elaborate a whole world around a simple theme. A dazzling world of counterpoint, ascending and descending harmonies, intervals, and polyphonies of which Bach's fugue is one of the miracles. Variation stretches time to infinity; it appeals to memory (of the theme) while constantly diverging from it. Variation introduces the new under cover of obedience to the old (theme—guardian of the temple); it is a pure improvisation in the guise of respect for ancient rules. It operates in secret, much like neurosis, but in exactly the opposite manner. When you are capable of variation, you escape repetition. For neurotic repetition (in your life) always appears in a new light, but, in reality, obeys a single scenario, indefinitely reprising the same pattern. Repetition in our lives never proclaims itself as such; the combinatory logic that governs the tragic apparatus never lets itself be discovered so easily; beneath the contingencies of the real (many prefer to say "life") there is a prohibition upon inventing variants, escaping the circle. Abandonment leads to abandonment, violence to violence, melancholy to melancholy. How to invent an outside? An elsewhere? "What gives sense," Deleuze recalls, "is not repetition but difference, modulation, alteration, what Doubrovsky called the *false note* yesterday—in a word, variation, even in its most elementary form. It would be pleasant to think that the role of the critic, like the musician, is to interpret variations."[1]

If metaphor is a variation whose vocation is to efface its provenance, the point is never to let the principal theme be divined, to act as if the image could replace the original idea with an apparatus of constant displacement, a vectorization, in a certain sense, an idealization.

"The only thing we ever live is metamorphosis," writes Aby Warburg in his notebook.[2] Difference, divergence, variation: these motifs are embroidered, unembroidered, untrussed, front and back, with a vertiginous window open on the real. Variation is also formal—that is, literature, poetry, and creation. "By *form*," writes Elie During, "I don't mean a determinate configuration, nor a principle of the global organization of meaning, nor yet a structure or regime of signs, but something like an invariance, an invariant determined in *dynamic* fashion and liable *retrospectively* to give value to the deformations that leave it intact. . . . This form itself is inseparable from the transformations that open the way from one motif to another."[3] Variation is formal because it is an organization continually creative of other forms. Form is not a static given; it is that by which variation becomes visible; it is the frame of the image that traverses the same landscape over again, ceaselessly revealing it otherwise.

She has old woman's hands with long fingers and impeccable nails, red. The hands of a witch or a fairy, powerful. Joined. Clasped in what prayer? She is not in mourning.

"He was three-and-a-half years old," she says. "My mother's sister was driving. Veering off the road, they both died instantly in the accident, or so I'm told. Was my aunt perhaps still alive for a little while?" The question is left up in the air, with no apparent need for assent. "But my child . . . It is unbearable to survive him. Yet I have tried. I left his father, changed my country, profession. I used to be a teacher here. I moved to New York where my father lived. I have dual citizenship because I was born over there. I designed lamps, a bit randomly, and people liked them. With French taste, it seems you can get credit for almost anything . . . I stayed for two years before I could even begin to imagine coming back. And when I finally made a return visit, I didn't have the strength to leave again for New York as planned. I had my ticket, all set to leave in three days and instead I came to see you." She seemed not to expect any comforting from me. I didn't risk offering

any. I was, I believe, transfixed by the autonomous life of her prematurely aged hands—a sculpture. The face and the body of this woman, seemed to me, for their part, intact. What do you expect of me?, I felt like saying to her; but even that would have been obscene. I kept silent.

"I would like to understand what I'm doing here. Someone gave me your name. I don't expect anything from you; I gave up expecting anything on that day, once and for all, but yes, why . . ." She averted her eyes for a moment and added: "I wanted to disappear as well; but it didn't take hold, the wish to die. There is a difference, I knew at that very moment, between not wanting to live anymore and wanting to die. Nothing has changed since then even if everything in my life has changed."

Variation is a curlicue, a wisp of smoke, a diversion. Obsession is also a diversion. Whereas you seem to be subjected to the most rigid immobility, to be attacked from all sides with thoughts that inevitably drive you back to this immobile point, obsession is yet a strategy of avoidance—which spares you, by all means necessary, from thinking about something else, a thing that you must not and cannot think.

Was this woman in obsessional neurosis? Not even. Her dead child was still there, in her body and in her arms, held in her hands. I felt it. I almost could have traced the outline of his body, sensed his light weight, his slenderness, his blondness. I would have liked to share the burden with her, stay there, behind her shoulder, and relieve her a bit of this perpetual cradling.

"He is there with you," I said.

"Yes, all the time, night and day,"[4] *she pronounced. "I can't leave him, you understand . . ."*

This time, there was almost the beginning of a question to me, a slight breath in her voice. It made me think of the beautiful title of a novel by R. J. Ellory, A Quiet Belief in Angels. *How does one translate "a quiet belief" into French? Une croyance légère? She—this woman—came with her invisible child, but so alive in her, to see me. And her hands alone expressed her hurt, and her inability to give free rein to pain at the price of seeing vanish the final attestation of his presence. Only this present was left to her, the pure presence of her dead child, and this time no one would take him away.*

"You design lamps . . ."

Variation. At times, perhaps, that's what it is, a variation. A swerve in an incline, a wrinkle in a cloth, a random question, completely random.

She smiled.

"Yes, very simple lamps, made with materials that I'd often pick up on the street. Used, forgotten, discarded objects. I took pieces of these objects, put them together, folded them, cut them, and reshaped them. People told me that they looked like some kind of boats. They took me out to sea. While fabricating them, I

wouldn't think of anything else; I was caught up in a sort of movement and that was all I needed."

"You found a means of transport . . ."

"How so?"

I see that she is intrigued.

"You know in fairy tales every time there is a test to pass, helpers are required, a magic wand, a destiny, a charm against Baba Yaga, a magic comb, a piece of cloth, something, and for you it is lamps. Not to light the way but to navigate is why, I think, you found them.

"The only thing is that I'm not going anywhere. As soon as I think, as soon as I kiss someone, and even while I'm asleep, my dead child is there."

"But where would you like to go? Our existence is nothing but a voyage, the time of a more or less rough, more or less perilous route. Why is it necessary to go anywhere? Three and a half years is too short in relation to a 'normal' life, but who knows? What is a lifetime if not the intensity and radiance that it emits, what it shares, what it offers of the mystery from which it arises, that will never be given up to us."

"Do you mean stop trying to make sense of his death? That does nothing to console me."

"The last thing you'd want is to be consoled, right . . ."

She relaxed her hands for the first time. "Yes."

"And if you stopped being angry at yourself for carrying your child in you, close to you . . . If you stopped wanting, as it were, 'to be in mourning'?"

Variation solicits intelligence in order to escape a circle it has already gone all around, whose equinoxes are all familiar. Variation is a pause that is not spoken as such, an empty space, miraculously safe. We say that a thing varies in intensity. A light, for example. A navigation lamp.

"You can keep him," I added, "in you, with you. But you don't hold him back; if he wants to go, he will go and come back every now and then to watch over you. Don't you think so?"

In the cinema, a wide shot, Deleuze wrote, is a face. Skin is always a face. And the face is an unknown language that we overcome by touching it, hoping for it, discovering it. When we are lost, a face is what we seek to anchor us, any face whatsoever. Perhaps because we come from this infinite proximity, given by the face.

She didn't move and didn't look at me. Her hands were at rest against her, living their own life.

"I think I'm going to have to leave . . ."

I rose, as did she. I didn't ask which leaving she meant, but I believe I knew that she would return to New York, that she would go regain the slow, fragile, and industrious confection of her lamp boats; that she would forget our encounter and the impossible consolation that we shared for an instant. But something very imperceptible was displaced, who knows, a slight variation around the voyage— the one we afford ourselves and from which we never return, that of memory and forgetting, of possible hospitality to death as making up part, totally, of life. The voyage of a mother's hands.

Variation is not avoidance, even if there is some resemblance between them. It is a very formal art of chosen, and thus surmounted, repetition. Into repetition itself, it introduces an apparatus of supreme invention, I might almost say of diversion. Variation makes us believe that all might be lost just when it gently leads us by the hand back to the principal theme, only to drift away, imperceptibly, once again. In this navigation, instruments aren't used much for guidance, because the whole point is to try to lose sight of the shore, to get lost altogether, and to find along the path of this loss, the loop of an intact desire.

The Event: Hyperpresence

Risk creates events. It gives form to a pure singularity, to what will only arise a single time. The event undoes the temporality required to invent an other time, the time out of which an other world, an other gaze is inaugurated. This beginning is another name for risk. Without it, the invention of the world anew at every instant would not take place and the world as we know it would be already complete. This prodigious capacity to produce something outside any trace, the unrepresentable, sustains the very possibility of the world as we know it. The event, in this sense, is always catastrophic, like smoke that at first rises straight up before a delicate torsion takes over; it reaches the exact point where its trajectory breaks apart.

Risk precipitates the event in its corporeity, in what might cause you to say: look what happened. No reason will be able to dispel this sort of penumbra, which remains opaque to the subject. It is what makes the risk taker (although the taker is really the one taken by risk) into a gambler. The bettor wages hand-to-hand combat with the unknown in the hope of emerging more alive than before; and this gamble is what does honor to the act as a risk. What makes the amorous encounter into an event, for example, is desire. Desire in the intelligence and at every point in the body, hidden in the folds of being, in the impossible mystery of what hides away and yet begins precisely there. This thing that takes place in secret, from which neither protagonist will recover, arises because both of them, without knowing it, without foreseeing it, risked themselves, something in them that committed for life to this event that took place. The event of an encounter is an elusive object. It must be thought from its almost inaudible beginnings. I see you, I recognize you, I brush against you, and in these two or three openings love crystallizes with astonishing speed, my hand, your gesture, your response delayed for a few seconds by emotion, the silence that falls between our bodies like a prohibition to go any further. Cultivating self-critique or derision, at such a point, serves no purpose, no more than the suffering you inflict on yourself by way of the real, so diligent to use our fears as weapons.

The subject of Descartes's *Meditations* becomes present to himself through the event of doubt. Derrida proposes that this doubt, from the outset, is the mark of a subject traversed by madness. This is, in a certain respect, where the Cartesian subject locates his reason, his knowledge, and his faith. Doubt, which Descartes thinks in its power (to suspend the real, to call it radically into question), is an experience that makes possible a credible world. I propose to name "hyperpresence" this capacity to arrive at oneself by the detour of "ravishment" by doubt. This experience might come by accident, at a decisive moment of life or even of contemplation: in such an event, you are "extraordinarily" there—that is, no longer entirely the same. And this hyperpresence, in fact, is quite rare in existence.

The event gives us embodiment, perception, emotion, and affects. One of the only ways we can relate to traumatism is through "disembodied" memory (that is, literally dis-incarnated, because really to *think* trauma—if we consider "thinking" as a form of living—would trigger it afresh), which allows us to make reference to it as something that, in some sense, happened to "someone else." At the same time, nothing of trauma can be captured, in order to traverse it and be delivered from it, unless we *re-embody* it—unless it becomes an event once again for us, unless we take this risk, consciously, presently.

It seems to me that the event in a political or cultural sense works in roughly the same manner. If something took place, it took place with the body, not only the physical body (of a dancer, for instance) but also perhaps the body of an artwork, or an installation. And this is perhaps the danger of "eventness"; the temptation would be perhaps to outsource the process, to posit the most perfect horizon possible, to recreate the whole protocol, the conditions of the happening of the event, and thereby, in fact, essentially to repress it. The more you are engaged in self-presence and in the entire world, the more the outcome will be, paradoxically, unpredictable—on a collective level as well. Why does hyperpresence constitute an event? Is it because a certain quality of being—in the sense in which one speaks of the quality of a sound, or the intensity of light—imposes and provokes, as in the experience of Cartesian doubt, a sort of epiphany, I mean, a coincidence of act and being.

Intimate Prophecy

Why are we in advance of ourselves? Who guides us, in this way, into the night of our unconsciousness and gives us an experience of the truth even before it becomes conceivable? Is there an agency in us that might gain intelligence of the future before we get there, a sort of sentinel on permanent alert? This is what I would interrogate in the course of three dreams because to my mind they are what guided one analysis to a specific conclusion, and only the dreamer himself held the key to this path. Neither he nor I would have been able to imagine what the dream's *insight*[1] revealed.

Why at certain moments of our lives are we in advance of ourselves? I would like to be able to think the psychic reserve in us whereby we gain access to the future beyond the narrow confines of our consciousness, our class, our education, our fears, and our inability to confront alterity. This ability would be—such is, at least, the hypothesis that I am developing here—a sort of unconscious turned toward the future, toward the promise, toward what portends itself. What derails neurosis—the "always already known," the "been there done that"—is the possibility within us of opening to something hitherto unsuspected, to a different time. Why, for instance, in an analytic session, does a patient mired within an inextricable life situation suddenly, calmly—albeit, in a certain manner, without understanding it himself—proclaim the conditions of his own emancipation, his liberation? He knows it, then, and cannot make use of knowledge, as if were madness or a delusion. It's the hidden face of this "knowledge without knowledge" that can be expressed collectively in revolts, revolutions, movements of anticipation or the avant-garde that announce a step beyond the present time or generalized servitude, bringing about a secondary "collective consciousness."

Philosophers and writers have interrogated this figure of the time to come, the unhoped for, the time that outstrips fatality, or the simple reduplication of the past, without, however, making recourse to messianism. I believe that, if there is an intimate prophecy in the speech or the life of any given subject, then this vision, no matter what it is, opens toward art; it necessarily entails a language; and this language [*langage*], even if not yet literature—that is, repetition, retreading, return to the source—necessarily says something in a new idiom [*langue*].

To prophesize is to say what is coming. It is to think and predict, to be in time in a particular manner, as if time might belong to thought, might open to it and in it. Philosophy, however, invites us to doubt, from the outset to distrust the term *prophetic*, which belongs to the lexicon of religion. Even so, it is extremely rich in meaning for research on the inner sense of time, or what might also be called *seeing* (the root of the word *theoria*—vision). What is the "seeing what is" that sometimes opens up to us? Must the self be outside itself, drawn toward some ecstasy or divine vision, simply delusional, or commanded by a *daimon* as Socrates believed himself to be, in order for a *vision* to take place? "When speech becomes prophetic," Blanchot writes, "it is not the future that is given, it is the present that is taken away, and with it any possibility of a firm, stable, lasting presence . . . Prophetic speech is a wandering speech that returns to the original demand of movement by opposing all stillness, any taking root that would be rest."[2]

At first, by his own account, he was a gambler. Everything that he lived, experienced, what pushed him out of himself, wounded him, his fury, his blasphemies, his shame—he gambled on them. Poker was his passion; the cards were an extension of his own body, a movement inseparable from his being. And yet he had a strange, unusual relation to loss. Even when strapped for cash, he always set aside enough to ante up at a table. One of his brothers died in an accident; the other committed suicide. He didn't emerge from it all in bad shape, he said, his absent alcoholic father's oscillation between love and violence, an overwhelmed, exhausted mother, left alone early on with three children, without the inner resources to face up to this solitude. He excelled in school, which was his escape hatch, his only oxygen; and games were the only way to prevail on his Baba Yaga of a grandmother, to get her to show him a modicum of benevolence. Only in college did he begin to become unhinged, to drift. How did he end up on the couch? A girlfriend (because he was surrounded by women and loved by them) urged him to come, alarmed by his delusional states. He was a witty person with a good sense of humor, often skewering people and the epoch with equal finesse. Never did he feel sorry for himself, as if his own neurosis wasn't a concern; he was, one might say, pitiless. After trying to scare me by painting himself as an unsavory figure doubled by a potentially dangerous person when on drugs or out of his mind, which I never really believed, he lowered his weapons, and something like an analysis had begun.

But why, here, speak of intimate prophecy?

One day, he had a dream. He dreamed that a white tiger was swimming in a little aquarium like the one that his father gave him as a present just before he left for good or, as they say, with no forwarding address (until seventeen years later when he was found dead, homeless, on the street). In the dream, he went up and plunged his hand in the water to save the tiger, afraid that he might drown but also afraid to get bitten. The tiger curled up in the palm of his hand and fell asleep. The following night, in a second dream, he was playing cards and could hear music that was faint at first but got louder and louder, so loud that it disturbed the game, to such an extent that no one could play their hand; he rose from the table in a fit of anger, dashing the cards and the money. On the third night, another dream. I should specify that this was a man who never remembered his dreams and during the first six months of analysis hardly made any associations or spontaneously recalled any memories from his past. In this final dream (there would be no others during that year) he entered a candlelit room; he couldn't discern where he was going, but he knew that he was expected and it was important not to be late; the light was very beautiful, although too bright; he tried at once to shield his eyes (from the glare) and to discern what was ahead of him. He realized then that he was afraid.

Let's call this man Jean. He is at a moment in his life when everything is falling apart; his daily life has become erratic; he hangs out at poker games and describes himself as a man at his wit's end. His associations around the first dream put him in contact with what Native Americans might call his "spirit animal," the quasi-totemic animal that connotes both power and rarity (the white tiger), resistance to cold or polar temperatures (trauma?) but also the quasi-amniotic fragility of an animal lost in a pocket of soft water where it evolves. It is a "self," potentially quite powerful but still enclosed within the mother and in the water of dreams, certainly a domesticated body of water (aquarium), at the mercy of the dreamer himself. The dreamer grabs the animal, takes it out of the water, and, despite his fear of being attacked, watches it snuggle up in his palm. Jean interprets this dream as an encounter with his animal self, with a piece of the psychic and instinctual power of which he is becoming conscious or literally "apprehending," no doubt literally for the first time. In the second dream, he is in the situation that he knows best, the poker game, which is at once his passion and his downfall. Music, he says, can be heard. No tiger here, just sounds. Why music? This simple question, for Jean, will reopen an abyss.

What is the psychic space that since Freud is called the "unconscious," which mainly works unbeknownst to the subject or the psychic agency that governs the desire of the subject? It is difficult to describe this psychic space without making reference, I dare say, to the spiritual. What is this "vaster region," which we have trouble qualifying more precisely, except in terms of its extremely acute relation to the real, time, and the other, as if we might suddenly be liberated of all our superegoic loyalties and the weight of the past in order to seize hold, at last, of the present time with all its potential for a future, a future that hasn't already been mortgaged. From what perspective should this psychic space be judged, if it actually exists? What if it can only be measured by its effects, after the fact, in the real? We come to adulthood with a more or less available stock of memories, certain of which will appear in analysis, reopening the archives of our identity. We do not falsify our past but give it a new contour; we discover in it zones of possible survival, words of life or of death. As Nestor Braunstein writes so marvelously, the dream is an intimate prophecy of what fashioned us, of our unconscious desire.[3] The dream is caught up in fright and the capacity to surmount this fright, to dance around it, to make images for it on the basis of scraps and fissures.

The psychic space that never came into being for this man was music. He absorbed a lot of music very young because his father, before sinking into alcoholism, was a nightclub pianist and would take him on tour. Even before he learned how to read, very precociously he knew how to decipher sheet music. Music caused him such emotion that he would go numb, and he became afraid to listen to any piece in its entirety. And, in fact, after these dreams, I didn't see him again for a month. He complained of unavoidable money problems, then came back. He had been prowling around the Beuscher piano store, he told me, before finally going in. One of the young students who demonstrated the instruments for customers showed him various pianos; the two of them hit it off. Jean had troubles of two orders: the first linked to the music that aggressively burst into his dream (disturbing the poker game), the second was the emotion elicited by the young man toward whom he felt an undefinable attraction. Never having had a homosexual relationship, not even adolescent games with boys, he was at once bewildered and ashamed. When we encounter a dormant but highly invested polarity of our being, like a precious mineral deposit brutally extracted from the earth (sleep) where it lay buried, I believe that the person who occasions this intrapsychic encounter with the object that personalizes it (here, the piano) becomes, in turn, amorously invested. What might be taken for the actualization of a latent homosexual desire does not pertain exclusively to this order. From the moment when this encounter took place, Jean recognized what he had by turns desired and dreaded, the intrusion of this music within his gambler's universe. But the music in question was not external but rather an internal capacity to "become" music (or a musician).

To question the relationship between psychic space and truth is to think that, in all of us *qua* subjects, there is a relationship to what I call an "intimate prophecy." If at certain moments we are able to "see" what's inchoate, what's in the offing, is it because we are questing after a truth that goes beyond and overflows the usual dislocation of neurosis between reality and the pleasure principle? Does the space of analysis, at a specific moment, allow for existence to echo this insight, this gap, to capture a foreign language as if it were the most natural thing in the world? Intimate prophecy would be the capacity, within us, to bear witness to what is coming. Jan Patocka amply spoke of life as the inherent capacity to experience limits, to allow for the unreconciled to be risked in us. To be sentinels at the outposts of time (Kierkegaard) or visionaries (Rimbaud) or bridges above the abyss (Nietzsche). To forge new paths is a difficult matter, a continual rupture with old alphabets and sluggish circumlocutions. It is a matter of being contratemporal, attentive to the "crumbs" (Kierkegaard again) on the bypaths, to broken equilibriums, to the order in which things appear . . .

After eight years of unstinting work, day and night, Jean became a pianist. In a certain respect, he did nothing but rejoin and repeat his father's trajectory, avoiding failure at the price of a fraudulent resemblance. Perhaps . . . The repetition compulsion, in the loop of fatality from which it proceeds, insists just on the hither side of freedom; it abuts freedom on a common and endlessly threatened border.

His first recording, of nocturnes, was dedicated to the memory of his father.

Intimate prophecy becomes perceptible via an inner voice to the poet, to the delusional, or to the hand of the painter that traces, even before he sees it, a line dividing the visible and the invisible; it is the mark of apparition. But any apparition, no matter how spectral, is a gift, which we can always refuse or else yield to. No matter how shattering the consequences, she who sets out to encounter her own being is, secretly, a visionary.

At the Risk of Bedazzlement

To see is also, and above all, to be able to stop seeing. To shut your eye-lids. No longer to let the world in, to close your eyes, curtain. Sudden quietude, penumbra. When they reopen, bedazzlement. Very quickly, the night light mix is restored, outlines regain their sharpness, and the world is back where it should be, all in a matter of moments—nothing but an instant. The brighter the light, the more bedazzlement is certain. But what happens in us during the fraction of a second when we can't see from see-ing too much? Are there also moments when the psyche thus receives very bright thoughts, which it dispatches for an instant, in order, a few fractions of a second later, to let itself be ravished anew? Is this what's called delu-sion, hallucination? Is this the moment when thinking confronted with too much truth gives way and returns to the penumbra in order not to understand what, in reality, it knows? Thoughts without a thinker pursue the thinker, said the genial clinician Wilfred Bion. What obsesses us is the relic of a never pacified combat.

Delusion says the too much of the real. To be able to see is still and also to be able not to see. To close your eyes in time, before total bedazzle-ment, blindness. Closed up in black again. Delusion says the spilled milk, the palm of a child holding a pebble tight, a cry, terror without echo, two guitars in tune, a phantom from among the dead, forgotten, ignored, without tombs or names; delusion speaks of an impending blizzard, jaguars and wolves in conversation on the couch. Exultation. Jubilation. Bedazzlement. You must be able—yes, just a little—gently to open your eyelids, to let the day and its flood of light filter in. Forge an alliance with terror and fear, control your flight response and to get closer to what emerges as the source. Because terror also comes from deliverance. Maledictions create delusions, but no one dares to ask: what do these delusions actually say?

She drew roses, overlapping roses with long bright thorns that striated the drawing like a cry. Roses and only roses. As I watched her draw, I remembered what a nun once told me when I was little, that life is not a rose garden.

"Oh I see," I say, peering at the drawing. "It's a rose garden, so special."

The little girl looks up: "Have you ever seen one?"

"Yes, in Morocco, there was rose nursery and there's one not far from here as well. But the roses in Morocco had a scent, an especially strong scent that stuck with me."

"Ah!" said the little girl as she added some black to the edge of a thorn. "This one is poisoned, can you see?"

"Oh really?"

"Are you going to ask why?"

"I don't believe in why so much," I say. "That's definitely my problem."

The little girl smiles, indulgent. Her hand moves, the marker along with it. A sun appears, a moon by its side. Right by its side.

"The sun is a star, the moon is a planet," says the grown-up.

"Yes," says the little girl.

"Oh really! Do you know that already? I wanted to impress you but I guess it didn't work."

"No it didn't but I like how you look, so I am going to tell you. The poison, I put it there myself to protect the rose because it doesn't know how to."

"We never really know what to do to defend ourselves, do we?"

The little girl is suddenly alarmed and urges: "... yes, especially against birds, birds that carry them back to their nests and eat them before their rosy time is up."

"Then just too bad for the bird if it gets poisoned?"

"The bird," responds the little girl, quite seriously, "is in my head, and in yours as well. Didn't you know that, too?"

"No I didn't. I'll pay closer attention."

"Promise?"

"I promise."

The psychologist who referred the little girl had forewarned me that she was in a psychotic state with occasional delusions. She was unbearable with others, a real demon. She had been pulled out of school. A diagnosis of autism didn't hold up. Too precocious, no mutism. On the contrary, an impressive vocabulary. Her parents and caregivers no longer knew what to do. Delusion has no age. But there must be times when it can emerge in childhood, to splatter its raw, violent truth all over the place, to arise in nightmares, drawings, stories, or else delusions will come back to haunt so-called adult life, embroiling it in old nightmares. And because no one is going to ask where delusion comes from, everything will quickly end up within the four white walls of a hospital. Echoless, or almost.

To risk bedazzlement is sometimes to go in search of the unnameable, knowing that ultimately you will come out alive. What happens to our confidence in speech when it has been taken away, betrayed? Travestied, constrained, perverted? Speech arises like a bedazzlement to expose the bare life of terror and dreams. It is the first combat, an exposure that counters the terror of the world, opening the possibility of a gentleness without combat. To risk your word, this is sometimes the only act possible when you have been abandoned without recourse, when you lose faith in all love; the trustworthiness of the spoken word is then your sole refuge. As when you murmur in the ear of a frightened animal, a scant few words might unveil what space of recognition still remains. A language must then be reinvented, a possibility of resonance, a first imprint.

To risk speech, in analysis, is to hope that someone hears you . . . in spite of the bedazzlement that took hold of you one day because you closed your eyes too fast, too soon, in the face of the unbearable, and also because you reopened them. To see rather than to die psychically is a form of resistance. To seek the penumbra is only ineffective medication, at best. *Sorrow*, to use an English word, is a mix of sadness and disenchantment.

Risking bedazzlement means agreeing to glimpse truth for a second at the risk of losing your vision, because only there can you possibly stay alive. Only there, as well, can you possibly oppose perversion and lies. The excess of light also affects creation and love, which share the same essence, the same secret entry. Someone who can't be dazzled—going blind for an instant after a huge influx of light or suddenly, an abrupt plunge into blackness—has no access to delusion. By "access" I mean the sort of second order truth that only delusion can transmit. To risk bedazzlement is dangerous because in the too much of light or of truth there resides the possibility of permanent, total blindness, life in a penumbra besieged by phantoms. But there, too, is the apparition of joy.

Desire, Body, Writing

[T]he prisoner himself contributes most
of all to his own incarceration.

—PLATO, *Phaedo* [82D]

How to write desire? How to approach what moves us, each one of us, intrinsically, at the most intimate point of our lives, without metaphor, approximation, or stammering? How not to miss the point, fall short, how not to give up imagining the truth of the body around this elusive and unverifiable real? For desire is first and foremost the language of the body. A history of the body. The very cipher of the body, its secret passion, its genealogy. No body isn't sick with desire—that is, hampered, shackled, but also transported and galvanized. And once again it's the body that, by means of the symptom, shows that what traverses it is not known, or known very little, to the reason that claims to govern it. The language of the body is a half-saying, or a missaying, as Lacan enunciated it, because we have known for some time, in all latitudes, that desire is a history of chains, unchaining, and forming new chains link by link. With words, between words, and without words.

The effects of desire happen in the future anterior. If only we had known . . . From this misrecognition, from this irrecuperable belatedness thinking is born—by which I mean the faculty of thinking desire precisely at a place of lack. It is like a scarf that wafts through every hand that tries to snatch it and afterwards all we can do is exclaim: it was right there, I saw it. What is it about writing that retains desire? How is desire constituted as writing itself? For, desire, I believe, *writes itself*, and not only in books, but in everything that leaves a trace, inscription, memory, archives, everything that thereby opens a passage between the living and the dead.

When there is no longer access to desire, one dies; invisibly, everything loses its magnetism; your senses abandon you; tasks become mechanical exercises; even beloved faces are of no further help; they become burdensome, slowly but surely contaminated by anxiety itself. What can we say about such a life outside of desire, also known as depression? This is the extenuated desire that arrives at the semi-closed chamber of the analyst's office in the hope that it will ultimately become a space of possible deliverance or rebirth. The writing of desire is a talismanic space, a gage offered to death (but not yet), to love (yes, a little more), and to thought. Sometimes she who writes enters into the penumbra without knowing in advance exactly what is being written but with the confused understanding that it precedes her. What are the reasons that lead someone to write? Sometimes, perhaps, misunderstandings, requests from a friend or an editor, or things to share, articles, dream notebooks, little pads of unfiltered thoughts. The most mysterious, indeed, is the process whereby a hand extended by a pen or a computer commits to tracing, almost unbeknownst to us, what is written? For, in all writing, I believe, there is a text subjacent to the one that we plan ahead of time, that we master with more or less talent and force. This subtext—which the unconscious arms like it arms our dreams, our slips of the tongue, our bungled actions, the significant dates in our lives, our favorite names—there precisely, truly, desire is risked. In an analysis, it is difficult, disquieting, but wonderful to rely on writing as a *weapon*, or at least to offer it as a possibility, perhaps because it represents the risk of challenging, in a certain manner, the privilege of orality, the transience of the word that has been given, understood, and accepted.

She is a vascular surgeon and her analysis truly began at the interchange that carries blood from the arteries to the heart and vice versa, there where the scalpel almost always intervenes at the limits of life and death, where the vessel is strangulated—where blood no longer passes freely, nor desire. She presents the symptoms of recalcitrant melancholy, recalcitrant to both life and to death, confined to the space of a sterile room (the operating theater), the sole place where life remained possible for her. Every other place seemed scorched earth. To my attempts to bring up her childhood, she responded with: that doesn't interest me. I couldn't figure out how to modify this polite opposition to my questions. I had before me a young woman composed like a puzzle within a puzzle, a compact presence, considered formidably efficient by her colleagues and by the one who quickly became the only one who really existed in her eyes, and whose value grew the more she sacrificed for him—"but actually," she corrected herself, "there's nothing to sacrifice, no intimate life." To him she offered up her intelligence and a huge amount of work—that is, to a young research biologist whom she was helping apply for a patent. Everything related to the feminine could not be articulated, or only with frigid words. Her life was absurd, she said, outside of work and this friendship. She was a classic beauty but such a stranger to herself, to any possible acquiescence to this beauty, that she managed to make you forget about it. And yet, one day I suggested that she write something. Rarely, if ever, did I make such a demand: to solicit a text. But I was at a loss, incapable of helping this woman without any consciousness of her femininity, her fragility, her exceptional intelligence, and without any desire other than to operate (especially life-saving surgeries)—everything else expunged from the chessboard of her life. I became the witness to a patiently monitored anorexia of desire. Before the hatred enmeshed in the apparatus could be exposed, a great deal of time would be required… Ambivalence always takes time, which is what makes it extremely toxic. But there was something that I felt, a strange proximity in a surge of passion withheld by an overweening ideal, fixated in a coating of deadly surveillance. Her writings were akin to molten lava. Full of a vertiginous consciousness of the most intimate folds of the feminine heart. One might have believed that she spent her life in the waiting room of an analyst, a gynecologist, and a highly accomplished sociologist. Short sentences, vitriolic, devoid of pathos. She didn't comment on her own pages; as first, she resisted talking about them or offering associations, as if it was another woman who expressed herself in them. The analyst's office became the place for this deposition and little by little, affects began to intervene, like isolated blocks drifting on the surface of a precisely regulated discourse. Then came her dreams. Seething, very somber, full of murder and madness, amphitheaters rife with assassins, rapists, loiterers, open hearts, and eviscerated bellies. Desire here is nothing but writing. Diffracted in the violence of these imagined, written destinies, it begins to be able to begin to be said; and no one can say whether the splitting that shelters such passion will one day have another theater than these proffered pages, which absolutely deserve to be published without any further commentary. What does it mean for an analyst to be the keeper and thus temporarily the witness to this chain of unchained words, to such a fulgurant writing of desire?

Living is an invention wrested from terror. A terror that some appease in ever different embraces, others in alcohol, and others in unhealthy busyness; people are unequal before anxiety. One might think that each of a mother's caresses undoes a little of this anxiety in the body of her child, whom she thereby continues to bring into the world; that each word, each syllable sung, each rock she imparts on the cradle, relieves some of the world's strangeness and, in an archaic and absolutely vital sense, offers hospitality to the child. In this manner, she basically envelops the newborn in another body—a second, psychic body, made of the resonances that are perhaps the first codes transmitted to the child (as to the animal, in fact) in order to translate the irrational sonority of the world. Why are some people skinned alive by this strangeness—or, at least, why do they remain so? They are often creators, or end up succumbing—because anxiety is unbearable in high doses, for too long—or else they abdicate right away and cling to a life-saving object (the bottle, the syringe, the crisis), which alone purveys the possibility of a refuge that they didn't receive in the cradle, or that they didn't know how to receive. Why do others seem to have been immunized against anxiety from birth?

Another theater of writing. Another rebirth.

Already as a child, H was interested in weapons, in the whole theater of war. Later an actor, he got a job dubbing voices for films; and, over the months, this doubling of his voice became a sort of second identity that he offered to the "ogre" (in the title role of the film) as an accolade. The ogre was the shadow that he bore of a father who literally swallowed up his own daughter but never touched his son, leaving him both in the lurch and furious to regain paternal love on stage. Then he entered the business world, took a few directing jobs convinced that he was collaborating with the enemy by participating in the economic and mercantile logic that he sought to escape in the art world. His mother came from the North, from a bourgeois family of educators. When she got pregnant, the family spurned the lovers. The child was born and then, at six months, placed with a foster family, until the parents could find work as teachers, also until the grandparents could see fit to accept the union. H's parents will come looking for him and they will live together for a period in the North. Then a little sister will be born, the parents will separate. The father will go on to marry two other women; an inveterate seducer, he is the incestuous father whom H spends his whole life endowing with a certain force, an invulnerability, and the temperament of a gangster, for lack, quite simply, of a relation to the law. The mother would pass from crisis to crisis, threatening to kill herself, to abandon her children at least one per week, flying into a rage and then reassuring them of her eternal love. The little sister became bulimic anorexic, making various attempts at suicide, thereby passing to the very act that their mother was always threatening, upon the altar of an already consummated sacrifice.

When I saw H for the first time, he was crumbling—like a ramshackle house with nothing left but walls and a patch of the roof, still rather stately but worthless as shelter. He was mistrustful, cultivated, and came to ask for what he called a "true analysis."

"If only someone would tell me what a true analysis is," I retorted, "but, yes, we can try . . ."

He had already done an analysis with a "master" Lacanian, a practicing guru. H was visibly suffering and didn't seemed to believe anyone could do anything for him. But he said that he still wished to suffer less and he immediately began to tell me about the woman with whom it was one crisis of jealousy, desire, and violence after another, enough to make him bang his head against the wall, in order not to break it, or her. One day he came to the session with his head bandaged. A few months earlier, I had in some sense driven him back to his father, recommended that he see him again. Indeed, I upheld that he did have a father after all—even if a contemptible, and in his eyes incestuous, father, he was still his father. After which, he skipped four sessions. A little while later, he had breakfast with his father, who told him that the reason he left his mother was that he saw her smash the baby's head against the wall, which made him realize that "she was crazy." We know how perverts engender violence in others to echo their own, so firmly held in check, encased in good feelings: the right feelings for every situation. When the perversion of the father, taking advantage of his son's rapprochement, hastens to detail a terrible scene that absolves him of any major failing, his truth, alas, still becomes legible when H repeats it in his own body, harming himself each time he gets embroiled in a crisis with the woman he loves. Once again, I need to digress. There was once another woman in H's life, whom he had married and then left not long after the birth of their son, thereby reactivating his own parents' act of abandonment of him. With her usual finesse, Françoise Dolto writes of the reparation compulsion, a better term in her view than the repetition compulsion. For, she concludes, what we want, always and again, is to repair; and this is precisely what we must be cured of because the desire for reparation forces us to revive the scene of trauma (how else to repair it?) and in this scenario traumatic repetition often gains the upper hand.

With each woman he ever loved, H would provoke the same paroxysms of love and hate, to the point of making himself loathsome and contemptible in her eyes, killing her desire while exasperating his own. He thus "saved" his mother because love would drive each woman sooner or later to act like her. Impossible for him to mourn his mother, whom he saw for the final time six months before her death. I asked that he take note of this amount of time, six months, as if it were necessary for him to abandon her before her departure, in order not to relive his own abandonment over again. "But I didn't know she was going to die," he responded. This mother whom he would talk to in each church he passed, he who didn't believe in God. While working on this non-mourning, he took up writing again (having completed one manuscript in the past). While he no longer shied away from assuming political responsibilities, and to some extent gave up his addictive behaviors (alcohol, driving too fast, and so on), he got into financial trouble at his job as a film director, which was identified with his father's world, and which he increasingly felt to be a terrible compromise. It should also be added that his theater professor had been his lover a bit longer than a mere adolescent phase; and that he would only ever speak of this homosexual passage to the act to say that he had enjoyed being at this man's mercy, with whom once again he had put himself in a masochistic position.

In one decisive session, he announced that financially he couldn't afford to pay anymore and therefore had to stop the analysis. He spoke as though it was a wise and responsible decision, delicately reminding me that I had myself urged him to get his finances in order. After that, how could I reproach him for being realistic! Reality came crashing down on him, taxes as well, the whole backlog of his un-regulated life, which seemed both devastating and comforting to him. I responded that I would take him at his word; and that, if it were only a question of money, then no problem, he just wouldn't have to pay for his sessions until he was in better financial shape. Stupefied, he said that could never commit to pay back such a debt. But I noted that there was no need to pay back anything—if only he consented to keep coming for however long it might be necessary. Never had I proposed such a radical solution to one of my patients and God knows many of them were in more precarious situations than his. But I felt that he was on a tightrope . . . He accepted and during the four months that these free sessions lasted he gave me pages to read from a new novel, which opened with a war story. Later, he will decide to become an analyst. And he will love a woman with a pacified love. Only the maternal voice stayed with him.

The gesture of writing resembles a disenchantment, an oath of fidel-ity, but to whom? Does the writer know at the instant of writing? H's text, beyond its force and formal accomplishment, is one the furrows that occurs in the wake of a traumatic event; but, whereas the sea closes over every passing trace, the text is an address that is also an appeal, a provoca-tion to respond. If trauma provokes the possibility of sacrifice or renders it necessary, what remains of it can be recognized in the symbolic offerings of its witnesses. When the waters of the sea are furrowed, as we know, they soon appear never to have been breached by the bow of any boat; but, in a human life, what happens never closes. And when the furrow belongs to literature, even less so. For literature is a particular form of memory; fictive or poetic, it has no idea what it leaves to the survivors.

We don't know how to explain creation, and we shouldn't. But how to create a language against language, this, indeed, is a question that might be approachable. Against the strangeness of the world, writing invents a language to translate the untranslatable, to let the unnamable be heard and to inscribe it in a new form. Whence a language all to itself is born, to paraphrase Virginia Woolf, a special vicinity where the subject took refuge for a time to negotiate her passage into the torment of the real. She experiences the world out of a certain exile, imprinted in her very early as an intimate modification, in order to be free. This language is also the colors of a painter's palette, the notes and the hands of a musician, sculpted stone, every artwork, temporary installations and abstractions, architectural plans, and the silent spaces between barricades. But we must believe that reaching the limit of anxiety is a process that, even if it often restores your intelligence, is itself extenuating. It consumes you slowly. If the subject fails to rediscover the path of inner peace (but how?), if she enters into the exile that is creation, it is a many-headed hydra that she confronts. But she does confront it, indeed—and this combat is liable to endow her with an extreme life force. No work, however, can do away with it. Unless, as some have done, you have done with life, or with the work (which often for them comes down to the same thing). For those whom we call "creators" become, on top of everything else, responsible for others. Responsible for their own work and the voices that they bring to life, and responsible to those who read, listen, or discover their work, for whom life would not be the same without them. And the body is what upholds this fragile equilibrium between anxiety and the invention by language of a path out of anxiety. Sometimes this body is drugged, hypnotized (always a little), in a state of desire or alert, often exhausted. By alcohol, sex, or any number of addictive substances, or perhaps by a specific type of pen, this window, that patch of wall in a studio, this light, that sound quality in that recording studio—to everyone their talismans for not disappearing, and losing everything. Like, for example, on the first page of *In Search of Lost Time*, this marvel: "a truly dark darkness." This page, whose opening is well known, slips us into the fragility of sleep and goes on to deprive the "I" of its orientation and imaginary consistency; and this is how it discovers the disrobed—that is, truly dark—darkness of habit [*obscurité déshabillée de l'habitude*]. Beckett has a word for such darkness in *Worstword Ho*, where he speaks of "undimmed" things. This is the flimsy nothing of the expression, "as if it was nothing," the almost nothing that Bartleby will personify now and forever, the stubborn resistance to predigested thinking, to overused images, to the stupidity of everything that compels us to adhere or lapse into the game of the same, on an endless loop. This almost nothing is an indeterminate and indefinite but extraordinary displacement.

What writing is backed up against—anxiety—is only perpetuated because we struggle so mightily to extract ourselves from it. In order for the other to surge up anew, the unprecedented, and the unhoped for. What's liable to assail us is the weight of what might have been and was not . . . what wasn't born, what wasn't able to open and never ceases to manifest itself to us in the form of regret, oppression. When we suffer from something in the form of a symptom, we believe that this suffering prevents us from living, whereas, in reality, on our behalf it negotiates the price of reality. One adopts a symptom because, all things considered, it is less worse than betraying the primal fidelity that we knitted with the first bonds of love, a relation equated with our survival. The symptom is an attempt to stay upright in existence at the price of a suffering that closely resembles debt. Rather than creating, we renounce looking into what paralyzes us. And what is sacrificed in the process is a something of the body: vomit, hives, local paralysis, frigidity, insomnia—the logic being that it's better to sacrifice a battalion to the enemy but win the offensive than to lose the entire "armed corps" on the battlefield. Nothing can shake up this economy of the symptom, I believe, unless you first forge an alliance with it. And this is what dreams tell us. The problem with the symptom is being unsatisfied. There is little long-term neurotic equilibrium in the symptom; it is an ogre that always demands more of us. This hungry ogre is unsatisfied with what we offer (whence the point of analysis: to confront the monster rather than offer ever more fresh meat) because this sacrificial value is precisely what it feeds on—a price that the subject imagines must be paid for her desire.

The four months of total gratuity were liberating for H: "I never knew that there is such a thing as a bond or a pact established otherwise than in a deadly economy in which no account is ever paid up," he says to me. If payment—no way around it—is essential to the settlement, even partial, of debt to the analyst, I believe that in certain cases the economy of desire (and thus economy as such) is so rotten, gangrened, that it embroils everything in its perverse torsion, and so something else must be invented . . . Because H had already written and writing was, I might say, also my own symptom, it was on the terrain of written words that the territory devastated by trauma could perhaps regain a form. It took me some time to understand that the pages brought to each session took the place of payment; and not until vacation time did I realize that the "promised" pages were not in the mailbox—no session being able to take place. Not long after, his novel was accepted by a major publisher—with no endorsement other than its arrival in the mail—and published.

Desire, when it writes itself, gets close to death and joy. As writing, it navigates among the destinies of our dead, those whom we loved as well as those whose anarchic memory, in abeyance, remains at work within us, through us, by strange repetitions and strokes of luck that would almost suffice to make us believe in fatality, in the Greek sense. In reality, writing's way of opening a pathway is an art of refusing to suffer any longer. For, to give up suffering, that requires great courage.

Healing?

When everything has been stripped away from us, including the very possibility of speaking, what healing is possible? How would it be possible to recreate a lively trust in language, the laboratory of all mutations . . . The risk of healing implies that you agree to dispossess yourself of a certain knowledge, because, in a certain sense, it is this knowledge that has taken hold of you and not the inverse. Do you know when it becomes necessary to accept losing what had always been your bedrock (emotional, physical, material) in order to attain a vaster but still indeterminate and thus uncanny place?

His name is Ariel. Alcohol, violence, amnesia. Arrests, relapses. His devil is close at hand. A double life, of little account: family destroyed, humiliation, self-loathing. Exhausted myself by this interminable analysis, I ask him to try automatic writing, each night of insomnia without crossing out or censoring to write everything that comes. A feminine voice very quickly made itself heard and wouldn't go away. A hidden sister? A dead twin? Someone from a previous generation? Nothing . . . He gets caught up in the game, is astonished by this double snuck in. No homosexuality in the picture, nor any significant feminization. But there are tango classes taken by chance upon meeting a childhood friend who brought him along. He has a good time. He still drinks as much as ever, perhaps even more.

He drinks in order to lose control. Alcohol divorces him from himself, forces him to navigate, to dream, absolves him, makes him porous. He forces himself to go into gay bars, persuaded that this feminine voice reveals a taste for men that he refuses to recognize. I am skeptical. He explores increasingly hardcore joints, becomes a voyeur, acts like a regular, and emerges as one steps out of a boxing ring. He wishes to meet his fantasy in the raw state. But he doesn't meet anyone, not even himself. He stops going, veers in the opposite direction, meditates. He embraces asceticism, sculpts his body, becomes anorexic. I am troubled by how thin he becomes. He takes up automatic writing again and then finds that he can't bring himself to drink anymore, gets neither pleasure nor disgust, just a pure opacity. An effect of traversing the looking glass? My name is Alice, he decides. And this is how he tells friends to rebaptize him. An infinitely more powerful drug? Laughingly, he tells them: this is my American identity. His body's opposition to drink frightens him, as if it called for a reconciliation. I propose that he take quite a risk, asking him to drink just a little and no more, to make a rule of it. One gulp of poison each night—but to regain what? Was it dangerous? Perhaps, but what else to do? In a famous text, the German philosopher Peter Sloterdijk advocated intoxication as the only vaccine for evil itself. To self-inoculate with the virus, to make the site of adversity into the terrain of your own healing, is, he writes, the task of thinking,

Do not split in two, distrust the blacks and whites riddled with scars where neurosis is queen. Alice/Ariel, the fused brother/sister of the mother, incest buried in his history, every summer (for her) between ages sixteen and nineteen. One evening, she would explain to him, "You understand, between brother and sister it doesn't count." It's to Alice that she says this, because their incestuous games involved playing Alice in Wonderland, *out of the world and out of sight. The mother treats this as her artificial paradise, as she says herself, bewildered guilt, her brother's life cut short in a motorcycle accident at age thirty, circles and rings of destiny. Does it suffice to listen to the speech of what lies dormant like a poison in the body and today wants to confide its secret? Maternal amnesia and the silence upon these incestuous summers, the distilled excitation of the body unto thought, no interdict in sight.*

Bewildering attachment to our wounds. What we do in secret, the blows that we strike at ourselves, the nostalgia that rips the heart from a life that we could have or should have lived. This is precisely where Hell opens up, with a childhood dream relegated to the status of broken toys and old school photos. In addiction and melancholia, no forgetting is possible. No beneficent amnesia, only remorse. The avowal of their failure works as a solvent. But this is not the same as forgetting. They have a damaged childhood in their sleepless nights.

The toxic substance that Ariel ingested was no less deadly. He began at age sixteen (the same age as the first incestuous summers with his mother) with eau ecarlate. Scarlet is the water of rules and of life, birth and death, the bloody water of the first wound. The water of dreams and secret destinations, the water of voyages and failures, secret water. Alice/Ariel passes through the looking glass; his (her?) mother before him (her?) had explored the byways of a prohibited jouissance and kept within her the traces of a never revealed secret, without any link to her future life (or so she believed). With her brother dead—no further witness. When her son descended into the hell of alcohol dependency, the whole world fell silent. Our silences are testimony to what cannot be said; they make the bed of madness, but also, above all, of truth, sometimes at the price of death. Wounded angels in a body they don't understand, which never becomes their own, repositories like everyone of a history, but without heritage, neither in words nor in anything, they are left with this history at variance with their body, hopelessly exhausted, without recourse against an anxiety that never says whence it comes nor why. Because, for them, it is always too late . . . What to do with this impossible forgetting, beyond any consolation?

Ariel is the magician from Shakespeare's *Tempest*, the messenger. He who arises. Ariel delivers Alice; and Alice brings Ariel back from the other side of sleep . . . where hurried white rabbits know better days, where all that's left of the Cheshire cat is a bizarre smile that appears maybe to kill or maybe to give life. Alice awakens Ariel from a dream that is so much more real than his entire previous life, how could he not want to return—even at the risk of getting his head cut off? What to do when you believe that the secret of all metamorphosis lies hidden in a small bottle, that to gobble or to drink a little something is all it takes to be delivered from this body? Ariel no longer drinks; Alice knows she was dreaming; the mother delivered up a past of summers more violent than any future disappointment. Is this what's called "healing"?

An Other Language

Risk exists in proportion to the time it slices in two. Joyce and Lewis Carroll, and Melville, all explored the passage from dream to the real and back again—and, I would insist, they knew what they were doing. This is a traumatic literature, in the proper sense of the term. And so, this might be a good moment to speak of literature—or what goes by that name—as a figure of concerted risk-taking, that is, as an art of living. Is there life outside of literature? What other possibility do we have to inhabit language, assuming that this phrase implies a familiarity that is at once ingenuous and bewilderingly foreign?

The Joyce of *Ulysses* foregrounds the rustling constellation of what is called a "subject"; he makes audible the discontinuous voices of a wholly calculated savagery. Molly Bloom's monologue is a territory where we enter as into a *terra incognita* full of fear, attentiveness, and revulsion, and literally unable to stay the course, to endure it at length, while, at the same time, everything is fluid, calm, and free. Literature gives us to hear, whether we like it or not, the pure risk of language. It is the dissonance that breaks into a world of harmonies, I dare say, established in advance. There is no literary text that isn't necessary. In a certain absolute sense. And yet, to become embodied in language—that is, in an *other* language—is to betray the mother tongue. To disavow its vow of return to the same, to the mortiferous savagery that the maternal carries within itself, in spite of itself. There is no metaphor without the risk of madness. Madness is a metaphor that is never confined, that could never confine itself to anything. Something in language itself that goes mad.

In *Billy Bud, Sailor*, Melville tracks down the point of inversion in language where a single being becomes the repository of collective guilt, but also of a place where he abandons himself, undoes all identity in order to become what the Other wants. This point of inversion, in the form of sublime idiocy—from Casper Hauser to Prince Myshkin, from the hero of *The Trial*, to Bartleby and Don Quixote—grabs hold of a subject to deliver him over to the violence of social conventions, of bureaucracy erected, in the imaginary, as a fatal law, of the guilt for wars of hatred for the just, in order make us hear what in humanity will never consent to lie. Or not to risk the truth. A truth, at least, which the language of these texts carry to the point of incandescence. And of unreason, if reason is what we rely on to form judgments and to uphold common law, a transmissible certainty and an unequivocal knowledge.

Speaking of what she calls a *killer-text*, Avital Ronell investigates—for example, in Goethe's *Werther*, but also in *Madame Bovary* as a figure of addiction—the dangerousness and even the lethality of language used in a certain way. Not only to the one who uses it but also to the reader. This toxicity of the text is a necessary poison, a toxin ingested in order to muster a barrage—here again, a sort of vaccine whose dosage is uncertain and thus dangerous?—against a threadbare language that channels nothing within us except conventions, absences, or a void that leaves us hopeless. This defunct language, ours most of the time, which children and psychotics miraculously resuscitate, is a shroud spread over the real. In order to protect us . . . because the world in its raw state hits us too hard, leaves us unstable, disobedient, and unoccupied. Killer-texts get under our skin and contaminate us just as inevitably as a virus works to colonize cells. They modify our manner of being in the world, imperceptibly at first, but then more overtly the more we enter into concrete resonance with them. Reading is a laboratory with immeasurable outcomes, while it's supposed to be an inoffensive placidity that takes up no more than free time, stretches of the night, siestas, or tranquil mornings. In fact, it is exactly the opposite. While reading, what is mobilized in us does not appear, at least not immediately. The alteration it effects is continuous, well beyond the moment when our eyes roam across the page. This is why, at certain moments of existence and even in certain existences *tout court*, it is impossible to read. Truly to read. To enter, that is, into the zone of ravishment where something in us is affected that escapes us absolutely.

Risking Scandal

"Scandal" in Latin means stumbling block, something that trips you up, an obstacle.

"Ah, would the scandal vanish with my life, / How happy then were my ensuing death!" said the Duke of Lancaster on his deathbed while Richard II planned to help himself to his property. No matter how you attempt to write about scandal, every angle is impossible, obstructed. We swallow every object of scandal as soon as it appears. Is there no one who might finally, all alone, at a certain moment, and in a certain place, do as Christ did and incarnate scandal?

What, still today, remains scandalous, outrageous? Outrage is what unfolds beyond all norms of acceptable conduct. There was an era when outrage happened all the time. The excommunications by the surrealists, the violent happenings by American artists during the Vietnam War, extravagances, obstinate misbehavior . . . Ultimately, such trespasses, fastidious unreason, intransigent mutual hatred, dirty tricks, chicanery, and artificial paradises, were all judged severely. Judged for taking the risk of a combat lost in advance. And yet this was precisely the price of intellectual life. What remains of our indignation? What has become of our revolt? If it's now out of the question to expose the state of our souls, there is perhaps still time to restore scandal to its underlying purpose.

Joyce's language shatters the usual ways of listening; it does violence to you, much like Céline's or the harrowing language of Proust and Woolf, so that you can't think straight or stay on rhythm; it is always taking you somewhere else, tearing you away; such texts attack you, endlessly undoing your levees and refuges. Joyce denudes all the voices that constitute a being; he exposes the lines of demarcation, shatters each person's intrigues. The effraction is willed, the violence awaited. If these texts have become canonical, it is also perhaps to keep them quiet. Their universal recognition poorly conceals the uneasiness that they provoke, their obdurateness, their sovereign savagery, their frontal attack on sleep merchants and the traffic in brainless language.

Only a work of art can be truly scandalous, because it alone invents a new language. Sometimes, an act, an event, or a character can themselves become, "as performers," a work; they belong, in some sense, to the language of the world that they renew willy-nilly, without a clear consciousness of the importance of what they represent in history, at that very instant. Scandal contaminates; it provokes a crisis in our perception of the world that proves rampant, such that all censure is doomed to defeat because the world will rely upon this new language, whether or not it wishes to, many years later, to determine its identity and its openings. Today, we are afraid of scandal; and the apparent reign of non-censure is merely the cover for an era that is more reactionary than ever.

The vehicle of scandal may well be something that appears to be utterly inconsequential, in accord with things, a surface effect. Our era would like to smooth things over to the point that they disappear, to efface beings within situations, hierarchies, decisions, so that nothing causes a scandal, nothing becomes actionable. "The moment when you become most profoundly overwhelmed," writes Pierre Zaoui, "never are you more sensitive to surface events that occur simultaneously in the world and in yourself, the surface enveloping the world and the self, the spirit and the body, on the same plane."[1] For scandal is also everything that people align with the negative, sickness, and death. What cannot be amended, or justified. No imaginary reparation can bring a departed loved one back among the living; this isn't a scandal that you cause but one that slays you. Nothing is reconciled by its occurrence, nothing repaired; it is, in many respects, pure nonsense. How to praise such a scandal, to assign it a possible outcome or an intrinsic value? Should we tell ourselves that every event has a meaning, a horizon? Perhaps not.

Scandal is unappeasable, irreconcilable; it opens a line of flight that can't be closed. It's not an option that you can choose, prefer to another; it's not an object of choice, not even of wager; it can't be used or seized; it arises. It splatters reality all over, displaces reliable markers, reference points, barriers, thresholds, and alphabets; it is a widening circle whose outer limit cannot at any moment be traced in advance. Perhaps it is a space of thought retrieved from barbarism—that is, from indifference.

Taking the Risk of Childhood

To take the risk of childhood is never to forget that you were once a child. This remark appears so simple . . . We turn our backs on childhood; we remember it only so as the better to bury it in a bygone past. To return to childhood is to enter a world of disappointment, but also, and only here, a world of wonder. The childhood present in us as adults has nothing to do with the childhood in our past, the childhood of recollection that we cradled within ourselves, whose contours we carefully redrew, whose underpinnings we reconstructed, whose atmosphere we corrupted, whose chronology we rewrote with the help of family albums. That childhood isn't very complicated to retain; rather, it is burdensome, sometimes even dangerous, and always reinvented according to our need to accommodate the so-called adult world. The childhood alive in us is something else. It is an experience of pure intensity, a sort of rare drug, hard to forget once sampled. A shot of spirit that procures a lightness comparable to drunkenness and an intact creativity. This childhood, however, remains beyond the reach of most people. It is classified as a "military secret" in our archives and access to it is denied. There is no pass that would authorize even momentary access. A break-in is required. To intrude like a thief and steal its essence. *Reignite it.*[1] Even to speak of it is difficult because the words liable to evoke it come to us from an irremediable exile.

Why is access to it denied so categorically? Wherein resides its danger, its extreme inflammability, its power of contagion, its madness? Indeed, madness lurks in these parts—that is, disorder, incoherence, delusion, visions, the force of desire, but also insight, the immediate perception of the trustworthy and the equivocal, language's power to recreate, its capacity to inhabit the world at any point whatsoever. It is the risk of living inadvertently, leaving aside everything that would go on to constitute our desires, our confidence, our doubts, our reasonable feeling of knowing how to tell good apart from evil, if only a little . . . Outside of memory, this childhood is still always coming back; it impregnates our life like a fugitive rainstorm that, one summer evening, restores intact the scents and sensation of night without fatigue.

Childhood is the sole metaphysical experience that we all have while knowing that it's where, all of a sudden, our life turned inside out. We have seen the underside of the world. The hidden lining, backstage. Then, forgetting ensues. And adulthood that transfers the ideal to the side of the real, the hidden side of Plato's cave, the secret message in Proust's singular madeleine, the epigraph to every narrative. To have hoped with all your might for something to happen is to have been a child. A wondrous, unconscious, whimsical, irresolute child. A child braced up on a dream shared with her stuffed animals and the corner of a certain window.

Her secret is shared; she is confident. The world speaks to her and she speaks to the familiar world, and even to ghosts. The unknown can be tamed; she knows it. This inner security permits her to think, delivers her dreams and her expectations. And then something happens, like lightning in the summer sky . . . Danger rattles the foundations of the world that seemed stable. This vacillation is actually her own: at the confines of the world is something undomesticated, a space of pure savagery, which even words cannot captivate or capture. Lightning is not the name of a thing that the child was refused, but perhaps a "no" spoken almost inadvertently about the thing most important to her life at that instant, and that not only produces frustration or sorrow but, yes, singularly, another visage of the real. It might be a bicycle accident, a trip delayed for a few days, the unfulfilled promise of a story before bed; the importance of the event is not—for the most part—what marks childhood, but rather how it effects a sudden, vertiginous, fall outside the stable world. A crack that abruptly reveals, within a familiar landscape, a new horizon line. And here, in this literally unthinkable place, for a few seconds or a few hours, the child will *see*. She will be left alone with this now removed shelter. This experience, if it's true, and if it's not disavowed, negated, erased, or travestied, is foundational. Another world appears within the lining of the world, which had always been there, hidden within its very thickness, its gentleness, its protective envelope. Who could have believed that the genie would escape the bottle right where you are crying? The bicycle down on the ground—not easy to get up but then you're up; nothing seems to have happened and now off you go, without training wheels; you are free. It's exhilarating. Lightning waits inside us like a tiny crouching animal. Consolation becomes useless. And once aroused fright propagates like a trail of powder that bit by bit is going to contaminate the whole landscape, color it differently around the edges and environs. Reality will never again be the same.

Risking childhood does not exist, by which I mean childhood is risked in us. The question is: can we become hospitable to childhood? Lightning across a summer sky ushers us into a world where wonder becomes possible because something has been posited—there at the edge of the page, of the hillside, of your eyes, of your heart—which evokes the incompleteness of the world and of all desire, which speaks of weakness and forgiveness for weakness at the same time, and which tells you that losing isn't definitive even if painful; that equivocation and misunderstanding are at the heart of language but you can still speak; that you can be abandoned all the time and still breathe, and still love; that you will be forgiven in the least expected manner; and that, beyond all expectation, you can, you must, never give up hope.

I was always a well-behaved child . . .

How many times have I heard this phrase? Well-behaved for whom? With respect to what? What madness, what torments held in abeyance, what divined abysses? The prudence of a very small child is infinitely unsettling.

"I believe that I have believed in romantic love . . . But my life is totally different: I was always the best student in school, then became a professor, and said yes to the first boy who proposed to me because he accepted me. Everything frightened me, but I always stayed calm, so calm. Except on the day when my little brother ripped the eyes out of my doll. From then on, I knew that life would betray me; that was the beginning of the fall, and it hasn't stopped since. I didn't understand a thing— about drugs, about rock music, or about erotism, or desire. Why? My intelligence remains blank, functional, as effective as fire in a downpour; I have nothing to say to you, no hope. I have always been already an old woman. My life is cast in the mold of the past. You will not be able to give me a present."

Childhood is desperate. Without any possibility of return to the refuges we construct for it, it is a risk always to come.

Assiduity

We repeat the same theme with disarming assiduity; we invent new byways but deliberately turn around a fixed axis, as if tethered to it, which had prematurely spoken of the world to us, or spoken *the* world—and gave us the use of words—in order to attempt with all our might to overturn the mirror, to shatter it upon a breath and to explode all resemblance. We construct machinations for our desire that will come tumbling down with a single breath. And we seemed to be annihilated, burned up with the essence that whisked away our fragile shelter, our armor, and all recognition to come. Afterward comes the melancholy of waiting, a shadow that spreads toward he or she who might like to gather up its cloth, so light, the stuff of which our secret barbarisms are made.

We were once erotic children and don't know it any longer. We tasted the world, touched and were touched; we listened to a noise until it dissipated into the night and enveloped us like a wondrous Milky Way; we cradled a blade of grass, a pebble, a word, and piles of things impossible to cradle (but did it anyway); we kept watch beneath our half-closed eyelids for a sign of life on the other side; we constructed passageways, signs, alphabets; we tried to understand with our backs to the enigma, and to tell stories that make us less afraid. And we forgot about it all. All this crazy energy expended for nothing, for the sake of a few burning and fleeting sensations that remained beneath the skin like undeciphered auguries.

With the body of the newborn, separated from the mother at birth, with the first breaths rife with the pain of being separated, of being outside the waters of all memory, erotism is also born. It's the whole body that is erotic, the body that vibrates, feels, and thinks, that loves and despairs, that waits, that suffers and feels the intense, infinite pleasure of being enveloped, caught up in a loving gaze, or a breath that ever so quietly utters words of love. How is it possible to get back to yourself? How do you little by little de-eroticize a body wholly delivered unto the pure sensation of existing, by and for the other, and yet newly separated from her? Little by little, the body of the newborn is desensitized. It is wrapped up. Little by little, it closes upon itself. Sensations become concentrated around the mouth and the extremities of the body, around what become the so-called erotogenic zones. The memory of the body is thereby divided, dispersed, and forgotten; the entire vibrant body of the newborn goes away, effaced upon contact with the real; but it also lingers to watch over your dreams, your fears, your nightmares; it is lodged within the scents you love; it is suddenly exacerbated as you brush against a passerby; it is volatilized. We spend our lives dismantling this body and trying to recapture it, to rediscover its scent, the miraculous draught of an elixir of lost life. Deep inside, we know that it exists, but no longer dare to believe in it.

Assiduity is a loop of obsession—its obscure, pathological double. Obsession drives us mad; it keeps awake for entire nights, at odds with imaginary enemies, tormenting us with missed opportunities. In fact, obsession makes sure that we think about nothing else; it builds up our defenses the better to help us forget a secret agony. The only way to exit obsession is to will it. To commit to undoing it by exploring it to its outer edges, intensely, without ever letting up. Assiduity is the overturning of passivity into an act, but only because it urges us to take the risk of this passivity, of this renunciation of will, and because we let ourselves be traversed by something that it can't comprehend or contain.

People say, be assiduous, and they are thinking of the amorous posture of she who doesn't want to detach from her object of desire, and from her pleasure as well. The usual meaning of the word implies a sort of inconvenience, as if it constantly strained the limits of the possible or at least the desirable. It harbors the idea that an anticipated victory over someone or something for which assiduity is risked is always on the verge of falling apart, of leaving behind a battle put off for too long. But assiduity, like its

obscure sister, obsession, really acquires meaning, perhaps, only in relation to truth. In this precise respect, it turns into patience—silently, like
an augury. Assiduity ventures toward the truth (of our love, our thinking,
our acts) in order to test itself, obsession does so in order to save us from
it. Augury is the time we are immersed in, the time of the microruptures
and discontinuities that betray no design, no escape either, but in which
it remains possible to recognize the imprint of something we have always
borne inside, a spiritual hunger.

Risking the Future

Something that he distractedly and pusillanimously let pass in the
present that would open the future . . . One has to suspend the
course of time, to turn upon oneself: to convert or perhaps to dance.

—MARIA ZAMBRANO, *Los claros del bosque*

The "pure" future, we want no part of. Its extreme toxicity already overwhelms us like an unkept promise. In response, you get rid of something:
the joker. And you pull an excuse out of your sleeve, looking a bit sad. Taking the risk of what's to come is a prodigality that you don't permit yourself.
Because you might lose everything that you have painstakingly amassed:
habits, permissions, betrayed secrets, furtive pleasures, little arrangements
with the dead. To risk seeing all of your hiding places unmasked, without
assurance of being the least bit protected? No thank you. It's salutary to
take refuge wherever you can . . . isn't it?

Phenomenology, today, eschews the grand idea of time that carried
metaphysics up to the threshold of the twentieth century. Thinking the
totality (of time, of space, and of the world) is no longer done, it seems. We
have entered the era of open—which is to say, local or fractal—totality.
Totality has become a perspective that brings together the microdiscon-
tinuities and all of the lines of flight that make up our vision. Say hello to
kinetic civilization, our cut-up images spliced together in a rapid sequence
to shadow our acts, our intimations, and the words we speak in an ever-
present imaginary projection. There is no longer any clear delimitation

between the inside and the outside, between the private and the public, between the juridical and the social, or between the representation we form of our lives aligned to a sort of ideal of the multiple and the transparent. The flow of time, today, is composed of fragments and ultrarapid juxtapositions that can no longer be encompassed by a single panoptic vision. The future becomes a pure surface of projection made from the compossibility of the states of the real. "Everybody fears the irruption of the unexpected," writes Michela Marzano. "Our fear of the future is so great that we lapse into all sorts of compulsive behavior in order to neutralize anything perceived as dangerous. But the compulsive behaviors that are supposed to combat fear often end up engendering even greater anxiety."[1]

All misrecognition is future. A miniature act of barbarism signed by us. And yet we want to rediscover what made us live to such extremes. We prefer not to know, to imagine ourselves vanquished, and not to fight. Because fighting with no certain outcome, even without any battle plan, is absurd. This is, most of the time, how we consider the future. Unworthy of risk. Unless the future is conceived on the basis of the past, ours and that of our past ancestors; on the basis of the knowledge we have stockpiled within us just in case . . . whereby we gain some assurance that the territory up ahead won't be entirely unfamiliar.

To risk the future would perhaps be to ask how to linger a bit longer . . . indeed, to slow down, to lag just a little bit behind the mad rush of hours and days and months, programs and lists, everything still to get done that has already been accomplished without us even needing to be here. Risk is a negative capability (a term that I borrow from Adam Phillips[2]); and negative capability is like a path that you follow in the opposite direction from *Petit Poucet*, toward perdition (at last). To risk the future would thus be another possible opening for deceleration, for swerving, for what lingers in the wings, off camera, before everything rushes ahead, as in Alexander Sokurov's film, *The Russian Ark* (2002), composed of a single long take.

Tom is an architect. He works at a firm, busy with plans, dossiers, prizes. Upon arriving, he just says, "I'm tired." That's all. For several months, that is basically all. And then, one morning, he says, "I can't do it any longer, truly, you have to help me." He had a dream. He was in a house where he couldn't recognize any of the rooms. Into each one he went; and door after door opened to him. The dream became a nightmare. No exit from this opening to infinity that met his progression . . .

What unreachable shelter would provoke you to become a builder, the healer of others' houses, the one who invents a refuge for them that he refuses for himself? Tom awoke from his dream filled with indescribable anxiety. It took him a while before he could face the day, as if he was preparing for a catastrophe whose precursors he alone could see. But nothing. Only the memory of this indefinite opening of rooms into other rooms. He wanted to understand this horrific night spent in fear provoked by a nightmare without object or threatening figure, or any apparent malediction. It was at work, during a site visit, that the key to the dream came to him. He was renovating a wing of an eighteenth-century chateau in the Perigord Vert, proceeding carefully because there were reports of Roman ruins underneath. He discovered not ruins but a secret passage. A relatively recent tunnel connected the village and the chateau. Most likely, it dated from the war and a large portion of it was obstructed by weather damage. Once cleared, it led to a large vaulted room, a sort of cellar where papers and maps were still to be found. He examined them: all of the houses in the village, or almost all, had a secret entry; there was an entire social organization of clandestine life. He studied the history of the Resistance in this part of the country, its ramifications, its organization, and got caught up in the game, astonished at his own passion. This is how he learned that one family lost three sons, arrested a few days before the end of the war. He went to meet the family. And then nothing, for five years. When his grandfather died, he learned that during the war he had hidden his father and his father's little brother, who were Jews, at his house, passing them off as the youngest members of the family, and that his "real" grandparents had been sent to the camps. Civil status gone, everything gone. His father, for his part, came out rather well, aside from the cancer that took his life at age fifty. His uncle, the younger brother, became a drug addict. Homeless, found dead in a cellar. Of cold, of hunger? His body wasted, barely thirty years old. As for Tom-the-successful-architect, he spent his life building shelters, houses for others. Silence kills more unavoidably than any memory. Why wasn't he told anything? This he didn't have the courage, the strength, to ask his dying grandfather.

Not that our silence always kills. What does kill is our cowardice, I mean what we consign to silence. The alibi that we make it endorse. The Catholic grandfather adopted these two children in order to save them, but then to reveal the story was beyond his ken. He was an ordinary hero. Human beings do what they can with their history. With the traffic of feelings and lies. With a conscience rotten with false thoughts even when generosity wishes and ultimately makes it possible to save lives. "To translate past words into present acts is a form of combat. A combat that only makes sense if it saves us from our past and our fathers; if it tears us away from tradition and makes us survivors within our own language and culture," writes Frédéric Boyer.[3] Psychoanalysis is a practice of appropriation that fabricates the unprecedented. I speak to this other, the analyst, in order to metamorphose the heritage that is supposedly set aside for me. The necessity of psychoanalysis is first that of an intimate rupture. It is to accept the feeling of being an orphan in every language. In this sense, yes, it is a sort of survival pact. Not to go deeper into debt or to make things worse by forgetting, but rather, on the contrary, to leave the ruins behind or exit from silences.

At the Risk of Beauty

The emotion that beauty provokes is lightning bright. It reaches us in a place of our being that humans have perhaps designated as paradise. Beauty is characterized by the joy it gives us—a joy that comes over us, a dilation, an enlargement of being. It is an infinitely higher ordeal, if possible, than that of Hell. There is terror in beauty because its perfection arrests us, or rather suspends us, vertiginously, outside any material contingency. The section of a wall, white on white, the chalky light of evening. No more is required. A random face, perhaps. A harmony that might be qualified as unreal were it not precisely so real, so present, engraving itself this very instant like a promise. Beauty pertains to transcendence, whether or not you are a believer; or, at least, to a gap that points toward the thing it effectuates. It attains our inner chaos, the affliction of our relation to ourselves, the escheat of everything we left for naught. Beauty recalls us to an ancient order in which life came with the sensation of an other closer to us than ourselves, who carried us, lodged within the heart of another heart; and for nine months this miraculous equilibrium—and time itself— would go unbroken. The experience of the beautiful makes us believe in a saved or spared world, as if, far from all subjectivity, we might go toward an experience more sovereign than all intention. In beauty, however, there is also a horror, which an entire literature has spoken of. At the same time, it points to something that desists, constantly, all the time.

He possessed an incandescent beauty. As a dancer, he had experienced the grace of being a sort of angel for others, a man in a body as fine and limber as the body of the most beautiful women. When he showed up at my door, I was left speechless. Literally stupefied by the beauty of the young man in front of me. Troubled, I made him wait for a moment. Then follow into the room. A large window framed the branches of a chestnut tree. The lamplight accentuated the warmth of the space. But I couldn't shake my trouble. I no longer knew what to do with my own body, my own gaze—I who had seen so many beings and bodies traverse this space and lie down on the couch, day after day. Never had I been attracted to a patient; and on that evening as well it wasn't attraction that I felt but something more disquieting, more unresolved—something extra, I might have been able to say if I knew what was coalescing within me at that instant.

The young man spoke of his distress. Of existing nowhere, of feeling exiled in an unbroken solitude, and of his wish to be done with it all. He was almost beyond the demand; his appeal arose from the most incommunicable pain. His beauty was draped on him like a shroud. Never again would I see him like this. The second time he came to see me, I welcomed him without any trouble, looking forward to the lightness of his grace and to his face. But I sought to understand, in the feelings that had submerged me, what others felt when they looked at him, and the circle of solitude that he effortlessly accrued by virtue of a sort of perfection that would diminish with the years but at this moment didn't give way. Wouldn't give way. How might the intelligence of a body that knows how to dance take hold of space in order to produce yet more beauty, in order for the perfection of gestures to make it possible, perhaps, to forget the eminently singular thing that he bore within himself?

Beauty elevates, overwhelms. It fixes us to the spot, in something that does belong to us. Far from being the subject of beauty, she who experiences it in some sense becomes its thing, not an object so much as an effect of resonance that undoes any idea of belonging or subjectivity. Beauty is not personal and yet it can arise from what is most singular. It is the naked part of the revealed world, even when it is a face. You enter into beauty as into a cloister, when its measure repeats and yet differs; what elevates then—or, we should say, what lightens us—is the spirit at work in secret.

Beauty weaves an impossible, nearly unbearable alliance with the body. The body, here, is paradoxically censored. Inviting in all its splendor, it becomes literally unwatchable. The incarnation of beauty in a singular being makes it into an object of fantasy and thus the source of all solitude. A factor of illusion, its sensuousness is a principle of deviation and must be constantly realigned with the mathematical measure of truth. Most Greek thought—but not all—posited the body as a site of deviation and *hubris*. The cynics and the materialists, for instance, ardently sought to uphold the consistency of the body . . . When, later, religion eschews the kingdom of ideas in the name of the (oh so much less futile!) idea of God, it perpetuates the original distrust of everything that derives from the body; or, at least, it looks askance at any principle of knowledge that founds the measure of truth upon what affects the senses and the body. In this respect, Descartes posits the defining equation of Western modernity: if technology is what you want, then you must know how to examine every source of knowledge in order to extract—under the auspices of the divine—only the measurable quantum to which science will lay claim. Quietly the revolution will come—of the baroque, of planetary motion, of ellipses, of optics, and of modern science itself—and it will rely upon the Cartesian investigator-subject, will call him to witness. There is no limit to the religious ground that the heavens will cede to the orbits of the physicists. The revolution is the subject in perspective and the discovery that the true appears more true if the real is deformed. And what then remains of beauty? A simple metrics of harmony? A certain measure of a body, or an idea, attuned to truth? Since Nietzsche, we know that concepts have a genealogy, a history, and that the idea of truth is unstable, mobile, and—to use Deleuze's expression—deterritorializable.

The young man became a photographer, which required a long detour by way of the "outside" of the body, or rather a body seen from outside; and, within the freedom of the photographer's viewfinder, by way of the right not to be pinned like a butterfly in the other's gaze, and frozen in place just waiting to be devoured. This detour by way of the precise technique of a gesture and a moment, in the exactitude of a certain light or a place, the effort to find his own visibility in the other obliged him to break the frame of his own terror of being a pure object of "seeing" for the other. Neglected by his mother and left to fend for himself at dance school, which he did with a passion that was killing him for 15 years, to the point of burnout, with no other escape route, he believed, than skateboarding and life on the street, which he was contemplating when he entered analysis. His photography (odd collections of odd objects that quickly gained him renown in artistic circles) left him mistrustful of faces and extreme close-ups; but, most of all, it enabled him to decline any request that he be photographed himself, saving him from the exhibition to which his entire being had been reduced for many years. Beauty, here, ricocheted off the grain of the real; and between the floor barre exercises that contorted him and the frame of the photograph a world was assembled, recomposed.

Beauty beckons us toward a gap internal to the real itself, a gap that beauty itself cannot enclose or limit, no matter how close it comes to perfection. The risk of beauty obliges us to take into account the negative, the imperfect, what makes a line falter and come apart, without seeking to sublimate anything—neither aestheticism nor ornamentation. The movement of beauty, like a state of grace, remains incomplete. It is a verb more than a noun. It is, in this sense, perhaps a secret mathematics of the real, like the gesture of a photographer when he takes a picture: what he captures is already elsewhere, invisible in what he will give us to be seen.

At the Risk of Spirit

The spirit blows where it listeth, it is said. Spirit designates something that we don't know how to name among the visible things of the world; it names the part that it is withdrawn from the sensible world and that animates it from inside. Fathers are the guardians of the spirit. They can open a child's spirit, open her wings so that she may rise up or forbid her from doing so. For children, fathers are spiritual agents and thus dangerous. For the child who comes to interrogate the world through a father's eyes, the world gains an outline thanks to his vigilant attentiveness. Tell me about the world, the child asks at bedtime, hold me in your arms, in your words, in your faith, and take me with you, never let me go . . . And if this father doesn't open a path, if he doesn't listen to the child's bedtime prayer, if he doesn't keep his promise, spirit will be threatened. Spirit, indeed, but not necessarily the child. The spirit blows where it listeth; but if the passage of spirit is obstructed, the child is exiled from it, left alone with all her ghostly fears and sorrows fraught with uncertainty.

Why the father? Why not the mother, the educator, the faithful dog laying there, the house? All of this too, but after. The father might be dead, absent; he can have been unfaithful, devious, or violent, but the question is: does he remain a father? A father is someone who posits a living, plausible, and loving separation between the mother—the savage and matrixial mother—and the child; who lets the child know that the world outside the womb is possible and desirable; that there is much to learn and fun to have; that desire is permitted; that desire is infinite, inexhaustible; and that it carries you more than you carry it, much like spirit. The father is not necessarily real but he demands a space of recognition, within the mother and, somewhat differently, within the child. Within the most secret heart of hearts. There where the child can speak in a hushed voice, mutter and imagine. Life, all around, the landscape. Fathers are irreplaceable. Unfortunately, or fortunately, that's how it is. In this sense, the father is always a "risk," who, in order to anchor his power and/or his name, must be named by the mother, designated by her as such. Indeed, the father is named by the desire of a woman whom he makes a mother. Later, in the relation that unites him to his child, he might make it possible or forbidden, by a tacit order that is often obeyed, for this child to be visited or not by the spirit, the spirit that polarizes desire and sets it in motion.

When a father dreams upon a child, she will have a freer spirit. Otherwise, she will have to conquer him, become a soldier, and go to war. This is what Cervantes is all about, lost fathers and war, too. And battles won over perversion and madness. Our battles are often fought in the name of the father, but without our knowledge. We believe ourselves unarmed, on a solitary search, while, in fact, it's the shade of he who preceded us, to whom we also owe our lives, that we desire to attain.

The idea of spirit is that of a pure visitation. It is what migrates into us and convokes us; we possess no ways or means to make it an object (of thought), a relation (to the world), a project, or a vector; it can only be experienced in and through the freedom that pertains to it alone, absolutely. I have no wish to sacralize spirit by a sleight-of-hand that would transfer it from an order of worldly intelligence to that of a spiritual entity, and yet I still believe that only because spirit is a cradle much vaster than all culture, all orders of thought, and all belief, does it originally give us the possibility of being in relation to alterity.

Risking the Universal?

There is no humanity that doesn't participate
in the inhumanity that contains it.

—ANNIE LE BRUN

Any value given to the universal is inseparable from the duty constantly to remember and to attend to the singular—that is, to what tilts the concept, the ideal, the just, and the beautiful toward fragility, the "human all too human," toward what is neither defensible nor even, very often, representable. The defeat of the Kantian imperative—glorious as it may be—obliges us to think the universal in line with the Enlightenment but also on the margins, there where no words remain to defend it. Can the rights of man simply be absorbed into the tide of good feelings that riles up people raised on Western democracy? When it becomes a rhetorical weapon in social and political discourses on current events, the universal risks turning into a little empty shell, hardly more than a name. Does hospitality, for instance—a concept under whose protection I would place psychoanalysis in its entirety—remain a universal value? From the outset, it raises the question of who does or doesn't deserve it. To whom should we extend our pity, recognition, or distrust? Like Cerberus before the gates to the underworld, all of our guardian figures are rather terrifying. In our mythologies, they lend form to our fear of the wholly other—that is, first of all, our fear of the dead—standing between, presumably without any contamination,

164

the world of the living and that of potential revenants, phantoms, ghosts, and wanderers. For hospitality is all about the threshold. Delimiting an inside from an outside, it invites us to think about the transgression of this limit, but also aggression, invitation, exchange, everything that might take place at such a border. Psychoanalysis, as well, works at the threshold of a reason destabilized by the passions. It is an art of the between-two-deaths, of second birth, of wings and margins—in brief, all the spaces that prevent any knowledge or rule from bringing the world to a definitive close. Sometimes, only when a patient leans upon the universal can she emerge from her singular history, freer than before. But isn't the vocation of psychoanalysis to question the universal and, even more, to make it listen? To convoke the universal is to suppose that there is a point of transcendental support for the contingencies of the world. Does this support describe a structure of the human or a horizon of thought, a scientific hypothesis, or an ethics?

Our birth constitutes the first act of hospitality, not psychological, but ontological: we come from an other, we are carried, carried in our very constitution by a mother. The first hospitality occurs with birth. It is the very condition of life. We are mortal beings and our finitude makes us *passeurs* on earth. The act of hospitality, for Jan Patocka, only makes sense if this event doesn't belong to the one who hosts, to the one who welcomes, or to the one who arrives, but rather to the gesture whereby the one welcomes the other. If creating time, in Hebrew, is synonymous with inviting, then, in order to produce time, at least two are required.

Psychoanalysis takes hospitality to extremes, offering a space where— for the very first time in Freud's day—the doctor withdraws in order to let the patient become his own doctor. The time of the analytic session is a time where this movement of unconditional hospitality—whose only rule is to say "everything comes to you"—finds space for an unprecedented translation. Freud said that the goal of an analysis is to love and to work. A magnificent response, now and always. But we shouldn't forget that work, in the etymological sense, is not foreign to torture—that is, the destitution of the sovereign subject reduced to slavery. Such slavery submits the supposedly free subject to loyalties that "work it over," adorations that captivate her, hatreds that annihilate her, archives deposited in her as the ghostly reminder of an age without forgetting. I might evoke a fragment from an analysis that marked me because it had been difficult to understand what was happening; because I had to make do with being in the dark and not attempt to dispel it with imported knowledge, but rather to rely upon my strange trust in the possibility that my patient would be delivered from the predicament in which she found herself. In a letter sent two years after the end of her treatment, she attempted to put her version of events into words. She was what might be called "a battered woman," in the physical and moral sense of the phrase; and during the first months of her analysis, I felt like an impotent witness to her atrocious situation. She found every possible way to excuse her tormenter, an object of pleasure for this man whose abjection she was unwilling to see. Then one day she said to me, "It's over. He will never touch me again." And this is actually what happened. It took her another year before she separated from him for good, but she wasn't molested or harassed again during that time. Of this event, she was only able to say, "All of a sudden I realized that one does not beat *A Woman*. Never." And in this "a woman" resides the universal of human dignity. Her letter told me: "With your listening, you lent me a strength that I never had before, a horizon that I had stopped believing in, and a dignity that I had long since abdicated. This is what allowed me, one day, to rely on universal principle: one does not attack a woman or a child in the flesh. This was my first refuge and my first freedom."

Hauntings

To take the risk of allowing oneself to be haunted is a strange ordeal, to say the least . . . By what being, what thing, what event, first, are we haunted—and how precisely do we name this presence? If the measure of this risk is determined by the amount of danger confronted, in what sense does a visitation constitute a threat? And why would we *want* to be haunted?

What is haunting? Whether you are inhabited by a memory or visited by a voice that defies death, like the spectral apparitions in British novels from the beginning of the century, aren't you always haunted, ultimately, by yourself? That is, by your own double? Whether collective or individual, our hauntings poison our nights and infuse our love stories with savagery. In literature and cinema, the enigmatic figure of the double is what best expresses what I am approaching here under the title of haunting. "The theme of haunting merges," writes Elie During, "with the curious topological condition of a double that only doubles itself, that is nothing but a torsion upon itself."[1] To let ourselves be haunted is to admit that, at the most intimate point of ourselves, our own doubles overflow us; that, within us, a vampire lurks, feeds on our blood, our identity, profanes our chastity, and can't see his own image in the mirror. "Vampires, as everyone knows, have no specular image," During recalls. "As for doubles, they are said to be as insubstantial as virtual images floating in a mirror."[2] We are haunted and don't know it, or only slightly if our nightmares remind us from time to time, before they disappear anew into the disquieting folds of sleep.

To be haunted is to be at grips with a past that never ceases to return, making the present into an echo chamber, saturating it with variations that are incompatible with the pure present of the event, which it ceaselessly displaces . . . By what clairvoyance could we shed light on these vampiric shadows, these neglected specters, these shades deprived of any sepulchre? What is the intelligence that would allow us to advance toward the risk of being haunted? About the intuition that strikes to the heart of a philosophical doctrine, Bergson writes: "An image which is almost material in that it still allows itself to be seen, and almost spirit in that it no longer allows itself be touched—a phantom which haunts us while we turn about the doctrine and to which we must go in order to obtain the decisive sign, the indication of the attitude to take and of the point from which to look."[3] Might this intelligence of haunting be a gaze on something in darkness without any possibility of being illuminated, without shunning the negative?

One day I discovered a different way of working in an analysis that had already lasted three years. The patient had difficulty getting to her second session of each week (so much so, sometimes she couldn't even leave her house), which made me react. I proposed that she come two times in a row on the same day, first at the regular hour for her first session (say, at ten o'clock in the morning), after the session walk around or sit at a café downstairs for half an hour, and then return for the second session (at eleven). The insertion of an "empty" session between the two sessions—whether or not it was claimed by another patient—was something this patient very much appreciated, to an extent that surprised even her. Several dreams appeared that revolved around the figure a child whom she lost in a crowd or cared for so poorly that it died. Intrigued by the insistence of this figure (the patient had no children yet), I will ask her about her family genealogy and the order of births. Had a child been "forgotten"? What absence of a tomb haunted the nights of this young woman?

Several months later, in fact, it emerged that this intercalated session symbolized a lost child in her maternal lineage, a stillborn child whose place and sign she bore within herself. When we undo our maledictions, the order of absolute loyalty to absent ones—or to a parental sorrow?— are we thereby liberated from our lost or departed doubles, scrubbed from the archives and discourse, declared missing in action from the battlefield? To risk being haunted makes us *as well* into revenants, obliging us to re-open sepulchres and archives, and to convoke the living unto a potentially illusory but still necessary assent to their ancestral past. As for the inner pocket where our violences and maledictions are lodged, they will never be pacified, nor even perhaps reconciled. In a beautiful essay, Annie Le Brun writes that there is an irreducibility of the negative that cannot be transmuted into light and that we are also responsible for.[4] This untamable "blackness" does not distance terror but constrains it to come toward us and us to confront it. To risk being haunted is to walk right up to the border where life merges with death. But the value of this approach is its constant intensity, that of speech, a speech capable of dreaming. Blackness as blackness itself becomes an instrument of measure and exploration whereby we make ourselves into seers. The inhuman is what haunts us; it is what we keep trying to disavow, to ignore, and to set apart from our lives as if it should never enter the enchanted circle of consciousness.

Spirals, Ellipses, Metaphors, Anamorphoses

The ellipse is a very beautiful mathematical figure of evasion. An immobile vanishing point. A point of exit from the visible toward the invisible. A point of catastrophe—fractally speaking—in a universe of continuity: a volute. An ellipse has two foci, the one visible, the other invisible. It is opposed, without appearing to be, to all forms of authority; it opens oblique Baroque angles within perspectival space organized around a central subject; it is the slippage of death into the folding and unfolding of anamorphosis, the vertigo that, all of a sudden, opens a space under your feet. It is the spiral that launches the second focal point of the ellipse toward a never attained future. This is the movement that seems best to describe our relation to the past and, even more, to trauma. Reactualization in the present, at the same point on the axis but "on a higher level," offering a different access to the past, as if the repressed past were always seeking to be traversed anew, to be refigured at last.

What might it signify to take the risk of the ellipse? At once to return to a point where the past slips away, to cause it to be born or surge up anew; and, at the same time, structurally to adopt a vanishing point for yourself, a window on the checkerboard. Within an imposed figure, even

within a perverted, coercive power relationship, to imagine the very possibility of the existence of a Robinson Crusoe. I am thinking of beautiful
texts by Olivier Cadiot[1] and Jacques Derrida, who opens the second year
of his seminar, *The Beast and the Sovereign*, with the eminently elliptical
figure of Crusoe.[2] Because silence overflows the ellipse from all sides, the
discourse that would like to circumvent the figure ends up magnifying its
disquieting familiarity, its *Unheimlichkeit*. "Let us recall that the uncanny as
Freud defines it is not the coming to light of a buried secret, which would
be inherently foreign, but rather the return in foreign guise of something
known and familiar. The uncanny thing is not what returns but rather the
return itself—in other words, the ghostliness that has the effect of estrang-
ing everyday life: the return of the same as different (precisely because it
returns)."[3]

To take the risk of the ellipse, then, is to make room in yourself for a
vanishing point, a point of unconsciousness, of pure metaphor, whence
meaning ceaselessly escapes, untangles itself from its own support, and
slips away, both reproducing the model and driving a wedge into it, such
that the model is ceaselessly reinvented, and so on. This risk demands that
the assurance of the unity of consciousness in itself, the infallibility of the
experience of time and space, gives in to the vertigo of tottering supports,
loss of breath, and the dream pegged to the real. The shakiness, the eva-
siveness, and the withdrawal of the real are, for Plato, aligned with the
pure simulacrum: the minimal gap or warping of the real inserts a gap into
being, a self-inequality.

Metaphor (in Greek, *metaphorein*) means to transport. According to the
dictionary, metaphor is the use of a concrete term to express an abstract notion through analogical substitution, but without an element that formally
introduces a comparison. In Lacan, the process consists of the substitution
of one signifier for another, which thereby becomes its repressed. Metaphor invents within the space of language a movement, a dynamic, a ten-
sion between two terms that create new meanings. At the price, therefore,
of repression. In addition to transport, a word whose polyphony should be
sustained—in order to keep its amorous sense in play—metaphor entails
an art of substitution, the sleight-of-hand whereby a magician pulls a dove
out of a handkerchief. And this is how we might imagine the possibility
of a displacement, a sort of grace within language that envelops us in its
metamorphoses, making us into children dazzled by the spectacle of its
legerdemain.

Metaphor invents a space of meaning that didn't exist beforehand. Like
the ellipse, its visual sister, it is risk incarnated within language itself. This

space is, by definition, unprecedented; the proximity that metaphor creates between two terms acts just once, in a specific context, at a specific moment within a text or someone's speech. In this sense, metaphor bars any duplication of meaning, as if, with each transport, it opened a new icon on your computer screen; and yet, at the same time, metaphor incarnates the possibility of always and ever saying the same thing: wait for me, do you love me, I forgive you—over and over again in a thousand different ways—or so it seems. It establishes a link between two things, bringing them together, lifting a bit of meaning from the one in order to donate it to the other, and thus to imagine for both an augmented reality, a gentle astonishment. Does this process constitute an instance of repression? I am not so sure. For the work of metaphor does not result in effacement or forgetting, but rather leaves us caught between two worlds. The first term for which metaphor substitutes another, or many others, remains as a sort of invisible lining to the new term whose discovery it incarnates; and this term, in turn, no longer belongs entirely to the old world of the language that metaphor made it leave behind, and which isn't yet rooted in the image where it has taken up residence. Metaphor is a strange hospitality offered to language—because it also does violence to it. It speaks the point of upheaval in language itself that is the place of spirit. The place of a withdrawal, of a silence.

Metaphor is the first space of the dialectic, and of thirdness. A first term is compared to a second term; and then, the new sequence produced by the proximity between the two opens a meaning somehow "enriched" by this transference or transport of images. This is what happens, give or take a few details, in an analytic session. The subject position that you are constrained to occupy is replaced by a new (psychic) place into which the time of the session transports you, toward which you strain, without thereby repressing the position in which you had arrived. Metaphor is a violent act. Violent because it's irreversible. Nothing can undo the fact that one term was "compared" to another; and in the new term whereby the first was violently substituted, ousted, and traversed, will always remain the memory of an origin. Nonetheless, something will have been not repressed but lost. And in the possibility of such loss, there is life.

Anamorphosis thus conceals an image of the dead within what appears to be the figuration of pleasures and days; but nonetheless it resides in what it lets be seen between pleasure and finitude, between the outline of a skull and faces, chalices, fabrics, a resolutely living metaphor—that is, incarnated on the side of light.

Envisaging Night

The night is our secret amplitude. The space of our mute, inner madness. The night records our fears and delivers us from them, come day, thanks to a beneficial amnesia of which anxiety is the indivisible remainder. The night is our truth; it beckons us to rejoin a more ancient place sometimes called the soul, whose language remains undecipherable. We are strangers to the night and yet it convokes us to recognize it deep within ourselves as a sister, or a weapon.

To envisage the night is to wander off with Eurydice; to know the non-resolution of enigmas. It is to admit that the nonsense which plunges Alice into a labyrinth of roses painted red by gardeners who play out their lives at the whim of a mad queen is the exact flipside of our world of reason; and that, in our relation to chance, death, time, love, and especially to our birth, we must confront a degree of absurdity that will never be resolved in any system of knowledge, any given order, any secret, or any conspiracy. Envisaging the night dismantles us from within like on a stage set. But without any backstage or rehearsals, in the course of the play everything is exposed out in front. And the very pure line of the language that each actor speaks, a story from long ago and yet new each night, is reinvented during the play, undoing itself right before our eyes, magnificently.

It began as a children's game. Something like hopscotch. Feet together, hop, hop, and back again. Then it got out of control. The bottom fell out. She would come to see you as a last resort, much as one seeks a magician, a rainman in the middle of the desert. You would open your door without knowing her, without trying to find out who recommended that she come. She would take a seat in the armchair, almost facing the window that only let in a little light, a piece of sky peering through, slate colored. She would remain silent at first, not particularly encouraged by your silence. And then you would hear, from her, these few words: how to get back again?

How to get back, indeed, from such a long night that had swallowed up every-thing, markers of time and space, oaths of love and friendship, knowledge, law, the materiality of things, the cipher ("x") of desire—in brief, everything that might constitute, for you and I, normally, an existence.

You are not the type who is easily impressed, having spent a whole life listening to everything, complaints, savagery, expectations, as well as mad desire, irrever-ence—not enough, never enough—envy and risk. But now, all of a sudden, you no longer have any idea of what might protect this session, lead it to shore—any shore as long as it offers the glimpse of a foothold amidst the tumult of the river; you are disarmed by the night that you envisage. There, in the words uttered, very simple ones, by the woman come to speak to you.

You say to her: "But why seek an end when everything is just beginning? Don't you see it? Don't you understand that the beginning it actually what causes you such fear, you almost said 'us,' including yourself for a fraction of a second in this so essentially human fear, yes, don't you see, right now, that it's not tomorrow but at this instant that your life is coming back, starting up again, being invented, at the precise instant in which you speak to me of the impossibility of living, of continuing . . . But is it even a matter of continuing? Or perhaps the point is finally to dis-continue this continuation, to put an end not to existence, its sense or its blood, but rather to the same, the endless; to cease, yes, to cease to continue, to forge ahead, to lay down your weapons and armor from now on, to welcome the total night where you are, envisage this night as the very first, the night of your birth and all birth, the night of first beginnings, stammerings?"

She would stop crying. She would look at you like one looks at a madwoman, very attentively and with great gentleness. You, all of a sudden, yes, you are the one would have taken all madness within yourself, along with the danger it entails of losing life—that is, losing love. For love is what holds us upright in this life inun-dated by night until it no longer belongs to any possible horizon, any human word.

She would say to you: ". . . but that's not possible, you haven't understood a thing . . ."

"What do you wish me to understand? Those who have understood you have also left you in complete despair and perfect solitude. To understand is sometimes an insult to intelligence, the very poor conquest of a meaning retained at any price, possessed, but without any space around it. Without breathing room or mystery."

This time she would look at you differently and you would feel her fear. The fear that an animal experiences when she knows that you are opening up, with all the trust that she can have in you, a pact of freedom that she hadn't yet envisaged alone. And that, to enter into this pact, she would have to renounce believing herself forever alone.

Trust comes at this price. Exorbitant for those who have experienced such solitude. It cannot be renounced more than once. One would never survive.

She would say, "Very well, I would like to try, to learn how to do this with you, from you."

You would reach out your hands almost to touch her and would say, "You know, don't you, that I am not the one who will give this to you, you are the one who will enter into this night, I am very old and with me you will soon feel abandoned over again, and I don't want that for you. This one meeting will suffice."

"No, I could never do it without you," she would respond. "I need your presence. I beg of you to believe me, in your turn, just to go that far."

You would know, in your turn, that you couldn't say no; that, for a time, you should confront what had opened up, in order for her to regain trust, for her gaze to return, and for her heart to open.

In *Richard II*, Shakespeare represents a king who, rather than renege on his word, accepts destitution. In a sublime dialogue with Bolingbroke, the Duke of Lancaster, he stages the ordeal of a Beckettian stripping away in which the man outside the function that makes him a king, sovereignly deposes everything that properly constitutes him, except his life itself. This is our common night, this destitution. The stripping away of all functions, orders of recognition, and commodification, sends us back into the depth of night where we become recognizable only by the singularity of a voice, a body, or a presence. When a work is created, it brings forth a bit of this dangerous night of being merely indistinct, when you advance to the turning point of undoing yourself of yourself. It is not surprising that, in Shakespeare's time, royal power considered the play sufficiently dangerous to forbid any performance of it. To show a king who strips himself of his own royalty, a king turned into a "non-king," a miniscule point at the edge of the abyss, who doesn't defend himself, was too great a risk. To envisage the night does not allow for any recourse to a belated, salvific clarity. It offers no other point of resistance than its own secret density.

Revolutions

But what is essential in the revolutionary is not that
he overturns as such; it is rather that in overturning
he brings to light what is decisive and essential.

—MARTIN HEIDEGGER, *Nietzsche*

Before it takes the form of revolt, revolution announces that a world once
familiar has had its day [*révolu*]. Is our world over and done? If yes, which
world? The world of handwritten letters, of sextants, of ink, the world of
oaths spoken before altars and the belief that they would last a lifetime, the
world of slowness, penumbra and ambiguity? No, Bernard Stiegler tells us,
it is the world of consumption that is close to finished and we will be left to
deal with its consequences and the revolution to come. "We have wanted
it all—the overvaluation of money, sex, speed, transparency, and profit—
but, it can only keep working if we keep believing in it."[1] The horizon of
expectations might glow like a blue line graph on a trading floor, if there
is no belief in profit, the edifice crumbles bit by bit. If the banks no longer
invest, no longer take risks on the real world, but only on a purportedly
real world, then they build increasingly artificial powers upon merely possible margins, forgetting that at the other end of all the numbers there are
men and women in pain. And the end is in sight, already . . .

This is seductive, but is it true? Or rather, because truth is but a fragile
cursor that we use to serve our most immediate, most prosaic needs, and
that we affirm or recuse in direct proportion to its fluctuating value, is

it reasonable to think that the fall of our thoroughly capitalist era—this much is impossible to deny—would also be *predictable*? That we'll soon be done with the endless expansion of surplus value, the circulation of material goods ceaselessly revalued to purely speculative ends, simply because this doomed world would be nearly over and done [*serait quasi "révolu"*]? Which revolution will bring this about? The precursors of the future are less readable than is generally believed, which is why, most of the time, only a handful of artists and thinkers prove to be visionaries. "Today, psychic life knows that it will only be saved if it gives itself the time and space of revolt: to break off, remember, refashion. From prayer to dialogue, through art and analysis, the capital event is always the great infinitesimal emancipation: to be restarted unceasingly. Without it, all that globalization can do is calculate the growth rate and genetic probabilities."[2] As Zev Sternell recalls, the Revolution is a heritage of the Enlightenment, in that it is founded on a humanist universalism that refutes all forms of communitarianism and particularism—a thought of the universal that has since been thrown into question not only by nationalisms but also by what might be called the "spirit of peoples." To which Lévi-Strauss responds: "Despite its urgent necessity and the high moral goals it has set itself, the struggle against all forms of discrimination is part of the same movement that is carrying humanity toward a global civilization—a civilization that is the destroyer of those old particularisms, which had the honor of creating the aesthetic and spiritual values that make life worthwhile."[3] Lévi-Strauss is fighting a losing battle: soon, no "savage" or nomad peoples will remain untouched by the values and objects of our civilization. At the end of his life, the ethnologist who wrote *Tristes Tropiques*, a work of genius, no longer concerned himself with the great maneuvers of civilizations, but rather, as he noted himself, he became extremely attentive to very small things—to rocks and plants, to light, to all the things that we forget, or that we ignore because they seem much less grave than the worth of a human life.

Julia Kristeva writes: "The word 'revolt,' with its rich and complex etymology, acquired its current, distinctly political meaning with the French Revolution. Thus when we speak of revolt today we first understand a protest against already established norms, values, and powers. For more than two centuries, political revolt has represented the secular version of this negativity that characterizes the life of consciousness when it attempts to remain faithful to its profound logic. A synonym of dignity, revolt is our mysticism."[4] Revolution is a stellar movement, of those who turn back toward themselves before heading forth again. What memory or what return nourishes the revolt semantically inscribed in all revolution? If nothing is

ever over and done [*révolu*], then each movement coils within the movements that precede it in order to risk further what revolt conquers, a hitherto unrepresentable space of thinking. For this is, perhaps, where every
revolution is generated, in what we call technology, to the extent that human invention runs ahead of the representation of the world to which it
gives rise. As we see today, the movements of spontaneous revolution are
also the children of technical innovation and the avidity of a world that
endlessly swallows up its own children. No epithets or decrees announce
the coming of the revolution; it just comes and makes us answerable for
our ideals. We do not grasp that our objects of invention, it's true, will soon
enslave us. We dream of a world that revolves around an almost infantile
desire to possess everything, to know everything, like an ingenious feedback system, and not by the desire to "dwell," as Heidegger thought. The
revolution is ungraspable, an event that can really be thought only after
the fact; it comes into the world at the same time as these hybrid objects,
whereby it can be thought. Almost sensuously, it gives birth to a new world.
Accordingly, financial institutions—with all due respect to Stiegler—will
not meet their demise (bygone world) by turning from investment to pure
profit, thus opening the way for a revolution not of carnations but of the
new ecologists of a pure thought, politically delivered from all demons.
This is not, I don't believe, how things will go. The revolution will swallow up its own children, phagocytize their objects, and develop better per-
forming, faster, and more volatile objects that demand ever more virtuosic
adaptability—but for what other world? There is no easy way to divine;
it's hard to be contemporary with one's own time. The coming world will
speak a language to be produced by our new toys, our new words, our new
images, and our new codes, which will certainly take something from the
past but in order to swallow and reinvent it—by "touches," tactilely.

A world is disappearing before our eyes. We have trouble becoming
witnesses to this revolution; we oscillate between nostalgia, regret, and
expectation, our eyes riveted to the horizon without seeing that it moves
along with us, as intimate to our vision as to the real. To risk revolution is
perhaps, at a certain moment, to have reached the limit beyond which no
further thought, freedom, and love are possible, and where, in the movement of a *volt* that says no, a new language and a new day appear. What
makes a revolution is the consent to lose everything; and such moments
are rare because we are loathe to let go of anything and the status quo feeds
on this substantial economy, this slow devoration of ourselves by ourselves.
To enter into a movement where everything will perhaps be swept away
requires a madness, a vision, but mainly a solidarity without which revolt

can't start anything. First and foremost, technology will remain a relation of mastery and the exercise of power, although it is also susceptible to sudden shifts of allegiance, often serving the cause of those who depose tyrants and open up prisons. It is a relation of everyone to time, to the same time, to a commonality that speaks one and the same language; and it is as rare as a true encounter between two beings. This clearing of being (not necessarily in the Heideggerian sense) opens a second contemporaneity, an other tonality, a collective figure of jubilation that delivers huge amounts of energy which nothing can resist, not even revolution itself; and like all beginnings, it will be digested and then formatted and reeducated—and this will be yet another restoration. But nothing can make it not have happened. That it might happen is what we most lack today.

If revolution is and will remain our mysticism no matter the cruelty of the altars on which its ideals have been sacrificed, it is because it opens toward *an other side*, a negativity pregnant with an inalienable freedom that, at certain moments of history, we confront, we defend at peril to our lives. To risk one's life for the revolution is constitutive of our humanity; it cannot be otherwise, it seems to me, even when the peaceful skies of democracy seem to augur well far into the future.

At the Risk of Going Through Hell (Eurydice)

Pure love is naked, detached from everything. It pretends
nothing, expects nothing, and desires nothing; it cares
not for itself, nor its salvation, nor its perfection.

—JEANNE GUYON

We are all Eurydices. We carry her number and her name within us. We have loved and have been loved; and we have lost this love; we have disappeared very deep into the place called Hell, there where no one is even wept for. One day, someone came looking for us, braving night and desolation, and bringing us the chance to have a living, loved body—and to climb back toward life. Eurydice speaks of us; she is an absolutely modern figure, or rather, like all truly mythical figures, she belongs to no age. Every era has its own version of Hell; ours is not that of Bosch or of the prayer manuals, but rears its head, today, anytime that we desert our own humanity. Eurydice recalls that death can claim us at any moment, in any of its forms: from renunciation to sacrifice, from anesthesia to dereliction. It recalls that taking the risk of "not yet dying" is a gamble that we will always lose in the end, but only after traversing life with more or less plenitude, joy, and, most of all, intensity.

For Orpheus, to retrieve Eurydice was, perhaps, at a certain moment, to surrender to her voice calling out for him—but why, oh why? Couldn't he bring her back to life? Or was she still a dream, an illusion? But what the myth doesn't say is that Eurydice didn't return to Hell, because Hell is not the type of place that holds a place for you; Eurydice remains a wanderer between the living and the dead, for all time she who calls—for the beloved and for love. Come hell or high water. The story of this madness is what I want to speak of, a traversal of Hell—and after.

Is Eurydice the only one to migrate between the living and the dead? Are we guilty of no longer wanting to take such a risk, going to Hell in order to return to life? Eurydice came to know Hell as many women do because she lost her love and she had lost herself in this love; because such a loss of self leads through antechambers where all is but echoes, mirages, illusions, and devastation. Today, however, Hell is not a sad place; it is where, so you'll be told, all pain, regret, and trepidation will vanish; where you live in the effusion of the instant—all vows annulled, all rancor effaced, all crimes pardoned. The instant reigns supreme in the array of shimmering delights and trompe-l'œil skies. Hell has long since retired the cauldrons, torture, and hard labor. Now it's a lot of fun, not without elegance and a certain refinement in pleasure-seeking. The first thing that happened to Eurydice in Hell is that she was dispossessed of her deadly melancholy, her lovesickness, her despair. The memory of her lover became no more than a shadow on the wallpaper in a room. Welcome to the chambers of eternity! Here, everything is repeated in exquisite loops, without seriousness or sobbing. Oh no! No mourning here . . . it would be completely out of place. Levity is required and all arrivals are promptly unburdened of any past tinged with suspect violence or useless disquiet. Any effort to resuscitate such a past will be in vain. Eurydice will no longer remember the serpent's bite or her carnal love; she enters noiselessly into a space that offers, in its permanent savagery—all the same . . . the pure absence of a loved body.

Everyone in Hell is protected, or so they believe. No disorder, not tolerated. Voluntary servitude is the law; all, here, is calm. The quiet is deeper than in the acute care wing of a psychiatric hospital, except there is no need for medication; and, in Hell, no one exercises any constraint. No adjuvant to the law, not a single codex. No text, no sentences, no judges, no prisoners—nothing, here, ever transgressed. There is no other space. Transcendence is a flakey snowfall, melted on contact with the ground—a pure effect of whiteness. The horizon line loops upon itself. The very idea of an exit would be devastating and so doesn't exist. All that belongs to another time, immemorial.

Eurydice was loved by Orpheus, sung, and longed for. Dead, she is unbound. In Hell, time is no help; it doesn't filter things. Escape attempts are no good since "wanting" and "preferring" no longer have meaning here. Justice no longer matters because there is nothing to desire, to covet.

Because everything is already there, and you along with it, eternally, because possession is meaningless, dispossession is as well. Bodies are given and taken, all erotism gone; the very idea of desire is utterly out of place. Desiring goes along with flashes in the dark, lack, thirst, expectation, vertigo, skin, caresses, collapse, suspense. Hell is self-regulated by its very inhabitants without any need for an external monitor; the docility of souls is only rivaled by their vacuity. They have been unburdened of any useless sorrow, anxious expectation, and even melancholy; they hover, like dragonflies, in a perpetual present. No rush. The only violence is the absence of violence. In Hell, the name that everyone bears is borrowed; you can take it or leave it, or decide to adopt one of the indefinite pronouns—he, she, you, me. Nor do the ego's exploits last long; they dissolve into a lethargic benevolence—except for, here and there, a few combats perdure, for the sake of spectacle—which is needed—but are soon forgotten, each adversary already persuaded of their mutual error, and of the uselessness of their onslaught.

In Hell, the problem of the body has been solved, but speech not so much. Speech alone keeps going haunted by its own disappearance, words no longer attached to any effects of time, duration, or causality, turning upon themselves and upon lips in an incessant murmur. Everything here is meaningful. One sets about decoding conspiracies, understanding the meaning hidden behind anodyne information, flushing out falsehoods, double meanings, mirages. Nothing resists Hell better than the meaning given to things. Strangely, it's a land where the word ranks high; the death blow is given by the best at using language. All speech is susceptible to interpretation, and thus to being upended. You wear it you like clothing: a deadly phrase in a pocket, a funny quip in a shoulder strap, and a sentence already wound up in your mouth. Apathy is out of the question. Speech is a weapon. The only one here.

Eurydice distrusts words. Once she entered the song of Orpheus, once she heard his voice—his voice that delivered her from spells and spoke to the animate and inanimate worlds—she had less faith in speech. In Hell, the only silent one, she is seen to prefer the simple luminous echo of the glass walls that quite precisely reflect the light from outside. Hell, you see, is an exact replica of the living world where you and I live. A surface projected into a cardboard eternity, where eras are superimposed on one another, from reflection to reflection, the juxtaposition producing a kind of temporal continuity, as when a family album, quickly leafed through, gives the impression of a life pinned to A4 paper, from birth to death, with a lot of smiles and unhappy kids forced to stand for the camera.

Eurydice explores Hell. What remains of humanity? The sexuated body couples and uncouples; all sorts of alliances are conceived, envisaged, but, in reality, few venture to touch, whence the strange disincarnation of this place; the outcome is fully known in advance and *jouissance* is exhausted in the search for a border where it can break off. For a long time, Hell was subjected to the erotics of Bosch and Breughel, of bodies tortured with sadistic refinement, men with bird heads tearing at other bodies contorted amidst infernos rife with cries. But here (alas!) no such cuisine. Torture is the province of the living alone. Nothing of the kind in Hell. The unlimited doesn't call for crime but cruelty, or, at most, for a form of voyeurism constrained by indifference. Voluptuousness is without weight, bonds or vows. No betrayal because nothing is ever promised. Hell is a vague corridor with bluish floodlights. There is no determinate place, or anything like one, where to deposit your soul.

Eurydice, the world of the dead can't take you back, you went too close to the living, to the human voice. Technically speaking, you no longer exist. In your arms, your beloved now weighs nothing, the bonds of your memory no longer hold, and images, too, little by little, have vanished; all that remains is the certainty of having lived something like mad love. There you are now, among the departed. No more shades in this kingdom, nor penumbra, nor shadows, but only the blatant overexposure of forms, bodies, objects. You attempt to think, but there is no possible shelter for thought. Doesn't true thinking always occur in emergency, anxiety, the proximity of the event, and in expectation? Thinking has thus dissolved and, along with it, any idea of becoming contemporary with anything whatsoever. Finally, self-consciousness lacks grace, lightness, and you amuse yourself by imagining that the sort of effervescence that we call an idea is a bizarrerie that should be met with caution. Hell is a remote place and yet offers no refuge. You get used to it rather quickly. Getting rid of yourself is another matter . . . Everything reverberates in a loop here, like the refrains from childhood that crop up intact just when you thought it possible finally to outrun the predestination of your past, your family. Savagery resides in the almost absolute ignorance of bonds woven, emotions felt, things exchanged, things shared. Hell is an echoless world. Everyone sets out to finish and—albeit in vain—to speak—but to say what, to risk which truth, since the very idea of truth has disappeared and nothing resists the obsessive and corrosive metaphor of eternity? Savagery is the reign of everything outside the law, but here law itself is unthinkable. Law has no other reality than its own name; it proclaims itself and undoes itself. Savagery feeds bodies into a processor. Bodies deprived of all singularity, scent, silhouette, and tone of voice. Here again, everything is decomposed, recomposable. But the strange thing about Hell is that it retains the trace of things, indefinitely; an event doesn't come to pass—it passes in a loop until it gets worn out, until its taste, its language, whereby it signifies, no longer say anything to anyone; and then it comes undone, deteriorates.

You might say that Eurydice is sad, if that had the least meaning here, where sadness has no more reality than a poorly pronounced word. Sadness demands an intermediary space between the tragic and pleasure, a sort of antechamber of dereliction, where, in its characteristic minor key, it delivers up music in a kind of absence, recognizable anywhere. Savagery is also this: there is no sadness, or joy, or passage. Hell has no other side; it opens on nothing but itself, into the labyrinth of passions that it offers, into an obscene panoply that bends bodies to a savage law, that of pure pleasure; that is, also, to horror.

Eurydice, you have no idea what is wanted of you. If anything is even expected of you. Being expected is what keeps the living alive. The living that you used to be. In Hell, all expectations dissipate, a fine mist between words. No tomorrow to support the weight of their incandescence, their lightness. Hell is always a scene. Dramaturgy of a perpetual festival. A festival that has become a macabre order: never be bored. How to imagine that someone is looking for you? That he is coming down to take you in his arms? You used to have such a beloved lover. A snake bit you, consigning you to live among shades, in a liquid night indistinguishable from day. How to find the strength to hope? To continue when there is no other world, no other scenario, no backstage? Don't give up because then you would disappear, joining those whom Dante said no one would lament, the disappeared among the disappeared, not the least living memory to call up what they once were. Those for whom no one prays.

How to emerge from the shadows that spread indiscriminately over the living and the dead when they can't be dispersed? By what path of love could Eurydice be saved? Orpheus came down to Hell to get her. The most mysterious moment is—and remains—when he turns back. How to imagine it? All this effort to come get you, all the way down there, and suddenly he turns around and casts you back to Hell? Was it all a masquerade from the outset? A useless and cruel ordeal, a final offense? The order was given not to turn around. A single condition. Don't turn around. Orpheus said yes, anything for his love. Did he even hear what was asked of him?

Some have said that it was memory, the past. That to turn around is go down the path of deliverance in reverse. Some say that it was the irreversible, that this was the price of being human: we are mortals, neither in reversible time nor omnipotent, merely beings who tarry within range of a voice, within the tenuous miracle of presence. The trap would be to believe that Orpheus exists, that he was ever anything but a pure mirage. We never do anything but wait, wait for he who will return. The only word is: forgive me, take me back. Come look for me, children say, children think, children cry, until the day when they are consoled, when they forget, when they, too, recover. You, you obstinately believed it. That someone would come looking for you in Hell. And Orpheus did come; he passed through, traversed. And you did go up with him; or, more precisely, as the myth tells it, behind him. Myth is common speech, already reverberated, which belongs to everyone, escapes toward everyone. A speech that memorializes a time perhaps more ancient than humanity itself, a narrative speech that tells that Orpheus, in spite of his promise not to, turns around, casting terror upon love. Does it still count as turning around if she, the beloved, calls to you, calls to you out of the kingdom of the dead to which she still belongs?

Freedom accrues to those who desire it; it arrives in and through desire, a pure event, internal to desire itself. It can't be assigned to the will, being much more originary, as Spinoza knew, coiled inside the desiring mechanism, this marvelous little clock that makes us living beings. Is perseverance in being a matter of consent to the enlargement of being called "joy"? To climb out of Hell is to quit exile, to follow the thread of a voice that calls from furthest away; and this same voice that calls to you gives you a new body, a consistency, and a shelter. But then . . . Orpheus turns around and you receive a vision of his body, the fragility of his being alive that responds to the desire that you receive; and Hell knew this—it knew that he could never not turn around because he loved you. There was never any chance. That's what Hell is—time turned into fatality. Nonetheless, some unpredictability remains, because you didn't return to Hell, precisely because hell is a place that no one never exits. But responding to the call immediately got you out of Hell, even if you could never leave with him alive; and he believed that you were lost all over again and he slipped up. And he began to die, to the point of being torn to pieces by the furious Eumenides, jealous of his passion.

But where were you? Neither alive nor dead, you no longer had a place, not even the unlimited place, the place of pure and barbarous madness, the place of uncanny and infinite gentleness that is called Hell? You will enter a space between two worlds, exiled from both, belonging nowhere; and you cherish this freedom, but, like all prophetic voices, you will be alone; you will be the passerby whom no one recognizes but everyone has seen, a pure witness, if that's even possible, a silhouette floating in space, a solitary, weightless body.

Is the space of Eurydice internal to language itself, the beginning of all metaphor? A metaphor forged between the dead and the living, a myth whose memory convokes all femininity, in each woman who knows . . . You slipped into the space of the letter, between the walls and the territories within this gesture that opens toward a response; inside language you brought a passage to life where you are no longer completely alive but also no longer a dead woman amongst the dead; because nothing ever stops being written or forgotten. Even in the most jealously guarded archives, there remain undeciphered messages, letters under seal that never reached their addressee—and you watch over all of them. You, Eurydice, are she to whom death was refused, who was locked into rebirth. Eurydice, you entered into the secret of every single letter, whether it be effaced, discarded, delivered, past, or future . . . Eurydice as Hermes the voyager inhabits the only place where it's possible to reside, between words, between mortals and their dear departed, at this fugitive intersection. You forced entry into the unbound space of writing, at the point where the word encounters the real—whence appears the most evanescent thing of all, what's called desire. To risk the space of desire, by which I really mean its living metaphor, the space that separates it from what it languishes for—being, the body, memory, the meaning of life, healing, recognition. What metaphor opens toward is another space, a space of possible speech.

TRANSLATOR'S INTRODUCTION: THE RISK OF READING

1. Benoît Morenne and Megan Specia, "Philosopher Who Praised Risk Died Trying to Save Children from Drowning," *New York Times* (July 25, 2017).

2. For variations on the same theme, see Roisin O'Connor, "Anne Dufourmantelle dead: French philosopher who wrote book on risk-taking dies rescuing children," *Independent*, July 24, 2017; Amy Held, "French Philosopher Who Promoted Risk-Taking Dies Attempting Water Rescue," *NPR*, July 24, 2017; Alexandra Ma, "A French philosopher who called life a risk dies rescuing children on a beach near St. Tropez," *Business Insider*, July 25, 2017; Kyle Swenson, "A famous French thinker's philosophy was based on taking risks. And that's how she tragically died," *Washington Post*, July 25, 2017; George Michelsen Foy, "Death and the Risk-taker: Anne Dufourmantelle, who advocated taking chances, dies as she lived," *Psychology Today*, August 14, 2017.

3. "Now, although the actual manner of philosophers' deaths is not always as noble as Socrates, and the vile circumstances of Seneca's botched suicide will be described below, I want to defend the ideal of the philosophical death. In a world where the only metaphysics in which people believe is either money or medical science and where longevity is prized as an unquestioned good, I do not deny that this is a difficult ideal to defend. Yet, it is my belief that philosophy can teach a readiness for death without which any conception of contentment, let alone happiness, is illusory. Strange as it might sound, my constant concern in these seemingly morbid pages is the meaning and possibility of happiness" (Simon Critchley, *The Book of Dead Philosophers* [New York: Vintage, 2008], xvii).

4. On Hobbes's political theory, Leo Strauss writes: "Since only evil is limited, not the good, it follows that the conduct of life, the goal set to life, is conditioned by evil. The conduct of life takes on the character of foreseeing the greatest evil and taking precaution against it. Expectation of future evil is called fear. Fear is not only alarm and fright, but also distrust, suspicion,

caution, care lest one fear. Now it is not death in itself that can be avoided, but only death by violence, which is the greatest of possible evils. For life itself can be of such misery that death comes to be ranked with the good. In the final instance what is of primary concern is ensuring the continuance of life in the sense of ensuring defense against other men. Concern with self-protection is the fundamental consideration, the one most fully in accord with the human situation. This is the origin of the distinction made between (moral) good and (moral) evil. The fear of death, the fear of death by violence, is the source of all right, the primary basis of natural right . . . Radical thinking recognizes the superiority of the will to power over striving after reputation. From fear of death by violence, from love of security, men seek after peace, after an ordered society" (Leo Strauss, *Spinoza's Critique of Religion* [Chicago: University of Chicago Press, 1965], 93).

5. Like a range of French philosophers and psychoanalysts (Emmanuel Lévinas, Jacques Lacan, Jacques Derrida, Jean-François Lyotard, Catherine Malabou) much of Dufourmantelle's work—from her first book, *La vocation prophétique de la philosophie* (1997), to *La sauavgerie maternelle* (2000) and *La femme et le sacrifice* (2006)—is devoted to thinking with and beyond the logic of sacrifice (and masculine heroism) that governs Western philosophy, ethics, and politics.

6. For a related psychoanalytic reflection of the paradoxical relationship of life and not dying or "not-death," see Lana Lin, *Freud's Jaw and Other Lost Objects: Fractured Subjectivity in the Face of Cancer* (New York: Fordham University Press, 2017).

7. Cf. Shusaku Arakawa and Madeleine Gins, *Reversible Destiny* (New York: Harry N. Abrams, 1997); *Architectural Body* (Tuscaloosa: University of Alabama Press, 2002). Dufourmantelle's reflections on not dying might, in fact, open up a less naïve reading of the work of these fascinating artists, in which it becomes clear how the decision not to die is something other than the mere avoidance or disavowal of death.

8. Of the many places where Lacan discusses this concept, perhaps the most amusing and memorable occurs during his seminar on January 7, 1970, when he explicitly states that it's the patient and not the analyst who is supposed to know: "What is asked of the psychoanalyst, and this was already in my discourse last time, is certainly not what emerges from this subject supposed to know on which, by hearing it a little bit askew, as one usually does, it has been thought possible to found the transference. I have often insisted on the fact that we are not supposed to know very much at all. What analysis establishes is this, which is quite the opposite. The analyst says to whoever is about to begin—'Away you go, say whatever, it will be marvelous.' He is the one that the analyst institutes as subject supposed to know" (Jacques Lacan,

The Seminar of Jacques Lacan, Book XVII: The Other Side of Psychoanalysis, ed. Jacques-Alain Miller, trans. Russell Grigg [New York: Norton, 2007], 52).

9. Sigmund Freud, *The Standard Edition of the Complete Psychological Works of Sigmund Freud*, Vol. II, ed. and trans. James Strachey (London: Hogarth Press, 1953), 111. Future references to this title are abbreviated as *SE*.

10. Along similar lines, Catherine Malabou suggests that we should approach the death drive in terms of what she calls "destructive plasticity." Rather than the end of life, "death" becomes the name for a radical metamorphosis. In fact, for Malabou, this metamorphosis is the only death worthy of the name, because, rather than simply putting an end to a life that is otherwise left intact, it transforms this life beyond recognition, cuts it off from its own past. The paradigm of this transformation is the experience of brain damage: "Whereas the psychoanalytic narrative of the resistance of the indestructible within destruction privileges the persistence of childhood, the past, and psychic destiny, which become recognizable through the disturbance that solicits them, the neurological narrative of the destruction of the resistance to destruction stages the exhausted but surviving resources of a psyche that no longer recognizes itself . . . The writing of neurological suffering—the theater of absence or the novel of 'brain ache'—raises the vertiginous question of *the psyche's survival of its own annihilation*" (Catherine Malabou, *The New Wounded: From Neurosis to Brain Damage*, trans. Steven Miller [New York: Fordham University Press, 2012], 56). Accordingly, the potential for such transformation arises from an immemorial past: not the past of childhood, but the virtual or unlived history of the brain itself. There is a complex and fascinating discussion to be staged between Dufourmantelle and Malabou about what "childhood" means, as well as on the role of the past and the future in psychoanalysis.

11. Serge André, "Writing Begins Where Psychoanalysis Ends," trans. Steven Miller, *Umbr(a): A Journal of Culture and the Unconscious* (2006): 143–77.

12. In *Beyond the Pleasure Principle*, Freud writes: "The patient cannot remember the whole of what is repressed in him, and what he cannot remember may be precisely the essential part of it. Thus he acquires no sense of conviction of the correctness of the construction that has been communicated to him. He is obliged to *repeat* the repressed material as a contemporary experience instead of, as the physician would prefer to see, *remembering* it as something belonging to the past" (*SE* XVIII, 18). Likewise, in "A Child Is Being Beaten," Freud discovers the agency of a fantasy that the patient cannot remember because it was never conscious and therefore can only become accessible through construction in analysis: "But we may say of [this fantasy]

in a certain sense that *it has never had a real existence*. It is *never remembered*, it has never succeeded in becoming conscious. It is a construction of analysis, but it is no less necessary on that account" (*SE* XVII, 185; my emphasis). Freud's discovery that memory fragments are "more powerful and more enduring when the incident that left them behind was one that never entered consciousness" provides the basis for Benjamin to distinguish between an experience (*Erfahrung*) that comes to pass without becoming conscious and an experience (*Erlebnis*) that is assigned a precise moment in time. "The greater the share of the shock factor in particular impressions, the more constantly consciousness has to be alert as a screen against stimuli; the more efficiently it does so, the less do these impressions enter experience (*Erfahrung*), tending to remain in the sphere of a certain hour in one's life (*Erlebnis*)." (Walter Benjamin, *Illuminations*, trans. Harry Zohn [New York: Schocken Books, 1968], 163.) This distinction is congruent, in Benjamin's analysis, with that between the untimeliness of the calendar (broken up by festive days) and chronology of the clock (an endless succession of hours and seconds).

13. Freud, *SE* XXI, 226.

14. On this point, see Jacques Lacan, "Beyond the Reality Principle," in *Écrits*, trans. Bruch Fink (New York: Norton, 2007), 58–74; and Philippe van Haute's masterful commentary on Lacan, *Against Adaptation: Lacan's Subversion of the Subject* (New York: Other Press, 2001).

15. Philippe Petit, *On the High Wire*, trans. Paul Auster (New York: Random House, 1985), 20.

16. Cf. Tim Dean, *Unlimited Intimacy: Reflections on the Subculture of Barebacking* (Chicago: University of Chicago Press, 2009). This fascinating book can productively be read among the various works of psychoanalytic or political theory to build on Freud's foray into group psychology (Kelsen, Bion, Lacan, MacCannell, Derrida, and Balibar, among others). Dean employs the category of "intimacy" to displace common notions about the risk in play within barebacking subculture. Rather than the risk of transmitting disease, what drives the practice of barebacking is the risk of radical or "unlimited" intimacy, an encounter with the other that is not framed in terms of perception, consciousness, privacy, personality, or identity. What emerges from this exploration is an account of group formation through impersonal relationality rather than the development of the ego through identification. For another explicitly psychoanalytic reflection on intimacy, see Leo Bersani and Adam Phillips, *Intimacies* (Chicago: University of Chicago Press, 2010).

17. *Man on Wire*, dir. James Marsh (2008).

18. For a more developed version of this analysis, see Steven Miller, "The Coup: Behind the Scenes of the Act with Philippe Petit," *differences* 28, no. 2 (September 2017): 116–33.

EURYDICE SAVED

1. The legend of Orpheus and Eurydice is linked to the mystery religions. Son of King Oeagrus and the muse Calliope, Orpheus knew how to charm animals with the accents of his lyre and found a way to touch inanimate beings. Eurydice, on the day of their marriage, was bitten on the heel by a snake and died. Orpheus, after putting Cerberus and the terrible Eumenides to sleep with his music, could approach Hades. He convinced the god to let him leave with his beloved on condition that she would follow behind and that he wouldn't turn around or speak to her until they had both regained the world of the living. But just as they were emerging from Hell, Orpheus couldn't help turning around to Eurydice and she was taken from him again, this time forever. "They were approaching the upper rim when the lover,/Fearing for his partner and eager to see her,/Turned his eyes. She fell back at once,/Stretching out her arms, trying to catch and be caught,/And sorry to take hold of nothing but air" (Ovid, *Metamorphoses*, trans. Stanley Lombardo [Indianapolis: Hackett, 2010], X: 58–62). Orpheus was then inconsolable. The most common version of his death is that the Bacchants felt painful spite at seeing him remain faithful to Eurydice and tore him to pieces. The weeping Muses gathered up the parts of his body to bury them at the foot of Mount Olympus. This is the myth around which Orphism was founded.

2. In English in the original.—Trans.

VOLUNTARY SERVITUDE AND DISOBEDIENCE

1. The French word here translated as "damage waiver" is *rachat de franchise*, which the author comments is "so well named" [*si bien nommé*]. The comment underscores the fact that, literally translated (in either French or English), *rachat de franchise* would be something like a "freedom voucher," proof that one opted out of a certain security system. —Trans.

2. Annie Le Brun, *Si rien avait une forme, ce serait cela* (Paris: Gallimard, 2010).

AT THE RISK OF PASSION

1. Elie During, *Faux raccords: la coexistence des images* (Arles: Actes Sud, 2010).

2. In English in the original.—Trans.

3 In English in the original.—Trans.

FORGETTING, ANAMNESIS, DELIVERANCE

1. Friedrich Nietzsche, *The Genealogy of Morality*, ed. Keith Ansell Pearson, trans. Carol Diethe (Cambridge, UK: Cambridge University Press, 2007), 79.

2. Emmanuel Lévinas, *Time and the Other*, trans. Richard A. Cohen (Pittsburgh: Duquesne University Press, 1987), 51.

INCURABLE (IN)FIDELITIES
1. Cited in Jackie Pigeaud, *Que veulent les femmes?* (Paris: Rivages poche, 2010), 12.
2. Jack Kerouac, *On the Road* (New York: Penguin Books, 1999).

HOW (NOT) TO BECOME ONESELF . . .
1. Adam Phillips, *Trois capacités négatives* (Paris: Éditions de l'olivier, 2010); *On Balance* (New York: Farrar, Straus & Giroux, 2010), 169. I reference both the French and English texts here because citation from the French text does not exactly correspond to the text from the section of *On Balance* entitled "Negative Capabilities."—Trans.
2. Gilles Deleuze, *Pure Immanence: Essays on a Life*, trans. Anne Boyman, intro. John Rajchman (New York: Zone Books, 2001), 27. Translation slightly modified.

AT THE RISK OF BEING FREE
1. Emmanuel Lévinas, *Otherwise than Being or Beyond Essence*, trans. Alphonso Lingis (Pittsburgh: Duquesne University Press, 1981), 122.

THE TIME THEY CALL LOST
1. Maurice Blanchot, *The Book to Come*, trans. Charlotte Mandell (Stanford: Stanford University Press, 2003), 79.
2. Elie During, *Faux raccords: la coexistence des images*, 75.

OF A PERCEPTION INFINITELY VASTER . . .
1. Maurice Merleau-Ponty, *Phenomenology of Perception*, trans. Colin Smith (New York: Routledge, 1958), 493.
2. Gilles Deleuze, *Two Regimes of Madness: Texts and Interviews 1975–1995*, ed. David Lapoujade, trans. Ames Hodges and Mike Taormina (New York: Semiotext(e), 2006), 187.
3. Arthur Rimbaud, *Complete Works, Selected Letters*, trans. and intro. Wallace Fowlie (Chicago: University of Chicago Press, 2005), 371.
4. Gilles Deleuze, *Two Regimes of Madness*, 297–99.
5. Pierre Guyotat, "Interview with Laure Adler," *France Culture*, December 30, 2010.

ANXIETY, LACK—SPIRITUAL HUNGER?
1. Søren Kierkegaard was born in 1813, in Denmark, to a family that belonged to a very devout Pietist community. In 1831, the year of Hegel's

death, Kierkegaard began his studies in theology. Soon after, his mother, his three older sisters, and two of his brothers all died in succession. He plunged into a melancholy that became even more acute upon the death of his father in 1838. Two years later, he met the young Regina Olsen and became infatuated with her. One year later, he brutally ended their relationship. The same year, he successfully defended his doctoral thesis, *The Concept of Irony with Continual Reference to Socrates*, and decamped to Berlin, where he attended Schelling's lecture courses. In 1843, he published his first great book, *Either/Or*, under the pseudonym Victor Eremita and, giving up plans to become a pastor, entered into a period of intense philosophical production that resulted in *The Concept of Anxiety* (1844), *Stages on Life's Way* (1845), *Concluding Unscientific Postscript* (1846), and *The Sickness Unto Death* (1849). He died at the age of forty-two. Although Kierkegaard was opposed to Hegel's philosophy, he retained the notion of the "dialectic" in order to apply it to the reality of concrete existence with its unforeseen events, doubts, and torments. Kierkegaard positioned himself as the perpetuator of Socratic irony and defended the idea of absolute negation against the Hegelian system that aspires to subsume all negation within the third, speculative and positive moment of Spirit's advent. In *The Concept of Anxiety*, Kierkegaard explores the paradoxical way in which freedom attests to itself because only a free being can experience anxiety—an experience of freedom as burden and obstacle.

2. Søren Kierkegaard, *The Concept of Anxiety: A Simple Psychologically Orienting Deliberation on the Dogmatic Issue of Hereditary Sin*, ed. and trans. Reidar Thomte (Princeton: Princeton University Press, 1980), 44.

3. Ibid., 41

4. Françoise Davoine and Jean-Max Gaudillière, *History Beyond Trauma*, trans. Susan Fairfield (New York: Other Press, 2004).

5. Jacques Derrida, "Rams: Uninterrupted Dialogue—Between Two Infinities, the Poem," trans. Thomas Dutoit and Philippe Romanski, in *Sovereignties in Question: The Poetics of Paul Celan*, ed. Thomas Dutoit and Outi Pasanen (New York: Fordham University Press, 2005), 135–63.

6. Ibid., 160

LIFE—MINE, YOURS

1. Marie Depussé, *Dieu gît dans les détails* (Paris: P.O.L., 2002). The title cites a phrase from the work of Aby Warburg.

AT THE RISK OF BEING CARNAL

1. Gilles Deleuze, *Two Regimes of Madness*, 192.

2. Emmanuel Lévinas, *Time and the Other*, trans. Richard Cohen (Pittsburgh: Duquesne University Press, 1987), 89.

AT THE RISK OF SPEECH

1. Martin Heidegger, *Basic Writings*, trans. David Farrell Krell (New York: Harper Collins, 1993), 369. Translation modified.
2. Michel de Montaigne, "On Liars," in *The Complete Essays*, trans. James Screech (New York: Penguin Books, 1987).

LAUGHTER, DREAMING—BEYOND THE IMPASSE

1. Sigmund Freud, "Humor," *The Standard Edition of the Complete Works of Sigmund Freud*, ed. James Strachey (London: Hogarth Press, 1950), Vol. XXI, 161.
2. Gilles Deleuze, *Two Regimes of Madness*, 41.
3. *Standard Edition of the Complete Works of Sigmund Freud*, Vol. V, 525.
4. Henri Bergson, *Laughter: An Essay on the Meaning of the Comic*, trans. Cloudesley Brereton and Fred Rothwell (New York: Dover Publications, 2005), 10.
5. Ibid., 26–27.
6. Frédéric Boyer, *Gagmen* (Paris: P.O.L., 2002), 34.

ONCE UPON A TIME, THE "ATHENAEUM" . . .
OR, WHY RISK ROMANTICISM?

1. Annie Le Brun, *Si rien avait une forme, ce serait cela*, 103.
2. G. W. F. Hegel, *Hegel and the Human Spirit: A Translation of the Jena lectures on the Philosophy of Spirit* (1805–6) with Commentary, trans. Leo Rauch (Detroit: Wayne State University Press, 1983), 87.
3. Novalis, *Philosophical Writings*, trans. and ed., Margaret Mahony Stoljar (Albany: SUNY Press, 1997), 34.
4. Friedrich Schlegel, "*Athenaeum* Fragments," §116, in *Philosophical Fragments* (New York: University of Minnesota Press, 1991), 31.
5. There are a total of 451 fragments in all the issues of the *Athenaeum*.

RISKING VARIATION

1. Gilles Deleuze, *Two Regimes of Madness*, 35–36 (translation slightly modified).
2. Cited in Annie Le Brun, *Si rien avait une forme, ce serait cela*, 244.
3. Elie During, *Faux raccords: la coexistence des images*, 45–47.
4. The phrase "night and day" is in English in the original.—Trans.

INTIMATE PROPHECY

1. In English in the original.—Trans.
2. Maurice Blanchot, *The Book to Come*, 79.
3. Nestor Braunstein, *Les présages, ou le souvenir d'enfance retrouvé* (Paris: Stock, 2011).

RISKING SCANDAL

1. Pierre Zaoui, *La traversée des catastrophes* (Paris: Seuil, 2010), 113.

TAKING THE RISK OF CHILDHOOD

1. In English in the original.—Trans.

RISKING THE FUTURE

1. Michela Marzano, *Le contrat de defiance*, 18.

2. Cf. Adam Phillips, *On Balance.*

3. Cited in André Lassoudière, *Flâneries VI: Génération-Intellectuel* (Lille: TheBookEdition, 2016), 103.

HAUNTINGS

1. Elie During, *Faux raccords: la coexistence des images*, 42.

2. Ibid.

3. Henri Bergson, *The Creative Mind*, trans. Mabelle L. Andison (New York: Dover Books, 2007), 125.

4. Annie Le Brun, *Si le noir avait une forme ce serait cela.*

SPIRALS, ELLIPSES, METAPHORS, ANAMORPHOSES

1. Olivier Cadiot, *Retour définitif et durable de l'être aimé* (Paris: P.O.L., 2008) and *Un mage en été* (Paris: P.O.L., 2010).

2. Jacques Derrida, *The Beast and the Sovereign*, trans. Geoffrey Bennington (Chicago: University of Chicago Press, 2011).

3. Elie During, *Faux raccords: la coexistence des images*, 49

REVOLUTIONS

1. Bernard Stiegler, from an interview broadcast on France 3.

2. Julia Kristeva, *Intimate Revolt: The Powers and Limits of Psychoanalysis*, trans. Jeanine Herman (New York: Columbia University Press, 2003), 223.

3. Claude Lévi-Strauss, *The View from Afar*, trans. Joachim Neugroschel (Chicago: University of Chicago Press, 1992), 23.

4. Julia Kristeva, *Intimate Revolt*, 4.

ANNE DUFOURMANTELLE, philosopher and psychoanalyst, taught at the European Graduate School and wrote monthly columns for the Paris newspaper *Libération*. Her books in English include *Power of Gentleness: Meditations on the Risk of Being; Blind Date: Sex and Philosophy*; and, with Jacques Derrida, *Of Hospitality*.

STEVEN MILLER is Associate Professor of English and Director of the Center for Psychoanalysis and Culture at the University at Buffalo, SUNY. He is the author of *War After Death: On Violence and Its Limits* and translator of books by Jean-Luc Nancy, Catherine Malabou, and Étienne Balibar.